THE MATHEMATICS OF THE
BREATH AND THE WAY

The MATHEMATICS of the BREATH and the WAY

ON WRITERS AND WRITING

CHARLES BUKOWSKI

Edited by David Calonne

City Lights Books | San Francisco

Library of Congress Cataloging-in-Publication Data
Names: Bukowski, Charles, author. | Calonne, David Stephen, 1953– editor,
    writer of introduction.
Title: The mathematics of the breath and the way : on writers and writing /
    Charles Bukowski ; edited by David Calonne.
Other titles: Writers and writiing
Description: San Francisco : City Lights Books, [2018] | "The Mathematics of
    the Breath and the Way: On Writers and Writing presents a variety of
    Bukowski's introductions and essays on authors, explorations of his
    poetics, and other samples of the ways he continually incorporates
    writerly themes in his fiction" — Introduction. | Includes
    bibliographical references.
Identifiers: LCCN 2018000977 (print) | LCCN 2018009809 (ebook) | ISBN
    9780872867826 | ISBN 9780872867598
Subjects: LCSH: Authorship.
Classification: LCC PS3552.U4 (ebook) | LCC PS3552.U4 A6 2018 (print) |
DDC
    814/.54—dc23
LC record available at https://lccn.loc.gov/2018000977

City Lights Books are published at the City Lights Bookstore
261 Columbus Avenue, San Francisco, CA 94133
www.citylights.com

CONTENTS

INTRODUCTION

INTRODUCTIONS AND CRITICISM

INTERVIEWS

INTRODUCTION

"Now EAT YOUR SPINACH..."

Charles Bukowski on Writers and Writing

David Stephen Calonne

Although many modern authors have made writing itself a central theme in their works—"metafiction" is a ubiquitous example—Charles Bukowski was particularly obsessive in defining himself constantly as a writer in his texts while simultaneously questioning what this might signify: he exists in a purely literary universe that spins out of and around the idea of writing. Experience exists in order to be turned into poetry and prose, but he also is constantly mocking himself and the pretensions of the "artist." In *The Captain Is Out to Lunch and the Sailors Have Taken Over the Ship*, he tells us: "Old Writer puts on sweater, sits down, leers into computer screen and writes about life. How holy can we get?"—a scene masterfully portrayed by R. Crumb.[1] *The Mathematics of the Breath and the Way: On Writers and Writing* presents a variety of Bukowski's introductions and essays on authors, explorations of his poetics, and other samples of the ways he continually incorporates writerly themes in his fiction.

The earliest work included here—Bukowski's 1957 story "A Dollar for Carl Larsen"—is an example of his experimentation with combining fiction and illustration: he submitted several "graphic fictions" to Whit Burnett's celebrated *Story* magazine. While it ostensibly treats an encounter with a "big blonde" at the racetrack, the tale begins and ends with mysterious literary, extra-textual allusions. The epigraph reads: "dedicated to Carl Larsen, owed to Carl Larsen, paid to Carl Larsen," and at the close we are told: "I thought about Carl Larsen down at the beach rubbing the sand from between his toes and drinking stale beer with Curtis Zahn and J.B. May. I thought about the dollar I owed Larsen. I thought maybe I'd better pay it. He might tell J.B." Larsen was actually the publisher of *Existaria*, a little magazine in Hermosa Beach, Southern California, hence the "sand from between his toes"; three Bukowski poems appeared in the September/October 1957 issue. Later Larsen would launch Seven Poets Press, which published Bukowski's *Longshot Pomes for Broke Players* (1961).[2] Readers are left to speculate that Bukowski may have owed money to Larsen, perhaps for a subscription to *Existaria*. In any case, it is noteworthy that the intertextuality here to the little magazines is brought directly into the narrative, indicating Bukowski's later practice of constantly foregrounding the fact that for him, reality exists in order to be turned into literature. Another person mentioned—Curtis Zahn (1912–1990)—had been incarcerated for a year as a conscientious objector against WWII and was a journalist and playwright; John Boyer May (1904–1981) was the editor of *Trace* magazine—which began as a little magazine directory in 1951 in Los Angeles—until 1970.[3] Bukowski submitted several letters/brief essays to *Trace*, which was extremely important for him during his early career because this directory provided outlets to which he would send his poetry.

Bukowski also produced a number of literary "manifestoes," and "Upon the Mathematics of the Breath and the Way"—first published in Tony Quagliano's *Small Press Review* in 1973—is one the strongest essays in this genre, in which Bukowski explores the connections between daily life and the transformation of experience into poetry.[4] And in his several introductions to fellow poets' works, he often takes the opportunity not only to praise the author, but also to adumbrate further aspects of his own poetics. For example, in his introduction to Doug Blazek's *Skull Juices*, Bukowski declares:

> It is not easy to realize that you are dying in your
> twenties. It is much easier not to know that you
> are dying in your twenties as is the case with most
> young men, almost all young men, their faces already oaken slabs, shined puke. They only imagine
> that death might happen in some jungle war of
> nobody's business. Blazek can see death and life
> in a shabby piece of curling wallpaper, in a roach

wandering through the beercans of a tired and sad
and rented kitchen. Blazek, although he would be
the last to realize it and is not conscious of it at all,
is one of the leading, most mangling, most lovely
(yes, I said, "lovely")! Sledges of the new way—
The Poetic Revolution. It is difficult to say exactly
when the Revolution began, but roughly I'd judge
about 1955, which is more than ten years, and the
effect of it has reached into and over the sacred
ivy walls and even out into the streets of Man.
Poetry has turned from a diffuse and careful voice
of formula and studied ineffectiveness to a voice
of clarity and burnt toast and spilled olives and
me and you and the spider in the corner. By this, I
mean the most living poetry; there will always be
the other kind.

In announcing a new "Poetic Revolution," which he
dates as beginning in the mid-Fifties—interestingly, about
the time Allen Ginsberg's *Howl* appeared—Bukowski
is also describing the so-called "Meat School" of poetry
which began to loosely coalesce around him with the ap-
pearance of Blazek's *Ole* magazine and with which poets
William Wantling and Steve Richmond were associated. In
Ole Anthology (1967), Blazek declares the rationale for the
new poetry:

But remember, there are still things to celebrate &
the best celebration is expressed in song & the logi-
cal extension of song is a shout. So, don't be timid.
If you still care, if that goddamned sun strikes
you in the eye right & you feel jubilant, THEN
SHOUT! Put your teeth into those words. Lift some
weights. Get that blood to cooking. Sneak in a peek
between your crotch & see if you still have hair
there. If there *is* hair, *say* there is hair. Don't hide
the balls either. If there are balls then include the
balls & make them look like balls, know they are
balls. POETRY WITH BALLS! POETRY THAT IS

DANGEROUS! MEAT POETRY! Juice to make the
ears jump . . . SOMETHING! as Bukowski says.[5]

Although Bukowski himself never acknowledged being either a founder or member of such a movement, it
is clear that both he and the poets he inspired attempted
to loosely formulate an aesthetic position which distinguished them from the other "schools" of American poetry:
Confessional, Black Mountain, Deep Image, New York, Ob-
jectivist, Imagist.

Another distinguishing feature of Bukowski's autobiographical prose/fiction is its structure as an extended
roman à clef. Fellow writers continually appear under different names and he settles scores with them—as D.H.
Lawrence often did in his satirical portraits of friends and
acquaintances—while also often portraying himself in the
worst possible light. For example, "Tony Kinnard" is Kenneth Patchen, and although the story carried a disclaimer—
"Note: There is no intent to hurt or malign living persons
with this story. I am sincere when I say this. There is enough
hurt now. I doubt that anything happened as happened in
this story. The author was only caught in the inventiveness
of his own mind. If this is a sin, then all creators of all times
have sinned . . . c.b."—Kenneth Rexroth was reportedly in-
furiated by the tale, vowing that he would cause physical
injury to Bukowski were they ever to meet.[6] Bukowski's
relationship with another poet—William Wantling, here
named "Jim"—forms the background of the story involving the woman "Helen," actually Ruth Wantling, the poet's
widow. Bukowski picks Helen up at the airport and then
spends several odd days and nights in boorish emotional combat with her. Again, Bukowski describes his own
boorish behavior as he attempts to get Helen into bed. Yet
another example is the story about "June" and "Clyde,"
editors of the magazine *Dustbird*—clearly Jon and Louise
"Gypsy Lou" Webb, editors of *The Outsider* and publishers
of two Bukowski poetry collections, *It Catches My Heart in
Its Hands* (1963) and *Crucifix in a Deathhand* (1965).[7] Here
again he makes a pass at Gypsy Lou, another widow of a

close friend. In other stories not included in this volume, John Bryan—editor of *Open City*—is pilloried, as is Harold Norse. Clearly, Bukowski lavishly criticizes others, but he also holds himself up for ridicule. Like Henry Miller, he enjoys magnifying his faults and madness, delighting in caricatures of sins of all kinds.

During the early 1970s, Bukowski's fame increased following the premiere of Taylor Hackford's documentary on public television and his readings in San Francisco. Linda King figures in the story describing his reading at City Lights: here literary figures again proliferate as we find allusions to Ginsberg, McClure, and Ferlinghetti. Furthermore, a story dealing with the early days of his relationship with Linda King—some of which reappears in Bukowski's novel *Women* (1977)—is entirely composed and shaped within a literary framework. The tale begins with an allusion to W. Somerset Maugham's *The Razor's Edge* and to the composition of Bukowski's first novel, *Post Office*; he then meets Linda at a poetry reading. King has read Bukowski's writings about women and critiqued them; they write letters to each other; he writes a poem about her; and finally writes the story itself. In fact, several of the most important women in Bukowski's life were connected to him through his writing. Barbara Frye was editor of *Harlequin*, where his early work was published; Frances Smith was herself a poet who became curious about him after reading his work; Linda Lee Beighle also knew of Bukowski through his writings and met him for the first time at a poetry reading.

After quitting his job at the post office, Bukowski began to earn his living by giving poetry readings, as well as from his royalties, book sales, and writing for periodicals. His account describing two readings at university campuses, which appeared in *Candid Press*, December 20, 1970, opens with a bravura non-stop paragraph containing not a single period: "I swung three deep out of Vacantsville, like bursting out of a herd of cow, and next thing I knew we had set down, the bird burst its stupid stewardesses, and I was the last man out, to meet a teacher-student in a shag of yellow and he said, you, Bukowski, and there was something about his car needing oil . . ." and the energetic sentence continues unimpeded on its way. Several of our selections depict him in a typical scenario: arriving on a college or university campus, drinking, giving his reading, and ending up in bed with a usually admiring female. Again the role of "writer" is both celebrated and lampooned as he exaggerates, jokes, and gives comical answers to ponderous questions: "I mean, I write poems, stories, novels. The poems are basically true, the rest is truth mixed with fiction. Do you know what fiction is? . . . Fiction is an improvement on life." The poetry reading becomes the scene of raucous insults and the post-reading party provides opportunities for the lofty poetic impulse to be brought back down to one of its purposes: the song, like a bird's, to attract a female.

Bukowski the journalist and book reviewer is also represented in these selections. In one of his earliest columns for the *Los Angeles Free Press,* on March 17, 1967—"Bukowski Meets a Merry Drunk"—the narrator reveals at the close that his "little talk" with the "merry drunk" might appear in the *LAFP.*[8] In his essay concerning the Rolling Stones, we can see Bukowski the journalist at work. He also reviewed a Rolling Stones concert in "Jaggernaut," an essay published in *Creem*: here he narrates the same event but takes a different approach, dramatizing the experience from a fresh angle.[9] This is of course his method as an autobiographical writer: he constantly tells and retells his life history from a variety of viewpoints throughout his prose and poetry. Bukowski describes his adventures writing for erotic magazines, describing a trip to an adult bookstore where he is nonplussed by the sophomoric level of the content of these productions, while in "Politics and Love," he depicts a hapless journalist sent to interview a violent South American dictator.

Ernest Hemingway returns like a leitmotif throughout Bukowski's work. In his "Introduction" to *Horsemeat,* Bukowski points out that "Hemingway liked the bullfights, right? He saw the life-death factors out there. He saw men reacting to these factors with style—or the other way. Dostoevsky needed the roulette wheel even though it always took his meager royalties and he ended up subsisting on milk." This theme returns in a seminal essay "Upon the Mathematics of the Breath and the Way," a central document of Bukowski's poetics in which he speaks of the centrality of the struggle of the horserace as metaphor for the act of creation. In the preface to one of his early plays, William Saroyan—an influence on Bukowski and an author to whom he frequently alludes—noted that the writer "must put his inner force, and the inner force of all living and all energy into the contest with non-existence. He simply must do so."[10] For Bukowski, Saroyan's "contest with non-existence" is the horserace, which confronts him with the contingency of chance and luck in their confrontation with free will, determinism, and the mystery of time. In his review of Hemingway's posthumously published *Islands in the Stream* (1970), Bukowski asserts: "This book does not make it. I wanted this book to make it. I have been pulling for Hemingway to hit one out of the lot for a long time now. I wanted another novel like *The Sun Also Rises*, *A Farewell to Arms*, or *To Have and Have Not*. I've been waiting a long time. . . ."[11] Bukowski admired the later section *Islands in the Stream*, which he calls "the best part of the book"—the section chasing the German submarine—and presciently remarks that "there's a movie in this part, and a good one": the novel was indeed made into a film starring George C. Scott in 1977, seven years after his review appeared. Hemingway was a wounded man whose work charts a continual drama of revealing and concealing his own vulnerability, a clear pattern in Bukowski as well.[12]

Bukowski also produced a number of essays, reviews, and introductions to the work of other writers. As we have seen above, he often used his introductions as places to espouse his own poetics. For example, in his "Introduction" to Jory Sherman's *My Face in Wax*, Bukowski writes: "When I run my hand across a page of poetry, I do not want oil or onionskin. I do not want slick bullshit; I want my hand to come away with blood on it. And goddamn you if you are otherwise." One of Bukowski's finest essays on poetry is his introduction to Steve Richmond's *Hitler Painted Roses*.

Richmond earned a law degree from UCLA , worked in his father's lucrative real estate business in Santa Monica, became friends with Jim Morrison, and published Bukowski in his magazine *Earth Rose*. Here again, Bukowski declares: "There is just one man thrown upon the earth, belly-naked, and seeing with his eye. Yes, I said 'eye.' Most of us are born poets. It is only when our elders get to us and begin to teach us what they teach us that the poet dies."[13] Bukowski also composed two essays celebrating d.a. levy, a central poet of the mimeograph revolution who committed suicide. levy's 7 Flowers Press in Cleveland had published Bukowski's *The Genius of the Crowd* (1966), and when levy was indicted for "obscenity," Bukowski responded with two essays registering strong support of his bravery.[14] Bukowski also admired Canadian poets Irving Layton and Al Purdy as well as the work of actor Macdonald Carey, for whose book *Beyond That Further Hill* he contributed a "Foreword." Bukowski's preface to *The Cockroach Hotel* by "Willie" requires a brief explanation: "Willie" is William Hageman, with whom Bukowski corresponded and who appears in Bukowski's short story "Beer and Poets and Talk."

Bukowski was consistent through the years in his list of favorite writers: Hemingway, Hamsun, Céline, and the early work of William Saroyan. Saroyan appears in "Hell Yes, the Hydrogen Bomb"—first published in *Quixote* in 1958—along with a fugitive allusion to the Czech writer Karel Čapek (1890–1938). As we see in his review of *Islands in the Stream*, and in scattered comments throughout the essays and stories presented here, he objected to Hemingway's lack of humor. Bukowski was also heavily influenced by the Russians Dostoevsky, Turgenev, and Gorky, as well as by Knut Hamsun's *Hunger*, in which the protagonist wanders the streets of Kristiania on the verge of starvation. The novel opens: "It was in those days when I wandered about hungry in Kristiania, that strange city which no one leaves before it has set its mark upon him." Bukowski's many poems about his hellish encounters with landladies also find an analogue in Hamsun as we learn in *Hunger* that our starving writer "stole quietly down the stairs to avoid attracting the attention of my landlady; my rent had been due a few days ago and I had nothing to pay her with anymore."[15] *Hunger* became a central text for Bukowski, who himself recounts eating candy bars in a floorless tar-paper shack in Atlanta and writing his stories on the edges of newspapers. In his essay "About Aftermath," we see how Bukowski recounted his early years of starving and writing. William Saroyan's famous short story "The Daring Young Man on the Flying Trapeze" and Arturo Bandini in John Fante's *Ask the Dust* continue this line of sensitive, impoverished writers who provided models for the ways Bukowski would portray himself. Starving leaves no room for self-delusion: one encounters the bedrock self which engenders a bedrock literary style.

In the interviews we also learn about Bukowski's writing rituals: symphony music on the radio, a bottle of wine and cigarettes nearby. In his interview with Chris Hodenfield, he reveals how much of the screenplay of *Barfly* was indebted to his times in that famous bar in Philadelphia where "We had a roaring time. And we'd be sitting there, eight guys. And suddenly somebody would make a statement, a sentence. And it would glue everything we were doing together. It would fit the outside world in—just a flick of a thing, then we'd smile and go back to our drinking. Say nothing. It was an honorable place, with a high sense of honor, and it was intelligent. Strangely intelligent. Those minds were quick. But given up on life. They weren't in it, but they knew something. I got a screenplay out of it and never thought I would, sitting there." Bukowski often affirmed that he did not want to be taken as a guru, and in his *Lizard's Eyelid* interview, he declares: "I have no message to the world. I am not wise enough to lead, yet I am wise enough not to follow." Bukowski also describes his life during the early seventies when he began work on his second novel:

> It's called *Factotum*, and it's about my ten years on the bum. I read *Down and Out in Paris and London* by George Orwell, and it's a pretty good book, but

I said "This guy hasn't been through anything—I can play the piano better than that, as far as experience goes." He had some rough trips but he didn't have as many as I did. So, it'll be an interesting book, I think. We'll see. So I've been making it on my writing the last three years, since I quit the Post Office. It's all right, I can't complain. Little checks come in, royalties . . . I'm a professional writer, man, get up at noon, get up at six, get up at three, hell, my life's my own. But that can get rough too, you know, you have to face yourself, it's all sitting on you. But it's lively.

Thus we can see how throughout his work, Bukowski's first love perhaps was neither women nor alcohol, but rather writing. From his very first short story, "Aftermath of a Lengthy Rejection Slip," to his final poems, stories, and essays, he returns obsessively to the primal question: "Old Writer puts on sweater, sits down, leers into computer screen and writes about life. How holy can we get?"

INTRODUCTION NOTES

1. Charles Bukowski, *The Captain Is Out to Lunch and the Sailors Have Taken Over the Ship* (Santa Rosa, CA: Black Sparrow Press, 1998).

2. On Bukowski and *Trace*, see David Stephen Calonne, *Charles Bukowski* (London: Reaktion Books, 2012), 42.

3. On Zahn, see Brian Kim Stefans, "Los Angeles Poetry from the McCarthy to the Punk Eras" in *A History of California Literature*, ed. Blake Allmendinger (New York: Cambridge University Press, 2015), 264-65; James Boyer May, "On *Trace*" in *The Little Magazine in America: A Modern Documentary History*, eds. Elliott Anderson and Mary Kinzie (Yonkers, NY: The Pushcart Press, 1978), 376-387. Also see Bill Mohr, "Scenes and Movements in Southern California Poetry" in *The Cambridge Companion to the Literature of Los Angeles*, ed. Kevin R. McNamara (New York: Cambridge University Press, 2010), 158; and Bill Mohr, *Hold-Outs: The Los Angeles Poetry Renaissance, 1948–1992* (Iowa City: University of Iowa Press, 2011), 37-9.

4. On Bukowski's manifestoes, see *Portions from a Wine-Stained Notebook: Uncollected Stories and Essays*, ed. David Stephen Calonne (San Francisco: City Lights, 2008), "Introduction," xii-xiii.

5. *Ole Anthology*, 6, ed. Doug Blazek, 1967.

6. Rexroth had reviewed Bukowski's *It Catches My Heart in Its Hands* in the *New York Times Book Review*, calling him a "substantial writer." He told James Laughlin, publisher of New Directions in a letter of July 25, 1967: "Why don't you publish [Charles] Bukowski? He is by far the best to come up in recent years, though he's near as old as you. I think he is great and would love to do an introduction." See *Kenneth Rexroth and James Laughlin: Selected Letters*, ed. Lee Bartlett (New York: W.W. Norton, 1991), 242. On the episode involving Ruth Wantling, see Howard Sounes, *Charles Bukowski: Locked in the Arms of a Crazy Life* (Edinburgh: Canongate, 2010), 137-39.

7. On the Webbs, see Jeff Weddle, *Bohemian New Orleans: The Story of* The Outsider *and Loujon Press* (Jackson: University Press of Mississippi, 2007).

8. See *Portions from a Wine-Stained Notebook*, ed. David Stephen Calonne (San Francisco: City Lights, 2008), 49-53.

9. *Ibid.*, "Jaggernaut," 156-61.

10. William Saroyan, "Preface" to *Opera, Opera* in *Razzle-Dazzle* (New York: Harcourt Brace, 1942), 118.

11. Previously, Bukowski had reviewed A.E. Hotchner's *Papa Hemingway* (New York: Random House, 1966). See "An Old Drunk Who Ran Out of Luck," *Portions from a Wine-Stained Notebook*," 54-56.

12. Hemingway was significant in the work of several poets. See Ron McFarland, "Hemingway and the Poets," *The Hemingway Review*, Vol. 20, no. 2, Spring 2001.

13. On Richmond, see *Gagaku Reader: The Life and Poetry of Steve Richmond* (Smithville, TX: Busted Dharma Books, 2016).

14. *The Buddhist Third Class Junkmail Oracle: The Selected Poetry & Art of d.a. levy*, ed. Mike Golden (New York: Seven Stories Press, 1999). Also see Len Fulton, "Anima Rising: Little Magazines in the Sixties" in *Print, Image and Sound: Essays on Media*, ed. John Gordon Burke (Chicago: American Library Association, 1972), 128-29, 134; Gary Snyder, "The Dharma Eye of d.a. levy" in *The Old Ways* (San Francisco: City Lights, 1977). For Bukowski's other (untitled) essay on levy, see *Absence of the Hero*, ed. David Stephen Calonne (San Francisco: City Lights, 2010), 115-16.

15. Knut Hamsun, *Hunger*, trans. Sverre Lyngstad (New York: Penguin, 1998), 3, 5.

MANIFESTO

Upon the Mathematics of the Breath and the Way

I was going to begin this with a little rundown on the female but since the smoke on the local battlefront has
cleared a bit I will relent, but there are 50,000 men in this
nation who must sleep on their bellies for fear of losing
their parts to women with wild-glazed eyes and knives.
Brothers and sisters, I am 52 and there is a trail of females
behind me, enough for five men's lives. Some of the ladies
have claimed that I have betrayed them for drink; well, I'd
like to see any man stick his pecker into a fifth of whiskey.
Of course, you can get your tongue in there but the bottle
doesn't respond. Well, haha among the trumpets, let's get
back to the word.

The word. I'm on my way to the track, opening day at
Hollywood Park, but I'll tell you about the word. To get the
word down proper, that takes courage, seeing the form, living the life, and getting it into the line. Hemingway takes
his critical blows now from people who can't write. There
are hundreds of thousands of people who *think* they can
write. They are the critics, the bellyachers and the mock-
ers. To point to a good writer and call him a hunk of shit
helps satisfy their loss as creators, and the better a man
gets the more he is envied and, in turn, hated. You ought to
hear them razz and demean Pincay and Shoemaker, two of
the greatest jocks ever to steer a horse. There's a little man
outside our local tracks who sells newspapers and he says,
"Get your paper, get your info on Shoemaker the Faker."
Here he is calling a man who has ridden more winners than
any other jock alive (and he's still riding and riding well)
and here's this newspaper guy selling papers for a dime
and calling the Shoe a fraud. The Shoe is a millionaire, not
that that's important, but he did get it with his talent and
he could buy this guy's newspapers, all of them, for the rest
of this guy's life and into a half-dozen eternities. Hemingway, too, gets the sneers from the newspaper boys and girls

of writing. They didn't like his exit. I thought his exit was
quite fine. He created his own mercy killing. And he created some writing. Some of it depended too much on style
but it was a style he broke through with; a style that ruined
thousands of writers who attempted to use any portion of
it. Once a style is evolved it is thought of as a simple thing,
but style not only evolves through a method, it evolves
through feeling, it is like laying a brush to canvas in a certain way and if you're not living along the path of power
and flow, style vanishes. Hemingway's style did tend to
vanish toward the end, progressively, but that's because he
let down his guard and let people do things to him. But he
gave us more than plenty. There is a minor poet I know who
came over the other night. He is a learned man, and clever,
he lets the ladies support him so you know he's good at
something. He is a very powerful figure of a man growing soft around the edges, looks quite literary and carries
these black notebooks around with him and he reads to you
from them. This boy told me the other night, "Bukowski,
I can write like you but you can't write like me." I didn't
answer him because he needs his self-glory, but really, he
only *thinks* he can write like me. Genius could be the ability
to say a profound thing in a simple way, or even to say a
simple thing in a simpler way. Oh, by the way, if you want
to get one angle on a minor writer, it is one who throws a
party or gets one thrown for him when his book comes out.

Hemingway studied the bullfights for form and meaning and courage and failure and the way. I go to boxing
matches and attend horse races for the same reason. There
is a feeling at the wrists and the shoulders and the temples.
There is a manner of watching and recording that grows
into the line and the form and the act and the fact and the
flower, and the dog walking and the dirty panties under
the bed, and the sound of the typewriter as you're sitting
there, that's the big sound, the biggest sound in the world,
when you're getting it down in your way, the right way,
and no beautiful woman counts before it and nothing that
you could paint or sculpt counts before it; it is the final art,
this writing down of the word, and the reason for valor

is all there; it is the finest gamble ever arranged and not many win.

Somebody asked me, "Bukowski, if you taught a course in writing what would you ask them to do?" I answered, "I'd send them all to the racetrack and force them to bet $5 on each race." This ass thought I was joking. The human race is very good at treachery and cheating and modifying a position. What people who want to be writers need is to be put in an area that they cannot maneuver out of by weak and dirty play. This is why groups of people at parties are so disgusting: all their envy and smallness and trickery surfaces. If you want to find out who your friends are you can do two things: invite them to a party or go to jail. You will soon find that you don't have any friends.

If you think I am wandering here, hold your tits or your balls or hold somebody else's. Everything fits here.

And since I must presume (I haven't seen any of it) that I am being honored and criticized in this issue I should say something about the little magazines, although I might have said some of it elsewhere?—at least over a row of beer bottles. Little magazines are useless perpetuators of useless talent. Back in the '20s and '30s there was not an abundance of littles. A little magazine was an event, not a calamity. One could trace the names from the littles and up through literary history; I mean, they began there and they went *up*, they became. They became books, novels, things. Now most little magazine people begin little and remain little. There are always exceptions. For instance, I remember first reading Truman Capote in a little named *Decade*, and I thought here is a man with some briskness, style and fairly original energy. But basically, like it or not, the large slick magazines print a much higher level of work than the littles—and most especially in *prose*. Every jackass in America pumps out countless and ineffectual poems. And a large number of them are published in the littles. Tra la la, another edition. Give us a grant, see what we are doing! I receive countless little magazines through the mail, unsolicited, un-asked-for. I flip through them. Arid vast nothingness. I think that the miracle of our times is that so many people can write down so many words that mean absolutely nothing, but they can do it, and they do it continually and relentlessly. I put out 3 issues of a little, *Laugh Literary and Man the Humping Guns*. The material received was so totally inept that the other editor and myself were forced to write most of the poems. He'd write the first half of one poem, then I'd finish it. Then I'd go the first half of another and he'd finish it. Then we'd sit around and get to the names: "Let's see, whatta we gonna call this cocksucker?"

And with the discovery of the mimeo machine everybody became an editor, all with great flair, very little expense and no results at all. *Ole* was an early exception and I might grant you one or two other exceptions if you corner me with the facts. As per the better printed (non-mimeo) mags one must grant *The Wormwood Review* (one-half hundred issues now) as the outstanding work of our time in that area. Quietly and without weeping or ranting or bitching or quitting or pausing, or without writing braggadocio letters (as most do) about being arrested for driving drunk on a bicycle in Pacific Palisades or corn-holing one of the National Endowment for the Arts editors in a Portland hotel room, Malone has simply gone on and on and compiled an exact and lively talent, issue after issue after issue. Malone lets his issues speak for themselves and remains invisible. You won't find him beating on your door one night with a huge jug of cheap port wine saying, "Hey, I'm Marvin Malone, I printed your poem *Catshit in a Bird's Nest* in my last issue. I think I'm gonna kick me some ass. Ya got anything for me to fuck around here?"

A vast grinding lonely hearts club of no-talents, that's what the littles have evolved to, with the editors a worse breed than the writers. If you are a writer seriously interested in creating art instead of foolishness, then there are, at any moment, a few littles to submit to, where the editing is professional instead of personal. I haven't read the mag that this piece is submitted to but I would suggest, along with *Wormwood*, as decent arenas: *The New York Quarterly*, *Event*, *Second Aeon*, *Joe DiMaggio*, *Second Coming*, *The Little Magazine*, and *Hearse*.

"You're supposed to be a writer," she says, "if you put all the energy into writing that you put into the racetrack you'd be great." I think of something Wallace Stevens once said, "Success as a result of industry is a peasant's ideal." Or if he didn't say that he said something close to that. The writing arrives when it wants to. There is nothing you can do about it. You can't squeeze more writing out of the living than is there. Any attempt to do so creates a panic in the soul, diffuses and jars the line. There are stories that Hemingway would get up early in the morning and have all his work done at noon, but though I never met him personally I feel as if Hemingway were an alcoholic who wanted to get his work out of the way so he could get drunk.

What I have seen evolve in the littles with most new and fresh talent is an interesting first splash. I think, ah, here's finally one. Maybe we have something now. But the same mechanism begins over and over again. The fresh new talent, having splashed, begins to appear everywhere. He sleeps and bathes with the goddamned typewriter and it's running all the time. His name is in every mimeo from Maine to Mexico and the work grows weaker and weaker and weaker and continues to appear. Somebody gets a book out for him (or her) and then they are reading at your local university. They read the 6 or 7 good early poems and all the bad ones. Then you have another little magazine "name." But what has happened is that instead of trying to create the poem they try for as many little mag appearances in as many little magazines as possible. It becomes a contest of publication rather than creation. This diffusion of talent usually occurs among writers in their twenties who don't have enough experience, who don't have enough meat to pick off the bone. You can't write without living and writing all the time is not living. Nor does drinking create a writer or brawling create a writer, and although I've done plenty of both, it's merely a fallacy and a sick romanticism to assume that these actions will make a better writer of one. Of course, there are times when you have to fight and times when you have to drink, but these times are really anti-creative and there's nothing you can do about them.

Writing, finally, even becomes *work* especially if you are trying to pay the rent and child support with it. But it is the finest work and the only work, and it's a work that boosts your ability to live and your ability to live pays you back with your ability to create. One feeds the other; it is all very magic. I quit a very dull job at the age of 50 (twas said I had security for life, ah!) and I sat down in front of the typewriter. There's no better way. There are moments of total flaming hell when you feel as if you're going mad; there are moments, days, weeks of no word, no sound, as if it had all vanished. Then it arrives and you sit smoking, pounding, pounding, it rolls and roars. You can get up at noon, you can work until 3 a.m. Some people will bother you. They will not understand what you are trying to do. They will knock on your door and sit in a chair and eat up your hours while giving you nothing. When too many nothing people arrive and keep arriving you must be cruel to them for they are being cruel to you. You must run their asses out on the street. There are some people who pay their way, they bring their own energy and their own light but most of the others are useless both to you and to themselves. It is not being humane to tolerate the dead, it only increases their deadness and they always leave plenty of it with you after they are gone.

And then, of course, there are the ladies. The ladies would rather go to bed with a poet than anything, even a German police dog, though I knew one lady who took very much delight in claiming she had fucked one President Kennedy. I had no way of knowing. So, if you're a good poet, I'd suggest you learn to be a good lover too, this is a creative act in itself, being a good lover, so learn how, learn how to do it very well because if you're a good poet you're going to get many opportunities, and though it's not like being a rock star, it will come along, so don't waste it like rock stars waste it by going at it rote and half-assed. Let the ladies know that you are really there. Then, of course, they will keep buying your books.

And let this be enough advice for a little while. Oh yes, I won $180 opening day, dropped $80 yesterday, so today is the day that counts. It's ten minutes to eleven. First post 2 p.m. I must start lining up my horse genes. There was a guy out there yesterday with a heart machine attached to himself and he was sitting in a wheelchair. He was making bets. Put him in a rest home and he'll be dead overnight. Saw another guy out there, blind. He must have had a better day than I did yesterday. I've got to phone Quagliano and tell him I've finished this article. Now there's a very strange son of a bitch. I don't know *how* he makes it and he won't tell me. I see him at the boxing matches sitting there with a beer and looking very relaxed. I wonder what he's got going. He's got me worried. . . .

Small Press Review, Vol. 4, no. 4, 1973

TALES

A Dollar for Carl Larsen

dedicated to Carl Larsen
owed to Carl Larsen
paid to Carl Larsen

. . . it was a lazy day and a lousy day to work, and it seemed that even spiders hadn't thrown out their webs. And when I got to the railroad yards I found out that Henderson was the new foreman.

The old Mexican, Al or Abe or somebody had retired or died or gone insane. The boys were matching pennies down by the barn when Henderson called me over.

"Gaines," he said, "Gaines, I understand you're somewhat of a playboy. Well, that's all right. I don't mind a little horseplay now and then, but we'll get our work done first and then we'll play."

"Just like recess at school, eh, coach?"

Henderson put his face real close to mine. I put mine real close to his.

"Or haven't you *been* to school, Hendy?"

I could look right down into his red mouth and his frog jaws as he spoke: "I can tie the can to you, boy."

"Proving what?" I asked.

"Proving you are out of position."

Which was a pretty good answer, and a pretty good criticism: I was always out of position.

I took a nickel out of my pocket and flipped it to the cement where the boys were lagging to the line. They stood back stunned, looking from the nickel to me. I turned and walked the hell out of there.

II

I lay up in my room and studied the *Racing Form* for a couple of hours and knocked off half a bottle of leftover wine. Then I got into my '38 Ford and headed for the track. . . .

I wrote the morning line down on my program and

35

walked over to the bar where I noticed a big blonde about 35, and alone—well, about as alone as a big babe like that can get in amongst 8,000 men. She was trying her damnedest to burst and pop out of her clothes, and you stood there watching her, wondering which part would pop out first. It was sheer madness, and every time she moved you could feel the electricity running up the steel girders. And perched on top of all this madness was a face that really had some type of royalty in it. I mean, there was a kind of stateliness, like she'd lived beyond it all. I mean, there were some women who could simply make damned fools out of men without making any type of statement, or movement, or demand—they could simply stand there and the men would simply feel like damned fools and that was all there was to it. This was one of those women.

I looked up from my drink as if it didn't matter and as if she were anybody else, and as if I were a pretty jaded type (which, to tell the truth, I was) and said, "How you been doin' . . . with the ponies, I mean?"

"All right," she said.

I'd expected something else. I don't know what. But the "all right" sounded good, though.

I was about half-gone on the wine and felt I owned the world, including the blonde.

"I used to be a jockey," I told her.

"You're pretty big for a jock."

"210, solid muscle," I said.

"And belly," she said, looking right above my belt.

We both kinda laughed and I moved closer.

"You want the winner of the first race? To kinda start you off right?"

"Sure," she said, "sure," and I just felt that big hip-flank touch the upper side of my leg a moment and I felt on fire.

I smelled perfume, and imagined waterfalls and forests and throwing scraps to fine dogs, and furniture soft as clouds and never awakening to an alarm clock.

I drained my drink. "Try six," I said. "Number six: *Cat'shead.*"

"*Cat'shead?*"

Just then somebody tapped me. I should say—rapped me on the back of one of my shoulder blades.

c.D.

"*Boy*," this voice said, "get *lost!*"

I stared down into my drink waiting for *her* to send this stranger away.

"I *said*," the voice got a little louder, "run along and play with your marbles!"

As I stared down into my drink I realized it was empty.

"I don't like to play marbles," I told the voice.

I motioned to the bartender. "Two more—for the lady and myself."

I felt it in my back then: the sure, superior nudge of a peerless and no doubt highly efficient automatic.

"Learn," said the voice, "learn to *like* to play marbles!"

"I'm going right away," I said. "I brought my agate. I hear there's a big game under the grandstand."

I turned and caught a look at him as he slid into my seat, and I'd always thought *I* was the meanest-looking son of a bitch in the world.

"Tommy," I heard her tell him, "I want you to play a hundred on the nose for me."

"Sure. On who?"

"Number six."

"Number SIX??"

"Yes: six."

"But that stiff is 10 to 1!"

"Play it."

"O.K., baby, O.K., but . . ."

"Play it."

"Can I finish my drink?"

"Sure."

I walked over to the two-dollar win window.

"Number six," I said, "once."

It was my last two dollars. . . .

Six paid $23.40.

I watched my horse go down into the Winner's Circle like I do all my winners, and I felt as proud of him as if I had ridden him or raised him. I felt like cheering and telling everybody he was the greatest horse that had ever lived, and I felt like reaching out and grabbing him around the neck, even though I was two or three hundred feet away.

But I lit a cigarette and pretended I was bored. . . .

Then I headed back to the bar, kind of to see how she took it, intending to stay pretty far away. But they weren't there.

I ordered a double backed by a beer, drank both, ordered up again and drank at leisure, studying the next race. When the five-minute warning blew, they still hadn't shown and I went off to place my bet.

I blew it. I blew them all. They never showed. At the end of the last race I had 35 cents, a 1938 Ford, about two gallons of gas, and one night's rent left.

I went into the men's room and stared at my face in disgust. I *looked* like I knew something, but it was a lie, I was a fake and there's nothing worse in the world than when a man suddenly realizes and admits to himself that he's a phony, after spending all that time up to then trying to convince himself that he wasn't. I noticed all the sinks and pipes and bowls and I felt like them, worse than them: I'd rather be them.

I swung out the door feeling like a hare or a tortoise or something, or somebody needing a good bath, and then I felt her swinging against me like the good part of myself

suddenly coming back with a rush. I noticed how green
her dress was, and I didn't care what happened: seeing her
again had made it O.K.

"Where've you been?" she said hurriedly. "I've been
looking all over for you!"

"What the hell is this?" I started to say, "I've been
looking—"

"Here comes *Tommy!*" she halted me, and then I felt
something in my hand and then she walked out, carefully, slowly to meet him. I jammed whatever it was into
my pocket and walked out toward the parking lot. I got
into my car, lit my next-to-last cigarette, leaned back and
dropped my hand into my pocket.

I unfolded five one hundred dollar bills, one fifty, two
tens, and a five. "Your half," the note said, "with thanks."
"Nicki." And then I saw the phone number.

I sat there and watched all the cars leave, I sat there
and watched the sun completely disappear; I sat there and
watched a man change a flat tire, and then I drove out of
there slowly, like an old man, letting it hit me, inch by inch,
and scared to death I'd run somebody over or be unable
to stop for a red light. Then I thought about the nickel I'd
thrown away and I started to laugh like crazy. I laughed
so hard I had to park the car. And when the guy who'd
changed his flat came by I saw his white blob of a face staring and I had to begin all over again. I even honked my
horn and hollered at him.

Poor devil: he had no soul.

Like me and one or two others. I thought about Carl
Larsen down at the beach rubbing the sand from between
his toes and drinking stale beer with Curtis Zahn and J.B.
May. I thought about the dollar I owed Larsen. I thought
maybe I'd better pay it. He might tell J.B.

Unpublished

Hell Yes, the Hydrogen Bomb

He felt tremendously bored and disgusted; his back ached from being in bed all morning. He folded the paper and threw it into the cubbyhole behind his desk. He tried the second best thing: he got up and opened all the drawers, took the papers out, and spread them on the bed. Sometimes on things you started and couldn't finish, sometimes you took two or three things like that, put them together, and by knocking off the edges you could get an unusual story—they'd never know, they'd think it was the same thing straight through. As long as the lines had blood in them. . . . Sometimes you could take all the lines that had blood in them . . . or you could get away from subjectiveness by making the musician a barber, and your lines of bemoaning would be forgiven because they'd think it was *he* instead of *you*.

He lit a cigarette and began to read the various sheets. There were dozens of them—wild scrawlings, neat printing, pencil, ink—and he'd forgotten most of them, and reading them again, there was something hellishly funny in them—one grows, you know, gets over extravagances. The drawers were always full because he was afraid to throw the stuff into the wastebaskets, and when he did, he tore the papers into very small sections and then swirled them all around with his hands:

. . . there's no telling when something will break. You can't believe the voices, or the faces of the voices . . .

. . . I said, automatic profusion

. . . I lit a cigarette but found it was an ember bud and threw it away.

. . . I cower before the look of eyes . . . this fat whore says, I've had nine glasses of port since this morning . . . the whore turns away, a little frozen . . . I shake my beer and look down into the glass . . . I phone my father from the Culver City Courthouse. I understand I am in the judge's chambers. The operator gives me the wrong number. A well-dressed woman stares at me. My hands tremble. I have a three-day beard and a hole in my pants . . .

. . . sickened, in a rage . . . rattle of glass . . . water pouring . . . her cough . . . footsteps . . . winding clock . . . washing dishes . . . eating . . . frying things . . . opening, closing drawers . . . vacuuming . . . strange sound, like a spray . . . night . . . snoring . . . her goddamned room, her pot lids, her spoons . . . that doesn't matter. She'll be dead by the time they get there. I don't want to wait till she's asleep . . . this is a thing to be done now . . . Rain. It rains. You'll see them hurrying in the rain . . .

. . . too often a brilliant mind makes a brilliant face, alas, alas. (These lines were underlined.)

. . . the guitar has been played too violently . . . lost another job drinking . . . 55 cents left . . . it's snowing and the want ads look terrible . . . Christ!—to be a fat, rich bastard with bullfrog eyes! . . . end product of American industry: the dead end: fear. 1931, 1932, 1933, 1934, 1935, 1936, 1937 . . . fear, fear, fear! . . . *everything* (march, boys!) to the job: the body, the voice, the soul . . . this type and nothing else . . . a suggestion of weariness . . . Hell yes, the hydrogen bomb! *Break* the tables, as N. said . . .

. . . Saroyan . . . didn't speak the truth . . . reason he didn't burn his 500 books in a tub when he was freezing in San Francisco was not because he saw value in the cheapest, most false book, but because he was afraid the fire would make the room too damned smoky and the landlady would raise hell . . . if he *had* 500 books and *did* think of burning them . . .

. . . Christ, what time is it? My feet are asleep!

. . . Iron Curtain, politics in Art . . . I, and them, and all, at last with pinch-bud faces, lost count, seeking electric altogether . . . brain suspends spirit like a hoyden insect . . . when waitress drops a plate I cry . . .

. . . he'd evidently had an education of some sort, and when I saw him there eating, I walked over and sat down across from him, "What are you doing in a dump like this?" . . . frightened, wild, unsteady eyes . . .

. . . Say words. Volcano. Interim. Daze.

... Battle plans

Sat. Sun.—$1.33 peanut butter 4.50 rent

bread

knife

newspaper leave—3

Thurs.—Dishwashing, anything. Gloves—75 cents.

Suit $8.00—Food—carfare—if money comes, keep suit.

Nxt. Wk. Fri.—1.00 (save 12 cents)

Sat.—Try Harry's credit

Sun.—Skip rent

Mon.—(Social sec.) get $20.00?

If not—*finis*

... drink goes well in novels ... or in magazine advertisements ... wrote home and asked his mother for money ... stood before the mirror ... posing wise and profligate—not quite bringing it off.

... too much electric altogether ... hoyden insect ... politics in Art ... politics in Science ... politics in breastplate ... asphalt, people, tracks ... Eve's infinite copulation ... say that Birdie told you so.

... easy does it, Charles. I am bored, a little dull and rather dissatisfied altogether.

what the hell's that noise?

a pipe

She always dreamed of lilies and loved Strauss (Blue Danube Strauss) quite so much

door slamming

feet, feet

how horrible, how mockingly

purposely horrible

I think

they enjoy it.

... Dear J—

I hate to be ridiculous—but could you loan me five bucks? I know this stuns you beyond measure—this encroachment, or what—but I've lost my job through drink, it's the night before Thanksgiving, everything's hocked and my landlady a pragmatic bitch.

I swear, sincerely, I'll repay you when I get over the

hump. Take a chance—the odds are good—and I'm really quite alone . . .

. . . he heard the voices downstairs, he heard the downstairs voices, he heard voices . . .

. . . Bar scene: a series of comments on . . . unfortunately . . . writers are mostly people with upper-strata jobs . . . English teachers . . . newspaper reporters . . . book reviewers . . . these people . . . attached to rather arched little physiognomies . . . brimstone eyes . . . or something . . . have a certain thing about them . . . sometimes claim they have washed dishes or boxed in the ring . . . generally it is a goddamned lie . . . and when they write their bar scenes . . . oh Jesus Christ! . . . few real men write . . . the living kills that . . .

. . . could try to escape by jumping from Russian trains . . . cold blood, areas of cold blood—rivers of dead, rivers . . . Karel Capek, *Benedicite coeli Domino* . . . today is a holiday of some sort. The people are singing and eating huge dinners.

. . . I got drunked-up and noticed a man next to me reading a sheet of music.

"Are you a music writer?" I asked him.

"Yes," he said . . .

. . . I'm done . . . through . . . botched it all up . . . Oh, if you could only know how terrible I feel . . . there are all these good people I hurt . . . good chances I've missed . . . chances, chances . . . little things, like Don putting the packages on my wrapping table—"*Happy Birthday!*"—and a little cake in there . . . and three cigars . . . Oh, I know this is wild, but it's the way I feel inside . . . let me speak a while, Father, there is nobody outside, there is no line . . .

. . . I could hear my mother in the kitchen, but the bedroom door was closed and I got up on the chair and peeked through the hole in the shade. The excitement flushed through me fiercely. What a break, what a *lucky* break! Miss Philippe-Cret, the new roomer, was in the garden swing. Her dress was high over her knees and as she rocked back and forth in the swing, the crossed legs changed their pose and I could see flashes of upper leg, where the stocking ended and the flesh began. I stood peering, my body tense, aching with excitement . . .

. . . You tell me to go out and get a job . . . why goddamn you man . . . where have you been living . . . don't you know when you've been drinking as long as I have you are just too goddamned nervous and frightened . . .

. . . he saw the sailors coming, five or six of them, wandering across the sidewalk, shouting, laughing over some ever-perpetual joke, mob-happy. He crossed to the other side of the street, but it was too late: there were whistles, shouts, as if to a passing girl, only with mocking intonations . . .

. . . Dear J—

Glad I'm not in L.A. now. Don't think I could swallow the "New Man." But I haven't given up on you yet: you're too inconsistent to maintain any attitudes for length . . . Political fervor is the blight of the young. History is too long— the tail swings the dog.

Well, bud, should you ever blow your top and throw in the towel as I have done, you are always welcome to join my troupe: voices out of air, worm's-eye of death, stockings of steel, wax bullets, creosote dawns, eternal confusion.

So your old man goes to the opera? Well, there are a few good ones. Do you think he's playing dilettante? I doubt if he amuses you as much as he irritates you. You laughter seems forced.

I'm still making plans to gorge myself on ancient literature, a study of the *Harvard Classics*—and so far, all I've read is a book on duck hunting. This, added to my former study on the operation of the mesocolon gives me a solid literary background . . .

There were more papers on the bed, but he didn't read them. It wasn't any good. Too disjointed. He went back to the desk, sat down, dipped his pen and wrote:

"A fit of terrible gloom came over him. It was Sunday, a cold, dark December Sunday and there wasn't any heat in the room. One shade was down, the other up; the electric lights were on but the room was full of shadow. Newspapers were all over the floor, covered with shoeprints, dirt; an empty cracker box, an unmade bed, the immense tick of clock. It was too cold to go out, he was broke, two bottles (empty of whisky) stood on the dresser. All his clothing was hocked, and open on the table was the 'Help Wanted' section of the newspaper, three or four ads circled. His back ached, he was sick: the rent was due, and it was cold, very cold.

"If I ever get over this, he thought, I'll save money. I'll get a nice apartment with a refrigerator. I'll cook, I'll drink fruit juices, I'll smoke a pipe, I'll wear clean, bright sweaters and buy rare and unusual books . . ."

He wrote on and on, and on.

Quixote 19, Autumn 1958

Dialogue: Dead Man on the Fence

Scene: cheap room, South Hollywood, 3rd floor, half-empty wine bottle, 3 or 4 books: *The Lives of the Composers*, Jeno Barcsay's *Anatomy for the Artist*, a watercolor painting "female figure" by Eric Heckel and another watercolor by Lee J. Wexler, 1952, a telephone, newspapers, correspondence, dirty stockings freckle the floor. The scene opens (and closes) in this room, between 2 writers, the first writer the owner (as long as the rent is paid) of the room and the second writer a visitor. . . .

Second writer (let's call him Karl Thornton): I sold this movie script to a producer. He thinks it's great. Can you imagine a surrealist Western? Can you imagine an abstract Western?

First writer (let's call him Henry Knapp): I can't imagine any kind of Western.

Karl: Now I've got this next one. It is about a bank hold-up. I've got 4 boys from Oxford, suave, who pull the job. I need some wild dialogue, way out. They told me you were the boy to do it. I've seen your poetry. It's the maddest thing since—since Rabelais shit on them and made them like it.

Henry: I know it sounds corny, but I cannot compromise.

Karl: That's just the *beauty* of it. You don't *have* to compromise! They don't know what the hell you're talking about. I have a negro running through the fields with his pants down, screaming, "Kiss my black ass!" You see what I mean?

Henry: No.

Karl: By the way, how did you come out on, well, how did it work out?

Henry: You mean the love affair with the 20-year-old negress?

Karl: Yeah.

Henry: I guess I told you about her when I was under the influence of a few beers.

Karl: You were drunk, man, plenty drunk.

Henry: (Pouring wine all around, draining his glass)

Well, she was only 20, and she was black, and she was the one who was *frightened*, not the whites but the blacks who would condone her for her act. Actually, and without being conceited, I think she cared, but not enough. None of them care enough—black or white.

Karl: You've had more damned affairs than a man of your age deserves.

Henry: Hold it, daddy, I'm 40, but I'm dying. You want some laughs?

Karl: I'd rather have a Hollywood script.

Henry: Well, this isn't Hollywood, it's life: for a short period, I was married to a semi-millionaire's daughter and I dabbled in her so-called magazine literary. And here came these sexy poems: YOU HAVE RUINED MY VAGINA; TAKE ME, LOVER; YOU, SEDUCER. As poetry it was less than fair.

Karl: But as an opportunity, it held all sorts of overtones.

Henry: And undertones.

Karl: You arranged a meeting, a literary meeting.

Henry: And found a 32-year-old virgin, well-read in the classics, ready to die, admirer of my mind and body, beautiful legs and hungry as a goldfish unfed 3 days.

Karl: What a spot.

Henry: I asked her to marry me.

Karl: You?

Henry: Hell yes—I've been married before. And I was married then.

Karl: And?

Henry: She had some type of incurable disease, and although she carried a Blue Cross card or something, it ended up to nearly $100 a month to the medics. Was my love that strong? Shit yes: for *horses*.

Karl: Tell me some more, baby. I'll work it into the script.

Henry: So women can go to hell, I'm going to get me a lamb like the old English sailors, or, yes, it was a sheep, or a nice young boy. Let me read you a letter I'm going to mail to this bitch today. Here goes, quote: "I don't want to hurt your feelings. My meetings with you down here were both physical and spiritual revelation that came at a time when I was very close to a foreboding finality. I've had another affair since then—she was only 20, much too young—"

Karl: That was the colored girl.

Henry: Shut up. "—that was less rewarding. I suppose it's thinking on this last affair, and Jane, and my X-wife, and some others, that shows me I'm simply a ladies' man. I don't know what's wrong and I much less give a damn. I've still got music and the horse, a drive down the coast and rotten alcohol for my shredded-wheat stomach. I've still got words to do and I've still got my pride, I still have my pride, and as Shakey said, 'I still have my death to do.'"

Karl: You're killing me, kid, but go on, round it off.

Henry: "And I can do without petticoats whether they be 20 or 40 or 60, rich or poor, sexy or cold, whether they live in Denver or Bermuda, East Kansas City or London, whether in the fog or the rain or the 9am sunlight—"

Karl: You're rolling daddy, hit it!

Henry: "Whether with cats on their laps or black boyfriends, whether letter-writers or screamers of arias, whether tall or short or pregnant, whether nun or nude or whether with breasts or without, whether resplendent with jewels and the image of love or whether wrinkled and grey and forgotten, whether riding places on oceanic steamers or shucking in a cow through the gate, whether ugly or beautiful, whether living or dead, rich or poor, the hags, the whores, the mirrors of my heart, may they all be damned and without

yours,
Henry Knapp."

Karl: Don't you think that's rather cruel? To a dying person? For $100 a month.

Henry: It certainly is, and that's just what happens when the words carry you and you forget the human side. Writers are all bastards, trying to knock off each other or some editor, or they, like I, throw dirt on the dying. I hate my guts.

Karl: Some others do too. They tell me that J. Karlton

Thrumbro thinks your stuff stinks. What have you got to say to this, Mr. Knapp?

Henry: I don't know. Why this eltchl, this conservative from the halls of the ikons and holy rollers, the pluckers of rondeaus and smellers of the lily, why this spalpeen should set himself up as a special critic of literary know-how is more than I can dispense with a quodlibet.

Karl: Let me fill in the rest?

Henry: The stage is yours. I've quite hogged it with my sloughed-off loves.

Karl: The field boils with literary journals, a great slough and pot wash of them for those who wish to continue on the descensive, whether they be gnostics, pansies, or grandmothers who keep canaries and goldfish. Why these reactionaries cannot be content with their lot, why they must lacerate us with their yellow-knuckled souls, the looming kraken of their god-head, is beyond me. I certainly do not give a magniloquent damn what they print in *their* journals. I beg no alms for modern verse. Yet they come bickering to us. Why? Because they smell life and cannot stand it, they want to plunge us into the same spume and sputum that has held them daft with the deism of stale 1890 verse.

Henry: Amen.

Karl: But what I'm getting at, are you going to help me with this script?

Henry: Buy me another bottle of wine and I'll think it over.

Karl: Your talent comes cheap.

Henry: What doesn't nowadays? (Looking around) Ring down the curtain! Ring down the goddamned curtain! I want to get drunk! Audience, go home! YOU'VE HAD YOUR INTELLECTUAL CHIT-CHAT, now clear the hell out: I've still got, I still *have*, plans for the 20-year-old negress!

end . . .

Autographical Statement

. . . Born 8-16-20, Andernach, Germany. Brought to America at age of 2. And for amateur psychiatrists who wonder what makes me scream in my poems: when I was a kid the old man bought me an Indian suit and headfeathers when he noticed all the other kids in the neighborhood were playing cowboy. I owe the old boy a lot but since he's dead I won't bother to square accounts.

. . . Los Angeles City College, journalism and art, but the closest I ever got to being a reporter was as an errand boy in the composing room of the *New Orleans Item*. Used to have nickel beers in a place out back and the nights passed quickly.

. . . Started out writing short stories in such places as Atlanta over the bridge, paper shack, no light, no water, no heat, peanut butter sandwiches or candy bars . . . or New Orleans or the stale rotten Village, or Philly, Miami Beach, hell, North Carolina, Frisco, Houston, you name it . . .

. . . Air mailing short stories to the *Atlantic Monthly* and if they didn't take them, tear them up. Finally heard of *Story* and Whit Burnett published my first. Appeared in international review, a ten buck rag, with Sartre, Lorca, everybody, then said to hell with it and got drunk for ten years.

. . . Ran errands for sandwiches and let the bartender beat me up—when I felt like it. I did work at times: dog biscuit factory, coconut man in a cake factory, shipping clerk, truck driver, stock boy for Sears-Roebuck, mailman, janitor, night watchman, dock hand, integral system player at your nearest track; hung posters in New York subways, god, I can't remember them all; don't want to. At the age of 35, sat down in front of a typewriter again and it all came out in poem form. To me, that is.

. . . But I found out that editors wanted everything in a cage. It was the same as punching the time clock or kidding the bartender out of a free drink. Boil it down, they said. You're all over the placenta. But I found out that all they wanted was dullness and the poetic pose.

. . . I sat through a poetry class once that I'll never forget, no matter how much dirt they throw on me. I mean burial, friend, not critical squirts across a verbal horizon.

. . . Well, I've just about said it, and there's really nothing to say, either the poem says it or it doesn't say it. I hold nothing against the boys who lucked it into the ivory and teach poetry classes. It's a way of eating and a way of talking but I don't think I could do it.

. . . If I have a god it is Robinson Jeffers, although I realize that I don't write as he does.

. . . Married once to Barbara Fry, editor of *Harlequin*. She could not stand me. Divorce.

. . . What else do you want to know . . . ?

Long Shot Pomes for Broke Players,
New York: 7 Poets Press, 1962

Bukowski Meets a Merry Drunk

"Getting drunk," he told me, "is something like committing suicide, only here, most of the time the suicide lasts but one night and you have a chance to return to life."

"How about grass?" I asked him.

"I'm not an expert on grass. I'd hate to get busted for grass; it seems so silly to get busted for so little. Grass is hardly that great. We all know that it is easier on the body and more often leads to a free and easy mellowness rather than violence. Drink tends to make asses of men more easily. Yet one's lawful and easy to buy and use; the other is not. Of course, the oddity is that they arrest you for being drunk. In a sense it's lawful to buy it but not to drink it. I've been in jail too much. And they make it rougher and rougher on the common drunk in Los Angeles. They used to just hold you overnight, then kick you out. Now there's jail. You arrive in court a couple of days later, sweating, wondering. You've got to face a judge. Everybody gets fined, at least. Sometimes you can get over 30 days or 60 days. You never know. I try to stay off the streets. It seems like every time you go out on the streets nowadays either the police get you or the citizens do. I mean the citizens roll you or beat you up. I stay in now. Lock all the doors. The bars are the worst places. The bartenders shortchange you. The whores look to roll you. The muggers look to mug you. Being drunk is a state wherein inferior men have a chance at you that they'd seldom otherwise get."

"Why do you continue to drink, then?"

"I don't know. They say alcoholism is a disease. I often feel like telling the judge when he sentences me, 'Your honor, medical authorities say that alcoholism is a disease. Would you fine or jail a man for having cancer?' Of course, if I did ask him this he'd throw the book at me. You and I know that courts have very little to do with justice."

"Are there any good sides at all to drinking?"

"Well, it breaks down the barriers to sexual intercourse on both sides. I've gotten a lot of sex through drinking that

I would not have otherwise gotten. Of course, the price is pretty high: you usually get rolled, especially here in Los Angeles. The Los Angeles ladies are the hardest in the world, a real iron-hearted and dollar-mad bunch."

"Anything else worthy in being an alcoholic?"

"Well, you usually don't have to live so long. Almost all my drinking buddies and my ladies are dead. The stuff is fairly destructive to the body. I have been in and out of hospitals all my life. But drink has allowed me to survive under conditions that are almost intolerable: rat-infested rooms, months of no income, no jobs. The pressure becomes almost unbearable. One could go mad thinking about his state of affairs. Yet if you are able to get hold of a bottle of wine, your worries decrease for a couple of hours."

"Was it because of drinking that you couldn't hold jobs or did being unemployed lead to drinking?"

"It works both ways. Who wants to work anyway? It's just a mutilation of your good hours."

"This wine is very strong."

"It's better chilled or with ice. Sorry, I don't have ice."

"That's all right."

"I guess the hangovers are the worst. You can get in a very depressive state lying in some bedbug bed two days behind in the rent and listening to the landlord's footsteps outside. There's hardly a chance in this land unless you have a definite trade. Being over 45 and not having a trade, you might as well be dead. A dishwasher's job is hardest to get. I used to show up at one of the big hotels downtown. About 50 of us showed up and they only took three or four. It was almost useless. Now they have dishwashing machines. All you need is the initial outlay and a little oil. I don't know what the rest of us are supposed to do. A lot of us can't do that bracero stuff. They ran the braceros off and what happened? They ran a lot of machinery in. Do I have a right to live or don't I have a right to live?"

"Some think you don't."

"I can't help getting scared sometimes. I can't help drinking myself sick. It's a very brutal and cruel situation. I thought maybe the Watts thing would open up doors for all of us but they only gave them a little sweettalk and wrote new manuals on how to break up riots."

"Are there any other jobs open to those at the end of the rope?"

"Yeah, there's a place you stand downtown and a truck comes and picks you up. They take you to a restaurant for a cup of coffee and a doughnut. Then they take you in this big room and everybody fights over the paper-carriers, those things you throw over your back. Then they take you back in the truck and dump you off at a corner with a little map. It's indicated where your papers are stacked. You walk around throwing these newspapers onto porches, newspapers filled with ads. When you're done you wait until the truck comes and picks you up. They take you back. The whole process takes about 12 hours. Then you wait until they call your name and then walk up and pick up the money. It's not very much. I think it was three dollars last time. I asked the guy, 'Don't you know the wage laws?' and he said, 'You're only paid on an estimate of your average actual working time. Also we deduct for transportation and food.' By food, he meant the coffee and doughnut. Most of them are glad to get the three dollars. You get four dollars for giving blood. Any other city in the country you get six dollars. Only in Los Angeles do you get four dollars. This is the coldest city in the world."

"I'm going to leave you with a couple of bucks for wine. And thanks for the talk. Have you ever heard of the *Los Angeles Free Press*?"

"No, I haven't."

"Well, our little talk might be in there."

"Will it do me any good?"

"No."

I put the money down and walked to the door.

"Are you a communist?"

"No."

"I don't want to appear in any communist newspaper! I still believe in America, this is my country. Things may get a little hard now and then but this is still my country!"

"Very noble," I told him, "although some people might consider you an asshole for a statement like that."

He lifted his wine glass and drained it.

"Ronald Reagan would love you," I said.

"OUT! GET OUT!"

I left him in there. My beloved patriot. I turned into the first bar for a scotch and water. "Hi, sweetie!" an old woman sitting at the bar smiled at me. I drank the scotch and got out.

L.A. Free Press, March 17, 1967

Notes of a Dirty Old Man

"Can't you keep those motherfuckers quiet?" he screams.

He gets up and knocks one of his kids for a loop.

Then she hits one of her kids.

They wear sweaters with each other's names on them. She had 4 kids. He has 3. He has just traded in his '67 Caddy for a '68.

"Read this," he says, "my new novel."

I sit there and begin reading.

He tells me, "We're going to knock out a back rear wall and make a large writing studio for me. It'll cost two thousand dollars to soundproof. I made 25 grand writing last year. How ya like the novel?"

"I've just begun."

"How do you like my new wife?"

"She looks good all right. You were always good with the ladies."

"But I still worry about Jeri."

"Why? You divorced her."

"Well, she's fucking this 22-year-old. I don't like it. I'm paying alimony, child support and every time I take the kids back there's this 22-year-old punk sitting on the couch."

"She's got to live too, Herm."

"But that 22-year-old kid's got no class. That's why I got the white Caddy, she sees me in the white Caddy, and she flips. She knows what she's missing."

"Maybe the kid's got a lot of string."

"Hey, that ain't funny! . . . How do ya like the novel?"

"Hard to read with all the noise."

"Hey, Toni, I TOLD you to keep those motherfuckers QUIET!"

"No," I said, "the noise: I mean us talking. . . ."

"Oh, yeah, well, anyhow, how are you doing?"

"Well, it's my hands, mostly."

"Yeah, hey, what ya doing with those gardener's gloves on?"

"Sores all over my hands. Can't type. Some kind of malady and madness. Then there's dizzy spells, insomnia, excessive fear, lack of sexual intercourse."

"Man, you're really fucked up! Hard to believe you were the one who wrote the foreword to my first book of poems!"

"Yes, isn't it?"

"How much did you make writing last year?"

"About the cost of stamps."

"How do you live?"

"In somebody's cellar."

"You're kidding. . . ."

"No, I'm not kidding. And I figure I'm very lucky."

"Well, O.K., but how do you like the novel?"

"Christ, what does it matter what I like as long as it sells?"

"Oh, it'll sell, all right, it'll sell! Hey, remember the old days when we used to drink together and you'd cuss me and I'd give you those karate shots over the eyes and across the neck? I could have killed you but I didn't."

"Thanks."

"Now I know all the big boys. I was on the Joe Pyne show a while back. I had coffee with Pyne before the show—I said, 'Listen, man, you mess with me and I'll rip you wide open!' He went easy on the show, did you see the show?"

"I don't have a TV."

"Oh, you're one of those Arty guys, eh? TV's too good for you?"

"I told you, I live in somebody's cellar."

"Man, I thought you were kidding!"

"No."

"Hell, you can stay here! You can help build my new studio! You can walk the dogs, drive the kids to school . . . no damn need to live in a cellar! I'll even pay you a bit! Why suffer?"

"I don't want to suffer."

"Then come live with us."

"I appreciate it, but let me think it over."

"Sure, sure, and I know I can trust you with Toni. I know you don't have a lot of string, and then too, you wrote the foreword to my first book of poems. And to think, I was just out of a madhouse then!"

"The poems were very good."

"And how about the novel? You been reading as we been talking. How do you like the novel?"

"I don't like it."

"It figures."

"Why?"

"Professional jealousy. Your eyes won't let your head see the greatness in the work. Professional jealousy."

"You might be right."

"I know damn well I'm right! You really don't like it?"

"Why do you keep asking me? I can't change my mind."

"Just like a cunt, eh? That's what you are, just like a cunt—can't change your mind!"

"I've got to go, Herm."

"You think a man's a bad writer because he makes money at it?"

"No, it works many ways. Tolstoy got bad when he gave up on money. Gorky stopped being an Artist when the revolution was won. A guy like Mailer just goes on and on in a kind of drizzling intermediate stream."

"And you live in a cellar and call my novels bad."

"Right."

"Get the hell out!"

"Going. Save the karate."

"Someday you'll know what it all means. Someday you'll know which of us was the writer!"

"I doubt it."

"Back to your damned basement!"

"Cellar."

"Back to your damned cellar!"

He slams the door behind me. Passion. The great ones always had passion. I always felt dead. Therefore, maybe I was. Too bad.

I pass his white Caddy and don't even spit upon it. I didn't even want it. I am 48 years old. He is 32. I walk away from his huge home. I walk toward my basement. I walk toward my cellar. Psychotic as my gardener's gloves.

National Underground Review, August 2–8, 1968

Bukowski's Gossip Column

Wonder if I could write a nice little gossip human column like the boys do?

Finally got my phone number today: BUKOWSKI. I had BUKOWSKI when I lived in Detroit and when I lived in Iowa. Dial BUKOWSKI and see what happens? Do you know what the Iowa State Flag is? See this column next week. . . .

My collection of UNKNOWN WRITERS OVER 45 will be out next week. You've never read anything like it . . . to officer Hanjob: Hanjob, you can take that traffic ticket and jam it up your cookie jar. Ticket #67834. Got it in your book there? Every time you guys see this beard on my face you go ape . . . lots of talk because Zigzag of the STOOPS finked on ape. What's wrong with a beard on the face/you guys don't seem to mind it someplace else. And skin pigment. Every time you guys see my wrinkled white skin, you go ape. Lots of talk because Zigzag of the STOOPS finked on his buddies on a Mary charge. The cops put him under the white light and he sang like he never sang before. He copped-out on Trenor, Asp, and Delirium Harry in that order. What's wrong with a guy copping out on his buddies? I think we are too hard on Zigzag. What's finking got to do with his music, his artistry? . . . At a Black Belt Karate tournament last Saturday I am sure I saw one of the Beatles mixing in with the crowd. He had on a boyscout uniform with green piping . . . Miracle Man Botello hung it out the window the other night and 8 full-grown women fainted. He lives on S. New Hampshire Street with an unlisted phone number. Weird cat. You go see him, he just sits in this broken overstuffed chair and leers out at you with slit-eyes and smiling . . . Woman saw me in the supermarket with my beard the other day. She spit on the floor and snarled, "oh you dirty, shit, why don't you wash your stockings?" Poor thing. I didn't have any stockings on . . . whatever happened to Tim Leary? I asked my girlfriend the other night, "whatever happened to Tim Leary?" and she started spitting hair and eggshells, "Oh SHUT UP! He's a great man, a wonderful man, a real man, a gorgeous man! All you little shits are always knocking his wondrous talents! What's wrong with him?" "Well," I said, "to begin with . . ." "Now, don't you say a goddamn word! If you didn't have that beard I'd leave you in a minute!" "All right, pass me that razor and a pack of Gillettes." . . . Russian horserace fix scandal. A former burglar nicknamed Intelligent and a furniture craftsman known as The Souse hanging around in a seedy café called The Contemporaries, fixing the races. They paid off and beat up the jocks, depending upon which way they went. One jock named Grechkin was so scared he guided his horse right off the track to make sure he didn't win. Intelligent and The Souse. For Christ's sake, can't they come up with better names than that? Hardly Hip at all, you know. And it's not just Russia. They tell me that in Europe that the best-known American writers are E.A. Poe and Jack London. I almost believe it . . . Dial Bukowski . . . "Listen," I ask my girlfriend, "why do these guys like Leary . . ." "There you GO again!" She starts throwing things. A real spitfire. Remember Lupe Velez? No, you're too young. "I mean," I said, "they wear these white bathrobes, with sashes, bathrobes that look like beachtowels . . ." "That's to center the SOUL, to let the SOUL breathe! Don't you understand, you ox? If you ever shave your beard, I'm leaving!" "You shave yours . . ." Pershing Square has not changed . . . I saw Tiny Tim buying bologna at the Invisible Market. God bless Tiny Tim . . . Saw an old Charlie Chaplin film the other night. As usual, it bored me. Made me seasick. It's like they weren't even trying. Very sloppy stuff. When we walked out of the theatre, my girlfriend said, "A great man. A wonderful man, a real man, a man, a gorgeous man, an artist!" "I'd like to see him in one of those beachtowel bathrobes." "There you GO again!" "Sorry dear, a bit jumpy, haven't had my 11 today." . . . I expect to be machinegunned, stepping out the front door by early July of this year. My column will be taken over by Matt Weinstock . . . Saw Tiny Tim at Barney's Beanery, eating sausage and eggs. God bless Tiny Tim . . . God might as well bless Maharishi and

John Thomas too . . . Steve Richmond—Earth Rose, Fuck-Hate Fame, and one Charles Bukowski have cut a record, Richmond reading his poetry on one side, Bukowski his poetry? On the other . . . will be released this week. See Earth Rose bookshop, Venice, one dollar. This beats buying an ad from Bryan . . . Jack Hirschman helping Bill Margolis edit new lit. mag. Send manus to Jack H 21 Quarter Deck, Venice . . . To the guy who wrote me about his brother dying and then finding all the Bukowski books and stuff at his place—this is straight—I lost your address somewhere, meant to respond to your letter but just can't find the thing. If you've been thinking me inhuman, I'm not. Entirely . . . To Milly Pavlick of N.Y.: I spent the dollar you sent me for soup on beer. Send more soup money . . . To King Arthur of N. Vine Street: no, I don't need any help writing this column, but will admit you sound more like a Dirty Old Man than I do. In fact, your whole wine-scrawled missile was nicely depraved. I admire you, but don't come around . . . To the doctor who showed up at my door a couple of times and offered to help me write my column, and wore those yellow-striped pants, and sent me all the little literary bits on slips of paper which fell to the floor from my hangover bed, you are also nicely depraved but not a very good writer, but keep subscribing to OPEN CITY. We need you. And I think that my hemorrhoids are coming back. God Bless Baron Manfred Von Richtofen. He did a good job . . . AT TERROR STREET AND AGONY WAY, poems, $4, Black Sparrow Press, p.o. box 25603, Los Angeles Calif. 90025. POEMS WRITTEN BEFORE LEAPING FROM AN 8 STORY WINDOW, $1, c/o Darrell and Litmus Press, 422 East Harvard, Glendale, Calif. Both books will be released early May, never mind the author. They released him last week . . . The Willie has hit the road again in a 1955 Cad. 2 jugs of stomach-murdering dago red 8 miles to the gallon. He left Rachel behind but I'm sure Rachel will not be lonely very long . . . People are always more clever than I am in conversation yet I always have this vague idea that they are not clever at all . . . God Bless Baron Manfred Von Richtofen's daughter who married D.H. Lawrence. That took a lot of guts . . . Extremism is a mind with but one eye but it often gets things done . . . I swear, I think the mini-skirts are getting shorter and I don't know what the next step can be, but whatever it is, I'm for it . . . Listen officer Hanjob, take that ticket and . . . Which reminds me, a friend of mine said he was stopped by a cop and given a ticket and the cop was so nice about it that my friend thanked him for the ticket. It's true. Some of those boys can really grease it in. But actually, I prefer the mid-thirties (you're too young) when a cop would stop you for speeding and come up ready to fight, strolling up, really *angry* saying, "Hey fucker! Where's the fire!" At least you knew who your enemy was still do but you know what I mean. Maybe I *do* need help writing this thing. SIT DOWN, King Arthur . . .

I once cleaned crappers for Chandler's TIMES at night. NOW look at me. Tomorrow the WORLD! Got fired for sleeping in the ladies' crapper. The L.A. TIMES simply doesn't appreciate talent . . .

Do you get uptight when you ask for cigarette papers? Tell them they are paper bandaids for the asshole of a cardboard bee you've designed for the state fair . . . There *is* something *very* discouraging about Bobby Kennedy but we don't want to admit it, not yet, right after old dull whipboy Johnson; but lord, lord, when's a man going to come along??? . . . This country, right now, on the point of revolution, can go any way, can go fascist, can go communist, socialist, can remain within the democratic mold with changes. But the whole thing reminds me of a headless horse running down a midnight street. And it's sad. For I live here and I want to see it go well . . . And let that be the end of this type of column for I have winded up with the deep deep blues. It's best to create the mold directly from life and let the others talk about it. Amen, men . . .

Open City, April 19–30, 1968

More Notes of a Dirty Old Man

You may not believe it but there's nothing as dull as tits and haunches and buttocks when you've seen enough of them and have seen them continually. Furthermore, there's nothing as sexless as a bathing suit: sand spread across the crotch, wrinkles under the butt, wrinkles above and below the hips, and also, here and there—warts, moles, and all the twitchy little infirmities the human body gathers. Look at that single long hair growing under her chin. Doesn't she see that? What's that blotch? And worse than a bathing beauty is a nude. If man has any imagination, he can forget it now. Look at her—whipped cream and pork rinds, soft balloons, and the sexual machinery in the center, almost a threat.

Sometimes, since I often write for the sex mags, I enter a mag store which deals exclusively with periodicals of that content. Since I create quite a realistic story I have to check the mags for their editorial courage. Here in Hollywood there are quite a few of these sex mag dungeons. So when was it? Saturday? Anyhow, I walk into one of these stores and I am stopped by a man who stands high in a pulpit-like structure.

"Psst!" he says, "Sir! Sir! Stop!"

"What's the matter?" I ask.

"It costs 50 cents to go in there," he tells me.

"But I don't want to buy a magazine," I say.

"That's just it. You gentlemen just come in here and look at the pictures. We have to protect ourselves. The 50 cents can be applied to the purchase of any magazine. We give you this returnable token."

I give him the 50 cents and he gives me the token. I am allowed to walk in.

The place is quite filled with men. The owner is the grand priest and the place does have the feeling of a temple. The men hardly move. They stand very quietly, turning pages. Some of the magazines feature men on the covers. On one, a photo of a penis, a diseased-looking and curved thing, pokes through some torn shorts. What the hell is this? I think. I walk around and don't know what to do. There is a glass case full of rubber penises. I look at them and walk on. Then, to give a façade of one belonging, I pick up a girly mag and finger through. The first photo I see puts me headlong into a gaping vagina. Has this been the object of so many of my pleasures? May the gods have mercy!

To resurrect myself, I pick up a more standard sex mag. Here she was on the cover—some lass with an I.Q. of 69 trying to leer back while seeming passionate. The faces of these cover dollies! Pancakes. A layer of skin with proper nose-size, proper lip-size, proper eye-size, proper ear-size, proper chin-size. That many men go to hell for these darlings is not my fault. I do suppose the photographers must realize that they are wasting flashbulbs upon female morons. But the editors, who write the copy under these photos, always attempt to invest these things with both intelligence and understanding. Soul, if you'll buy it.

Now, here's a shot of Lila. This time, just her head. She's pensive. She's so damned pensive that she's thrown her delicious head down into some green brush. That's getting there, think of it. But the eyebrows are plucked and the mascara is still there, even down in the green brush. All right, Lila, get up. That one's over. Now you see her leaning on a fence. She talks to animals. Mother Nature is her mother. Look at her in that Indian headdress! Jesus Christ. O, Lila, I'd like to have you in that Indian headdress! But what's that blotch on her back? How'd they let that get in there?

Now, here's Tanya. She loves water. First photo you see, there's water spilling all over her big tits. Wow. The next photo doesn't make much sense at all. Her butt is spread over a frog pond. She seems to be screaming. Constipated? Now she's standing behind a highly polished table. There are candles everywhere. Her tits hang down. She looks at you. What the hell? You think. What am I supposed to do? I'm told that she cries a lot for no seeming reason. Then one day she walks along under this raining sky and the sky opens a big hole right to the heavens and she gets the answer. She comes to California with her big tits and tail. She studies the dance. She's learned the discipline of Hatha Yoga. She's read Ayn Rand, the novelist. Tanya states: "The earth is in trouble." Profound.

And here's Clara. She hides behind rocks. Swims with the fishes. More of the water thing. Water's the thing, I guess. Keeps the body from stinking. Anyhow, she's a river-mermaid. She's an enchantress. She has large breasts also. The deeps of the river flash in her eyes, I'm told. Also, she gives her love to the lonely men who swim up the river at night. Too bad. Lonely men don't swim up rivers at night. They get drunk or kill themselves or go to a movie.

Here's Deedee. Deedee somehow came across a volume of and/or on Buddhism and came to Hollywood. Deedee wants to go back to nature. She's an expert on wild plants and herbs. She also has big tits. She likes the "Jefferson Airplane" but she also enjoys chewing birch bark. Her buttocks look fairly nice.

I have done my duty. I place the mag back in the rack. I am the last to arrive and now I am the first to leave. I walk toward the Hollywood night and the dark smoggy air. I am almost to the entrance.

"Hey, buddy!"

"Yes?"

"Aren't you gonna cash in on your token?"

"No."

"Why?"

"I don't know."

Immediately I see the fear and respect in his eyes. He thinks I am the heat.

I take out a pack of smokes, light one.

"Don't worry, I'll be back."

He stiffens and doesn't answer.

I walk to the parking lot, get into my car, and start the engine. As I do, I imagine one of the photo cover girls telling her shackjob:

"*Ladybug Magazine* was by today. They wanted to snap my snatch. I told them it would be a hundred bucks extra."

"Atta baby!" says the shackjob. They lean back and watch TV.

I drive on out, and as I take a left down Hollywood Blvd., I toss the 50-cent token out the window. The night takes it, and I am free.

Candid Press, November 29, 1970

More Notes of a Dirty Old Man

I was put in touch with them by somebody who had heard me at a poetry reading and so there I was driving around that part of Hollywood looking for a parking place, and it was hot. I was sweating, and I finally gave up and just drove four or five blocks off, parked and walked back. The walk wasn't bad because I was following this girl in the mini and she wiggled it at me, and I could have passed her but I didn't have the strength. She was good for three blocks, then turned into an apartment house. I walked the other block or so, uninspired. I walked up to the guard's gate. The old woman who ran the switchboard doubled as guard.

"Yeah?" she asked.

"My name's Bukowski. I have an appointment with Graf Productions at 3:30."

"Go on back to 172. Follow the numbers."

"Thank you."

The man, somebody named Eddie, had told me on the phone that I was to be considered as a narrator for a stag film. Since I made my living by the typewriter—a literary hustler—I was always in the mood for various considerations—anything but the eight-hour day and good honest labor. I was hungover (a more or less normal state) and I followed the numbers down. It was a long wooden porch, rotting, with offices or studios every 10 or 12 feet. Everything had been painted a chickencoop white—a long time ago. Since it was very hot, the doors were open and I could hear conversations:

"Now, look, Max, we've got to cut this thing down. There's too much overlap. Now take the central part. . . ."

At the next door:

"Well, hell, I don't know what to do. Do you think we can get away with it?"

Film hustlers, hanging to a shoestring, trying to break through.

I found 172. The door was open. I walked in. There was

a desk. On the desk I saw my paperback book of short stories, *Notes of A Dirty Old Man*. I was known. Fine. But that paperback had had one printing of 26,000 copies for which I had gotten a grand in front and the grand was long ago gone. A man had to keep writing and hustling right to the edge of the grave. It was a dirty game.

I whistled. Then hollered. "HEY, HEY, ANYBODY HERE? HELLO, HELLO!"

"In here," came the sound.

I walked into the other room. There was a pleasant and calm-looking young man behind a typewriter.

"Bukowski?"

"Yeh."

"Sit down."

"Where's the beer?" I asked.

"Beer?"

"The other guy, Eddie, said there'd be beer."

"Eddie!"

Eddie walked in. He was young too, dark-haired, the stuff hanging down, and a bit of a beard. He walked very stooped with his hands dangling in front.

"Bukowski," he said, "remember me?"

"Not from recent times."

"You were drunk. It was at this party."

"Okay, where's the beer?"

Eddie walked out and came back with a six-pack. He put it in front of me. I went to work.

The other guy explained to me what they wanted to do with the stag film. What the idea was, what the narrator was to do. It sounded like hard work. But so did standing around on skid row sound like hard work. I got around to the second beer. The sound would be dubbed in after the shooting of the film.

"We want to audition you. Turn on the tape, Eddie."

Eddie turned on the tape. Then he handed me an ad from one of the large weekly magazines. About how easy it was to make it by air and do the thing. Skiing on Mt. Zebralla is $337. Watching Elizabeth Taylor dip into the Spanish Castle River is $443. On and on. I had seen the type of ad before. They were written by subnormal boys who had flunked out of Harvard Law School and whose fathers owned ad agencies. I tried to read it, but I couldn't read it straight. The clever-flip slant was all too dull. I changed prices, names, words, cities as I went along. I cussed and laughed, gagged. They laughed too. But I knew I had flunked their audition.

"You need an actor," I said, "somebody without imagination, somebody with a healthy stomach."

"Wait now, the directors will want to hear this. We don't know."

"The directors?"

"Yes, we just write the script, shoot the film. We work for them."

"All right," I said.

"How about a walk-on part?"

"Wait a minute, let's go easy. I have a literary reputation."

Then they both laughed.

Just then two girls walked in with a guy with a beret on. The girls were laughing all the time.

"Come on," said Eddie, "we're going to shoot."

The girls looked good but they kept laughing. The guy with the beret didn't laugh at all.

We went into the other room, and they turned on the equipment. Eddie, myself, and the guy who wasn't Eddie sat behind the camera. Eddie worked the camera.

It opened with the guy in the beret wearing a smock and painting on canvas. There seemed to be much film wasted of just him painting. While he painted he sucked from a wine bottle. Then he stopped painting and just sat in a chair drinking from the wine bottle. Soon it was empty and he passed out.

The door opened and two girls ran in laughing. One of them looked at the empty wine bottle and laughed. Then the other reached down and pulled out the guy's penis and stroked it. The other girl began painting the penis on canvas. It was a large penis, on canvas and off. Then the painter awakened. He ran to the canvas and looked at it and seemed very angry. I couldn't understand why. Soon the girls were taking their clothes off (still laughing) and the painter was taking his clothes off too.

It's really silly, I thought.

Then they ran around assuming various positions, holding them for a while, then breaking off and assuming other positions. I was surprised how many positions one man and two women could assume. Some of them were simply ridiculous, and some of them were accidental, and some of them did have a bit of charm. Very much charm. How they went on! It must have gone on for 25 minutes. What a man he was. Suddenly the girls grabbed up their clothing and, still laughing, ran from the room. He leaped up, and as they ran off, gave himself a few last good strokes. Then it was over.

We walked into the other room. The girls came out, still laughing, only now they were dressed in their regular street clothes, minis and tight sweaters.

I got up and walked across to the one in the blue mini. I put my hand on her knee. The nylon was tight and hot. She kept laughing. I ran my hand up her leg. She laughed some more. I began to really heat up. I put my other hand on her other leg. I had both hands up near her ass, breathing heavily. Not my hands, me. She kept laughing. Suddenly she stopped laughing. She pushed me off.

"Hey, what's wrong with this guy? Is he a cube?"

Perhaps. . . .

The paper was thin. There seemed to be some writing on the back. I turned the paper over.

It said: $150.

I ripped the paper up, threw the bits on the grass, and got into my car, started it and began to drive toward my place.

I stopped at a signal at Melrose and Western.

Then I laughed.

Candid Press, December 13, 1970

More Notes of a Dirty Old Man

I swung three deep out of Vacantsville, like busting out of a herd of cow, and next thing I knew we had set down, the bird burst its stupid stewardesses, and I was the last man out, to meet a teacher-student in a shag of yellow and he said, you, Bukowski, and there was something about his car needing oil all along the way, 200 miles plus, and then I was standing in front of the students, drunk, and they all sat at little round tables, and I thought, shit, this is like any place else, and I hooked from the bottle and began on the poems, and I told them that I had death coming and that they had death coming but they didn't quite believe me, and I drank some more and I read them poems from way back and poems from recent and then I made one up, and it was dark in there, and I thought, this is lousy, I am reading at a university and I am getting away with everything, not because I am good but because nobody else is and there isn't anybody to correct me: wish Ezra were here or Confucius or somebody anybody to keep me in line—but there wasn't, so I read them my swill and they swallowed it, and then I grew weary and I said, let's take five.

Then I got down from the stage and walked over to one of the tables with my bottle. Some crazy-looking guy picked up my bottle and drank from it. I told him, take it easy, mother, I have 30 more minutes to go.

He picked up the bottle to hit it again. I ripped it out of his hand.

I told you, mother, the rest is mine.

They told me later that he was crazy, everybody was afraid of him, he was always on acid but hung around the university even though they had kicked him out.

That showed his weakness.

I took the bottle from him and climbed back on stage.

The second half was better than the first. They gave me good applause, even the crazy one.

Then I got on out. Almost. The teacher who'd brought me in knew a prof and the prof was at the reading, and the next thing I was at a party at the prof's house. Sell-out Bukowski. The guy who hated profs drinking with them.

I'd signed a contract to read at another college 150 or 200 miles away. Anyhow, I was a literary hustler and I was stuck with it. I stood around at the party because my ride was there, the young guy with the shag of yellow hair, the nice guy, and to help myself along I drank myself into a standing stupidity. I had a reading at this other place at 11:30 a.m. in the morning but you wouldn't have known it looking at me, peeling off tens and twenties: "Hey, man, go down to the liquor store and stock up for these good people. Looks like we're running short."

My host was an English teacher who looked just like Ernest Hemingway. Of course, he wasn't. But I was drunk.

"Ernie," I staggered up to him, "I'll be a son of a bitch in hell! I thought you blew your head off!"

My Hemingway was a staid and rather dull member of the English department.

He just stood there talking about poets and poetry. He was insane. I walked over to the couch and started necking with his wife. She didn't resist. He just stood there over us, talking about poets and poetry. I stuck my tongue deep into her mouth, mauled her breasts.

"T.S. Eliot," he said, "was entirely too safe."

I ran my hand up under her dress.

"Auden had no lasting power."

She stuck her tongue deep into my mouth.

The party went on and on, but for it all, I awakened in bed alone. I was in an upper bedroom, hungover and sick. I turned over to go back to sleep.

"Bukowski! Wake up!" somebody said.

"Go away," I said.

"We've got to make that 11:30 a.m. reading. It'll take us 2 or 3 hours."

"What time is it now?"

"8:30."

"God o mighty!"

I turned over and climbed out of bed. It was my nice guy with the flax of yellow. I dressed as best I could and followed him down the steps. The prof and his wife were down there.

"Want breakfast, Bukowski?"

"Please, no."

The prof started in on literature again. He was really crazy.

"Look," his wife said to him, "why don't you shut up a while?"

"Look, we've got to go," I said, "thanks for putting me up."

The prof and flax walked out the front door. The prof's wife walked up to me. We embraced. She really gave herself over. That kiss was better than many lays I had had. I walked out, got into the car. And then we were moving, out in the country again, the green trees, the lakes. The kid had a pint of scotch. And a thermos bottle to drink it out of. The next place, he told me was a little more conservative.

It was a goodly crowd and these hot lights were on. I was told I was to be put on videotape. I was too sick to care. I started reading. I read a while, then decided I'd better dare the scotch again. I tried it. It stayed down. The reading improved.

I tried some more. The reading improved some more. I took the five, came back, and finished them.

The kid and I walked back across campus.

"They'll mail you your check," he said.

"That's okay," I said. It was all over. Two readings. I'd picked up $375 in a night and a day.

We got back into the car. There were three or four hours before plane time, so we drove to his place out under the trees. His buddy followed us in his car. No women. Well.

We got there and drank beer all afternoon. Luckily they were easy fellows to like. They stayed away from literature and we talked about women and about survival. It was an easy afternoon and then we made the airport. I checked into the next flight and we sat at a table in the bar, and I bought the drinks. I'd made the money and felt obligated, besides, Flax had driven me all over the state, arranged the readings, propped me in front of the TV.

I kept imagining I heard my name over the intercom:

"C. Bukowski, C. Bukowski, please report . . ."

"Man," I said, "I must be going crazy. I keep hearing my name."

They laughed. Then we got up to go to the plane. It was just rolling down the runway.

I walked back to the ticket office, told them what had happened, and they put me on the next flight. We went back into the bar.

"I'd better make the next one," I said, "this can go on for years."

Well, I made it. We were in the air, and I was waiting on that first drink. They were quite slow about it. I looked in my flight bag. There were three or four warm bottles of beer in there. I opened one. The stewardess saw me.

"Sir," she said, "that's not allowed. We can put you off, you know."

The pilot had just announced that we were at 35,000 feet.

"You better give me that bottle," she said.

I gave her my bottle. I was a bad boy. Everybody stared at me. I felt like a killer or a child rapist.

Then they brought their bar around. THAT was okay. I had my scotch on rocks and looked out the window. Nothing out there. It was over: I was no longer the poet conning the crowd, I was just another lousy passenger going somewhere.

The cabby didn't know the town. Very few of them did. They couldn't even drive. The worst drivers in the world are the L.A. cab drivers. He made it on in without killing us so I gave him a good tip and there I was standing outside my beaten court, a couple more poetry readings behind me. Ski bum. One-nighter. Strictly vaudeville.

Candid Press, December 20, 1970

Notes of a Dirty Old Man

(Note: There is no intent to hurt or malign living persons with this story. I am sincere when I say this. There is enough hurt now. I doubt that anything happened as happened in this story. The author was only caught in the inventiveness of his own mind. If this is a sin, then all creators of all times have sinned. . . . c.b.)

Tony Kinnard was a great poet of the '50s. Well, maybe he wasn't great but he was interesting. He carried this halo of action with him; things seemed to be always going on around Tony. He was one of the first to read poetry with jazz. And he was strong, he was a man. Some of his poetry was soft but Tony was a man. One of the strongest men in America. I mean, physically. He assumed a kind of immortality while still alive, rather the type that is attached to Allen Ginsberg. Well, Tony was going along all right until one day he made the big mistake, as all strong men make that big mistake.

It was a pretty girl. She had jacked her car up and managed to change the flat tire all by herself but the jack was stuck and wouldn't go down. Bumper jacks have this habit of sticking. All you do is take off the brake and drive your car off the jack. It's simple. But Tony Kinnard was the strong man. And the girl was pretty. Tony told her he'd lift the car off the jack and all she had to do was pull the jack out.

"Really?" she asked, thinking, my god, what wouldn't it be to get fucked by a man that strong?

Tony backed to the bumper and lifted. The car rose. The girl took the jack out. Tony put the car back down. But he was frozen. He couldn't straighten his back up. The girl called an ambulance. They took Tony off. He hadn't even gotten the girl's phone number.

The troubles began at the hospital. The food wasn't right. The service was indecent. The doctors were hammerhead sharks. Well, anybody knows that doctors are hammerhead sharks. But Tony thought he had found out something new. Tony began fighting with the doctors and the nurses. After all, Tony was a poet and poets know things by instinct. He kept demanding new doctors. He changed hospitals. He was going to expose the whole medical profession. Somehow on the way to the x-ray room, being carried by two male nurses from the roller to the machine, they managed to drop Tony on his . . . back. You could hear him from Monterey to New Orleans. Tony entered a lawsuit for damages. They put him back in his bedroom. The medics wouldn't touch him. He lay there smoking pack after pack of Lucky Strikes and feeling bad.

At first Tony saw visitors and talked about his case. He had a nice wife, Clara, and they and his friends planned strategies. Benefits were set up and the money went to Tony. People would ring the doorbell and slip envelopes under the door. Envelopes full of money. Then, slowly, it seemed that Tony wasn't always in, or he was asleep or under sedative. Clara would answer the door . . . "I'm sorry, Tony can't be disturbed right now. . . ." The benefits kept coming but nobody saw Tony any more. Clara answered all the mail . . . "Tony and I are very grateful for your help. . . ." Tony stopped writing poems.

The shades went down and nobody answered the door or the phone. Clara responded to the mail.

It was some weeks later that Clara came in with the soup. Tony was dead. He was propped up against the pillows, and dead. Clara couldn't believe it. She refused to believe it. She had just spoken to him a moment ago. She opened his mouth and fed him the soup. Much of the soup wouldn't go in but she did the best she could.

"Now, Tony, stop it. Eat your soup."

There was roast beef for dinner. The roast beef was worse. Tony had seemed to have lost his appetite.

The days went on. Tony began to stink. Clara sprayed the air and bathed Tony. The process heightened. Chunks of flesh began to fall off. Clara flushed them down the toilet. Soon just the skeleton remained. Tony Kinnard had stopped writing poetry. Clara fed him soup, kissed him, and sang to him at night. Tony was silent.

The benefits went on. Money still arrived under the door. But the shades stayed down, the phone was not answered. The situation remained as was until one day Clara went to sleep on the couch while smoking a cigarette. The flames and smoke rose and somebody called the fire dept. The firemen broke down the door and put the couch out. Then one of the dudes had to use the bathroom to take a piss and as he walked by the bedroom the door was open. He never pissed. He saw Tony sitting up in bed there. The fireman walked out to the chief who was flirting with a 16-year-old girl outside.

"Chief," he said.

"Later, Henderson. . . ."

"Chief, I've got to tell you something."

"Listen, Henderson. . . ."

"There's a skeleton sitting up in bed in that house."

"What?"

"Yes. Just what I said."

The chief walked in. He went to the bedroom. There it was.

"Mrs. Kinnard."

"Yes?"

"What's this?"

"That's my husband."

"I see. . . ."

The chief dialed the police department. . . .

When Tony Kinnard was good he was very good. Much of his stuff was just a bit on the sweet side but when he hit it right he was on it. Like any other sensible man he seemed to ask for a better world. He didn't get it. We didn't either. I think it's time a large publisher put together a definitive collection of his work. After all, I sent some money up there myself. Mrs. Kinnard can be reached by THE FUND TO RELEASE MRS. KINNARD AND POETRY, box 2352 . . . Tony was given a burial by his friends. Almost all the great poets of the land were there. I couldn't make it. Somehow I kept wondering about the girl Tony lifted the car for. Think of the influence this girl had on world literature. And she's probably screwing some dumb-ass dude as I write this now. Well, the world has never been too happy a place, has it? My sympathies are with Tony Kinnard and Clara Kinnard, and with poetry. . . . Which of us will be next?

Nola Express 96, 1971

Notes of a Dirty Old Man

They'd been married 32 years, June and Clyde, and I guess of all the marriages I saw, they made it best. Close, that's what they were. Close, and I guess June cared more than Clyde, but they both cared and it lasted.

June was the extrovert. Clyde was the introvert, nobody much liked Clyde except June. In fact, they said, Clyde doesn't deserve June. I thought they deserved each other.

They battled, but in 32 years they only had one bad split . . . for a week. That's rather damned good. I think I fought with Clyde more than June did.

Clyde was the editor of the little magazine *Dustbird*, and he printed books, he printed a couple of mine, poetry; he had his own press and he did fine work, and lay around drinking beer and keeping them awake all night. They seemed to keep inviting me to whatever place and whatever city they were in, though, and I'd land and drink beer and flop around and start trouble . . . New Orleans, Tucson, Santa Fe, Las Vegas, there I'd be in their place, laying around and drinking their beer and arguing with them, and bringing dirty women in from the streets.

Listen, I got to know them. But this is not a story about me, it's a story about them, so let's go.

Close. He worked the press and she set the type and did the unglamorous work. They printed my poems on paper that was supposed to last 2,000 years. I told them that the paper was much better than the poetry but since they didn't pay me royalties I was going to eat all their food and stay drunk on beer and live in their goddamned place. "All right, all right," said Clyde, "only don't forget to sign those 3,000 pages in silver ink and make your nice little drawings . . ."

"Goddamn you, Clyde," I said, "you're living off my life blood. I'm outta beer. Gimme more money for beer . . ."

"All right, but only one more six-pack tonight . . ."

"Two six-packs or I don't sign any pages tonight . . ."

"You're a real rat, Bukowski. I don't understand how you can act like you do and still write like you do . . ."

"Come on, bloodsucker, I need two six-packs . . ."

Close. That's what they were.

"All right," Clyde said, "all right! Here's your god-damned beer money!"

Thirty-two years. And then Clyde got sick. We were in a southern town but they had a large hospital and I took some Alka-Seltzers and followed with a warm beer and drove Clyde in. June was worried. It was something about the neck. I don't know exactly what. One thing on one side of the neck was gone and now they had to operate on the other side, try to fix it.

It was to be a minor operation. June insisted on staying at the hospital. She was like a mad woman. She lay on the floor by Clyde's bed and they finally gave her a little mat to sleep on. I went on back to the place and looked for money for beer. I found some and drank up. I decided to help Clyde get rid of some of his piled up manuscripts. I drank beer and read and rejected them all and signed Clyde's name.

"You son of a bitch, you write poetry like riding a horse backwards. Give it up . . ."

"Dear sir: You'd make a better beet-picker in a hail storm. As a writer you succinctly stink of goat-shit. Give it up . . ."

"Madam: You might be a good lay (thanks for the nude photo) but I ain't gonna print this 9th-rate crap in order to get into your goddamned panties. I have some advice for you: give it up, and I don't mean copulating . . ."

I didn't sign any pages with my silver pen that night.

The next day I went to the hospital. I found they were going to operate on the following day. June was disturbed. About everything. "The potatoes had lumps in them . . . The ice water was warm . . . There weren't enough rest-rooms and there weren't enough doctors or nurses, and they didn't know what was wrong with Clyde, they didn't know what the hell they were doing, and here was some more money for beer, yeah, shut up, you signin' them pages? . . . They jam those tubes up Clyde's nostrils, how the hell's a man supposed to eat with those tubes up his nose. It's like trying to screw with a hose jammed up your ass . . ."

"I don't know," I said, "that might feel pretty good, especially if you turn the water on a bit."

"Look, I got a sick husband. I don't want no wise talk out of no half-ass poet . . ."

"Gimme the beer money and I'll lay off . . ."

"My god, and Clyde thinks you're better than Rimbaud."

"I am. Rimbaud sucked shit through his ears . . ."

"Here's the money . . . now go away . . . my husband's sick . . ."

"Give me a quarter for cigars . . ."

"All right! Here's your cigars! My god, you're as bad as these doctors!"

"Nobody can be as bad as these doctors . . ."

Well, something went wrong with the operation. The doctor told me that everything was all right, and then BINGO! Something seemed to go wrong. That's the way he described it.

Clyde went into a coma. One day, two days, three days . . . June stayed there, she slept on the mat, she prayed, she talked to Clyde.

"Clyde, honey, speak to me . . . Clyde, honey, I love you. Talk to me. Open your eyes, open those baby blue eyes . . ."

"June . . . June, " I said, "listen . . ."

"What do you want, you bastard?"

"Beer."

"My husband's dying and you want beer?"

"Yes, June."

"All right . . . *Here!* Beer money for you! Now go away, bastard vulture!"

"June, I'm washing the dishes, signing the pages in silver ink, I took out the garbage, I . . ."

"Just go away, please . . ."

The coma went into the 4th day, then the 5th. June stayed there, slept on the mat. "I'm praying for a miracle," she said.

"I am too," said the doctor. "I'm praying for a miracle. I'm praying that he dies . . ."

"You son of a bitch! You mean you're praying that he is going to die? What the hell kind of a doctor are you?"

"My dear, it he lives, he'll only have a part of his brain and he'll be partly paralyzed, he'll be like a baby . . ."

"So what the hell, I'll take care of him! You stop praying that he will die!"

I managed to get June out of that room and we took a walk around the grounds, sat on a bench in the shade. There was grass and quietness and you couldn't see the sick and the dying. Dying was such a struggle, such an inconvenience and it was expensive. The poor couldn't afford to die, that's why the poor lived longer.

When we got back the doctor was at the door to the room.

"He's gone," he told June, "he just passed this moment . . ."

"Lemme see!"

"Please *now*!"

June ran in. We followed.

"You pulled all the tubes outta him, no wonder he died! What'd you pull all the tubes out of him for?"

"Madam . . ."

"You let him die . . ."

"Please . . . ."

"What do I care if he was gonna be a baby? I like babies, he was my baby for 32 years, you let him die, you scum shit . . ."

"Please, madam . . ."

"I want his teeth . . ."

"Yes, what good are his teeth gonna do you? I can't let you have his teeth . . ."

"He was *my* husband . . . Listen, he's willed his body to the university for research . . . what the hell good are his teeth gonna do them? It's just his uppers . . . I want his uppers . . . see they're in that glass there . . ."

"I can't let you have them . . ."

"Like hell!"

June reached into the glass and then dropped the teeth into her purse.

"You just *try* to get my husband's teeth away from me, I'll kill you!"

"All right, madam, the teeth are yours . . ."

I sat drinking beer and June went over it.

"They let him die. They pulled those tubes out . . . those scum . . ."

"June, the dead are dead, there's nothing we can do about it. Let's go to bed . . ."

"Go to bed?"

"Yes, let's hit the sack, let's make it . . ."

"Make what?"

"I mean, let's forget, what the hell . . ."

"Listen, I knew Clyde for 32 years . . ."

"Clyde can't help you now . . ."

"His body's still warm, you bastard . . ."

"Mine's hot . . ."

"Stop it . . . ."

"Listen, June, you've still got it . . . after 32 years . . . and I've always been fond of you . . ."

"Let go of me . . . you're so disrespectful . . . let go!"

"Just a little kiss, baby . . ."

"I love Clyde . . ."

"You *loved* Clyde . . . He can't get it up now, baby . . ."

"Oh, you fiend . . . you stink . . . words can't describe you . . ."

"Try . . ."

"No, no, just stay away . . ."

A couple of days later June got to worrying about the body, what were they doing with the body? Exactly where was the body? Could we trust them? She wanted to see the body . . . she wanted to see it . . .

"Sometimes I get to thinking he ain't even dead."

I got on the phone. I phoned here and there. I located the body. We set up an appointment with the body. Then I hung up.

"They said you wouldn't be interested. They said it's just something in a plastic bag."

"Can I see it?"

"I've set up an appointment. Bring identification . . ."

Well, we got past the man at the desk and we went in to see Clyde. He was in a little round vault with a black plaque engraved with white letters over the opening. It hung from a gold chain that was screwed into the vault. June got out her fingernail file and tried to turn the screw.

"What are you doing? You can't get in that way . . . ."

"I know. I want this plaque . . ."

"You're crazy . . ."

"It's my husband . . ."

"It *was* . . . now he belongs to the university . . . they're going to chop him up like a frog . . . students will put his penis under their beds, they'll gouge his eyes out . . . chop off his balls . . . cut out his heart . . . slice his lungs . . . he'll be a eunuch, he'll be beefstew, garbage . . ."

"All for the good of Humanity . . ."

"Humanity? That gang? Piss on them . . ."

"Anyway, I want this plaque . . ."

I didn't think she could do it with the end of her nail-file but she did, she worked the screw out and dropped the nameplate in her purse. Then she tried to open the vault.

"Goddamn! Look at the size of that lock on there!"

They had a huge padlock on a chain that held the vault door closed. However, when you pulled at the door it did open about an inch and a half. June pulled at the door.

"Pew! It stinks!"

"Yes, he does . . ."

"Maybe I can work my hand into there . . ."

"June, let's go . . ."

"Look, I've got my hand in there . . . I can touch him . . ."

"Wonderful! Will you let me touch him?"

"No, he's my husband!"

"Come on, let me touch him!"

"No, I won't allow it, nothing doing . . ."

She touched him awhile and then we walked out . . .

I packed that night for the drive back to Los Angeles. June had stopped giving me beer money and she remained faithful to Clyde. She was a good woman. I tried to kiss her again that night but she fought me off . . .

"I'm the greatest poet since Rimbaud," I told her.

"You're shit," she said.

"All right," I said. I picked up my suitcase and walked to the door. There she sat next to those false teeth in the glass, those uppers. I'd watched her brush them. And outside the glass, sitting in front of the glass was the plaque—Name, Date of Birth, Date of Death, Donated to the University of . . .

Thirty-two years are hard to give up. Close, that's what they had been. Most marriages don't work. This had been the marriage of marriages, and all for the good of poetry too, most of it mine. I closed the door and got into the car and drove off. Well, he'd been a good editor, he'd discovered a great poet. That made a full lifetime for any man. It was nighttime. I turned on the car lights, turned on the radio and lit a cigar. A thousand women wanted to screw me but June had said no. Life was sad, death was sad. June and Clyde. And on the long trip to Los Angeles I decided that I would honor them both by writing about them.

epilogue:

I was recently paid a visit by Clyde's son. We had some beer and he told me that June returned to the University some months later and demanded the bones and the skull. She was very insistent. The University gave her the bones but kept the skull. I think that's fair.

L.A. Free Press, April 14, 1972

Notes of a Dirty Old Man

We walked in and our reservation was a nice table over the water and I sat down with her and there were six at the other table and they were all talking at once.

"They've come to see the STONES too," she told me.

The hostess came up. "Look," I said, "can't we get a table to ourselves, I mean, alone? I really don't need the ocean this bad."

"Surely, sir."

Suddenly there was silence at the other table. One of the men at the table made a polite remark about what a son of a bitch I was. The hostess seated us at a table further in the back, but elevated. The ocean was still there.

We had drinks and the lobster dinner. Unlike the people, the lobster dinner was perfect. But we hadn't paid for the people. We finished, got out of there, got in her car and drove toward the ROLLING STONES. . . .

Walking from the parking lot to the auditorium I realized that in order to get the performance down right there were several things I would have to realize. First, that rock had to have its values. It stimulated many people and what stimulated many people could also stimulate me. Just because I preferred classical music needn't make me a classical snob. Areas change, people change. I liked some rock, now and then. I disliked some classical music, now and then. It wasn't the form, then, it was the manner of doing.

Now there was also something else. Seeing a personality or a world-renowned group could make you accept things as holy and/or arty-worthy, whereas with a less advertised group it might even bore you. Then you have the reverse. Take anybody who has made it up to the top. There is always this group of untalented people who affect artistry and who say, "That's shit, that's shit! I can do better than that!" When, of course, they can't and never will.

To be a good critic is difficult. It would seem to me that it is far more difficult to be a good critic than a good artist
. . .

So I walked in with her and we had seats 10 rows from the stage, that's all right, you know, and there I was the oldest person in the building, hahaha, ha. There were little trebles of excitement winging through the air. I tried to grab some of them. I missed.

Four guys in front of us were smoking a joint. There were some attempts at seat-stealing. But it seemed so futile. Every seat was sold. It was the ROLLING STONES.

There was music over the intercom. People had waved at her as we had come in to sit down. Now she had to get up and go a few rows down and talk to some people.

Hell, I thought, don't they know who I am? I am one of the better horseplayers of the world. I almost break even.

She came back. I never worried about her. About other men, about phone calls, and how she got them by the dozens as I lay in her bed. Or the nights we decided to skip, I didn't worry about them either.

The intercom music was still on. I looked about. There were no empty seats. It was getting hot. Directly over top-stage was the upper balcony, which ran all around, but I could view the topstage balcony comfortably, and here was this young blonde in a tight-fitting dress, spangles and beads, she was built like an hourglass, she was sparkling and she was happy and the rhythms fell upon her like a shower of light rain, like blessings, the sound crawled around her and she voluted, but it was not a dance of sex to attract other men, it was a dance of joy, she voluted in joy, and her young man next to her, peering about through a spyglass was also happy, happy with her and with himself and happy with the music. . . .

The front show came on. Three black girls with a definite sense of beat. You had two girls who sang and one girl to fall in love with—the third one, long dark hair, eyes that threw the searchlights back. You could fall in love with her. I fell in love with her while waiting for the STONES.

Then there was the black strong male type, the garage mechanic type. Might be cruel. Beat his kids. Get drunk on Saturday night. Maybe even Thursday. Smoke shit. Sniff H.

He was all right. He sweated. It was hot under the lights.

His best key was a low beat down beat zombie zig. Like a lion trying to roar with his throat cut. But when he got on out he couldn't climb the ladder. He was just a drunken mechanic warbling under an oilchange job. He tried. Being blind didn't help. Maybe it did. He might not have been quite as good seeing everything. . . .

Then they said it: "THE STONES!"

Here he was. Mick Jagger. A little blue star pasted near each eye. An outfit on like your hip spade dude would be wearing tomorrow morning. His joint was showing through his tight hot jism pants, and he was dressed to fuck the world, but basically he had style, the style that comes with champions. I liked him right off and at the same time I thought, why does he have to fuck himself up like that?

He was the Light, he was the Cross, he was the Cunt and the Cock, he was wolves running across snow, the balling in Florida hotels where the sea is pink and green and filled with blood, he was the Monster with the inflamed TONSIL, and yet and yet, he was not that much. And I kept telling him:

do it,
do it, kid.
it can be done
light us all up
I am willing to be
lit
do it.

He had the energy, this Jagger I had never seen before, he was spartan, he drank little gulps of Coke to cool his throat while the U.S.C. football team threw his admirers back up the aisles.

He was good because he still had soul and he was reaching down into what was left of soul and he didn't need Beethoven and he didn't need Bach, he had his own gas and his own leverage and his own way, but he was tiring, it was like a shadow following, a shadow to an eternal doom of weariness where it finally didn't matter anymore, and maybe that was wisdom. I kept calling inside for him to come on, I said inside, Mick, forget my delicate little Chopin nocturnes that I listen to in roominghouses while two weeks behind in the rent, with suicide a spider's cunthair away. Mick, show me, show me, show me. . . .

He tried. And he was wonderful. He spilled more blood on that floor than a five-thousand-man army, but he didn't make it. He'd been tricked into acceptance, tricked just like they trick every artist. Or almost every artist. The others go into madness or kill themselves.

Mick tried. He tried very well. He did better than anybody watching him could. But it wasn't enough. He was tired. He was too much money in. He was too famous. He sucked at the crowd. He tried to remember how it was when he first worked it. How it was when he was really and purely real. It's difficult, too, it's so difficult. It comes to us and it leaves us. Imagine being the Pied Piper and losing your flute. Yet it happens to all and every. The remainder of us do the best we can. Mick was doing the best he could, which was very good but none of what any of us expected, which was more MIRACLE MIRACLE MIRACLE.

He finally took off his leather belt and flogged the floor, playing the sex maniac bit. It wasn't too bad. And at least the words were clear and the meaning.

(Let's get it all clear. There was only one champion in that place that night and that was Mick Jagger. People like this don't come along easily. Let's give him his money and his fame and his glory, because his glory is our glory no matter how much he laughs at us in back rooms. You did all right, Mick. I forgive you.)

Then there was the final bit. They were all supposed to go mad and clap. Show biz. The final number.

I wanted to be linked to and with all of them. The sound rose like ten thousand motherfucking sparrows masturbating in the dirt. I thought of all the wonderful and terrible things that had happened to me and you and the rest of us, the wars, the sell-outs, the political parties, the old cars rusting and smashed in the junkyards, everything so sad finally unless it's love, unless you can grab a little piece of love, not to say, that's mine but to say it's nice it's nice it's nice it's nice it's nice. . . .

We went back to the motel and we drank and we talked a long long time, mostly we talked, it was easy. And then we took a shower and I took a shower, and then we made love and then we made love and then me and she made love, and Mick took the next plane out, and we forgot about him and I remembered him and we each remembered many things about our lives, as we will do, and the sea beat up and down against us, and it was really peace at last, and for a classical guy I wanted to tell you what happened the night the STONES came to Long Beach, and after doing her in, in, in, I felt my piece in her mouth and they heard me all along the shore:

"I LOVE YOU, I LOVE YOU, I LOVE YOU!"

But I wasn't sure whether I was saying it to her or to all the women I've loved, or maybe to all the women I will love or should have loved, how can you tell?

Thanks for coming by, Mick. I admire you. And I admire you for everything you are or could have been. 90,000 temples ring for love or hope or kindness or realism. All our lives are set down to a singing that can never come true.

You sang us some good songs. This is my song back to you.

I get 20 dollars for writing this, Mick. You mustn't expect too much.

L.A. Free Press, June 23, 1972

Notes of a Dirty Old Man

I'm not in the mood for an immortal column today so I'll go into the chitchat bit that the others get away with, hope that it gets by D. Fife, and next week I'll be back with the good stuff, let's hope. . . .

The heaviest woman in the history of the world died the other day in Milwaukee. 46 years old, she weighed 880 pounds. According to the Guinness Book of Records, the former heaviest woman of all time weighed 850 pounds and died in Baltimore in 1888.

Our new record-holder was 6 feet tall and wore a size 62 dress. They said eight sheriff's deputies and several attendants were needed to carry the body into the morgue.

No offense to the lady, but knowing the human race I can't help imagining some of the comments that were made while they were carrying her in.

"Hey, her leg's slipping off here!"

"Christ, don't drop it!"

"Wonder how she ever sat on a toilet?"

"She dropped a *load*, you can bet!"

Me, of course, I wonder about her sex life, her possible loneliness. But I see she was listed as a Mrs. W_____. Mr. W_____, our condolences. . . .

There was this one lady, a friend of a friend, she was at the beach one day and felt the need to excrete and there weren't any restrooms about so her husband held a blanket around her and she did it in a bucket. She was a very heavy lady, damned fat to be explicit, and when she finished and rose the bucket was stuck to her behind, the fat mashed down there with the droppings plus the suction and she tugged and tugged but couldn't get the thing off her ass. . . . "Oh, Harry, what am I going to do?" and Harry said, "Well, there's only one thing to do!" and he dropped the blanket and with the lady standing there holding her dress up he tugged and tugged. It took some minutes, and then the bucket came off with an explosive sound and the turds and the seagulls whirled through the air. . . .

"Oh, I was *so* embarrassed!"

"Oh, I was so *embarrassed*!"

The lady laughs when she tells the story now, years later, she laughs the fat lady's laugh. . . . And if The League to Liberate the Obese is about to attack me, let me say that I weigh in at 220. Striped, stripped, or stoned. . . .

Was at Santa Anita this last Monday, the holiday, and I have this system I have been working on, based on the first flash of the board against general public information.

You see, anybody can lose at the track, I like to lose with method. The problem with systems is that few of us have the consistency or the character to ride them out. That 30-minute wait between races gives us too much time to think. Well, that's all right, let's look at the first race. I have all my figures before me. The board flashes, Sir Larry Jay is 20 on the line. The *Racing Form* has him at the bottom at 30 to one. The *L.A. Times* handicapper has him at 25. He opens up at 14 to one. That's my play. I mark it. Then during the betting Sir Larry rises to 35 to one. My mind cracks and I jump to Sake Tsuin at 7 to one. Sir Larry Jay is blocked at the 5/16th pole, Toro has to check him, that cost three lengths; he still comes on to win by a length at a payoff of $79.80. Sake Tsuin gets up for 3rd.

In the second race the system is no play. The first flash all goes on the favorite Money Truck, opening at 3/5 off a rating of 8/5, 5/2 over a morning line of 5/2. Too standard. I blow a deuce on Vicar General who places at 10 to one. Money Truck broke down and the favorite players' faces pinched up a little more.

In the 3rd race Glory Isle opens up at 18 off a morning line of 20, once again against public information, and then it rises up to 35 to one. They're not going to run in the same play twice in one day, I think. Glory Isle goes off the longest shot in the race and wins by three and a half lengths, paying $74.60.

I've got a saying that knowledge without follow-through

is worse than no knowledge at all. Because it hurts, that's why. So by the 4th race I am convinced. Broadway Frank, a name I like anyhow, rates 20-50 over a morning line of 15 and opens right on the line, 15. That's hidden action. B.F. hasn't been out for a year. No good workouts. The only other action is on Stand Straight who opens as the even money favorite. That's standard. I chance a deuce on B.F. who rises to 21 to one, is checked while blocked on the turn, came through the rail to win with authority at 45.80. The system stopped working there and I know why now, but this is hardly the place to mention it.

I've been asked, Bukowski, if you ever taught a writing class, what would you do? Well, besides staring up the legs of the girls in the front row and giving an A to every lady who went to bed with me, my first assignment would be to make every student go to the racetrack and make a $2 win bet on every race and then come back and tell me what they felt and what they had learned. The racetrack is a bloodpit almost everybody loses. The 15 percent take on the dollar is too much, plus just ordinary bad betting. And it's *boring*. The faces are boring, the 30-minute wait between races is boring, everybody is dying and desperate and insolent and dried-out and tired and lost and losing and stupid. They came to the track because they didn't know what to do. Well, over seven percent of their money (and mine) goes to state taxes, 25 cents for a little candy bar, 25 cents for a small cup of coffee, 50 cents for a hotdog, one dollar and a quarter for a sandwich, 35 cents for a coke, one dollar for a *Racing Form*, 35 cents for a program, 75 cents for parking, $2.25 to get in, then maybe you can bet. If you want a pack of cigarettes, it's 55 cents and you'd better ask for matches.

I once said to my girlfriend, "Horse players are the lowest of the breed."

"What are we doing out here?" she asked.

"Look," I said, "the four horse is getting unwarranted action. . . ."

The racetrack, though, is a place where you enter the arena and see the people, quite not like you see the people anywhere else. I believe it helps creation. Win or lose you have learned something or re-learned something. But I wouldn't suggest the track more than once a week unless you are on a winning streak. I can understand why Hemingway needed the bullring. It set the stage to move his people on. It was a quick review of death and life and movement. The boxing matches too are fine teachers, but only when you attend them live and get the smell and feeling of the crowd and fighters. Well, enough of that.

I left the track a small loser, falling into the exact trap which goes for $5 a ticket. I made it back to my '62 Comet and got in and here came a little old man with white hair and a shopping bag. I knew what he wanted. He ran up. "Listen, you going to Los Angeles?" "Listen, buddy," I said, "I don't have any auto insurance. If I crack you up and you're injured, you'll sue my ass."

I don't like little old men with white hair and shopping bags, I'm too close to that myself.

"I'll give you a dollar," he said, "a dollar for a ride."

"Get your head out of my window," I said, "I'm moving out."

Actually I don't mind the beaten and broke horseplayer too much but I've driven too many of them. I used to pick up an old guy at the Santa Monica entrance to the Hollywood freeway. He was bearded and in rags and slept in the bushes. His toes came out of his shoes and he stank. We made Los Alamitos almost every day. I haven't seen him lately. I think he finally died. He claimed the jocks got together in the jockey room every day and decided on a number, say number 5. He claimed they'd run in #5 almost all day long, just altering it enough so it wouldn't be obvious. Well, maybe he wasn't any crazier than the rest of us.

But the old boys with white hair and shopping bags *all* live downtown in those ancient hotels with the large plate glass windows and all those people sitting in the lobby waiting to die. The old boys talk horses all the way in: what they did do, what they will do, the time they hit the double at Bowie or Belmont or Turf Paradise for $725. They are mad, mad, mad! And I detest discussing horses vocally. And the last old guy I took down there, I got a flat tire at

5th and Spring and I vowed never to do it again. . . . What I am trying to say is that I lost at the races Monday and this is the long way to say it. But I've got a new system now. All you do is. . . .

If you think I've had some wild parties, they had one in Munich the other night. Five million people celebrated the marriage of King Ludwig I of Bavaria 138 years ago. It took them 16 days and nights. Despite police, the people stole over 200,000 one-liter beermugs. Over one million gallons of fortified beer were consumed, and over half a million grilled chickens were eaten. There were 500 arrests for fights, 15 purse snatchers caught, 399 Huns made the drunk tank, and around 250 were treated for injuries.

But I've had a few good nights off DeLongpre myself. One night I am passed out in the middle of the floor and somebody shakes me, "Hey, Bukowski, the cops are here!" I get up and one of the cops says to me, "Hey, buddy, do you own this place?" "No, I rent this place." "Well, keep the noise down. If I come back I'm throwing you in the slammer!" Another time they came riding shotgun. I'd run everybody off, which made a lot of noise and I was sitting there calmly listening to Shostakovich's 5th. "Hey, buddy," said the cop, "I know you. We've been here before." "What do you do for a living?" asked another cop. "I'm a writer." "A writer, huh?" "Yeh." "Ha, ha, ha," laughed the cop, "a writer, eh?" Then he walked over to my typewriter and began reading the sheet in there. It was part of my 5,000-word essay on The Meaning of Suicide. After searching under the bed and in the closets for dead bodies they drove off and I took a pint of scotch out from under the couch and finished it.

There are too many to remember but I suppose one of the best was once when I lived on the 4th floor of this hotel on Union Ave. And I was drinking in the afternoon with a male friend and two ladies. I forget what we were drinking but I felt that the party was getting very dull so I went to the window. Well, there were two windows together over the alley and I locked my legs around the centerpiece that separated the windows and hung over the alley upside down.

Soon I was almost hanging by my ankles. My friends were begging me to come back into the apartment. And when I looked down there was a crowd gathered in the alley. I'd heard that people were always encouraging near-suicidal acts, but it was a nice crowd down there. I could see their hands waving at me, I could see the tops of their palms, and several of them were saying at once, "Don't drop! Don't drop! Don't drop!" I got a very warm feeling from these gestures and decided to pull myself back into the apartment. But at first try I found that my legs wouldn't lift me. It wasn't a good feeling. Then gathering myself, I managed somehow to coil upwards and grab the centerpiece. I climbed back into the room. Everybody in there was saying over and over again, "Jesus Christ, Jesus Christ, Jesus Christ." I sat down and poured a drink. Then there was a knock on the door. I opened it. It was the manager.

"Was that you who was hanging out the window up here?"

"Yeh."

"What did you do it for?"

"I was bored."

"Well, listen, I want to tell you something."

"Yeh?"

"You do that one more time and I'm calling the police."

"O.K.," I said and closed the door.

It was one of those hotels where they didn't allow cooking. Every time you left your place they searched it for a hotplate. We used to buy weenies and heat them in the hot water in the wash basin in the crapper. It wasn't a very nice place.

Is this a column yet? . . .

"Oh yeah," said Neeli at one of the last parties, "tell the one about the guy."

"What guy?"

"The guy at Mad Jack's."

Well, Neeli was there. And me and Mad Jack and his girl. We were drinking beer and wine and screaming and playing the piano and I didn't know how to play the piano, and we were having a good time somehow and we went out for more to drink and in the liquor store this guy saw us laughing and he said, "You guys are having a good time, can I come along?" And I said, "Sure," and he went back with us and sat there and then he started bragging about how he had killed seven men in the war, he kept right on about his seven-man kill, nothing else, and finally I said, "Listen, that's not all that big—killing seven men in a war. It's sanctioned, it's blessed, it's no big thing. Now if you kill a man outside of a war, that might take a little guts."

"You don't like me, do you?"

"Not a bit."

He got up and left and we forgot about him. In about 10 minutes he was back. He had a gunbelt and a holster on and a gun was in the holster and there were bullets in the gun. He walked over to my chair. "You still don't like me, eh?"

"No."

He drew the gun and stuck it into my belly.

"I believe I am going to kill you."

"Listen, buddy," I said, "I've had a suicide complex for years. You'll be doing my ass a favor. But you're going to get life if you do this. Go ahead, pull the trigger. I don't believe you have the guts."

He just looked at me and kept the gun in my stomach. He had a stinking little yellow beard and yellow teeth and tiny hard eyes. I reached over for my glass and had a drink. Neeli, Mad Jack, and his girlfriend stood silent and watching. Then he pulled the gun out of my belly, put it back in the holster, walked to the door and down the steps. I walked over to the piano and began playing it. . . .

I really hate partie. . . .

This is a column.

Open City, November 3–16, 1972

Notes of a Dirty Old Man

I had given up on women. I mean, a man simply resigns and says, that's it, there's no going on with that. I mean, I had really gotten out of it, and at best it seemed as good a time as any. I passed the ladies on the street, and I mean, truly, they barely registered. They registered, say, as a tree or a phone pole might register. It was hardly a flaming life but it had its comforts. I remember the ending of *The Razor's Edge*, where the man had searched all through the world for meaning and found it by being a taxi car driver and giving up on women. I had had only one drunken affair in four years, had gone to bed with the lady, but had been too intoxicated to climax. I felt I had known enough women enough length of time to rate a retirement from that arena. I had quit a job of 11 years (Civil Service and security) and was sitting about writing dirty stories and immortal poems and giving poetry readings for the rent and beer and child support. It was a different life and in the leisure hours drink began to take over. Mostly beer, but I was able to create under the influence of many bottles of beer. I worked and drank most of the night while listening to symphony music and smoking cheap cigars. I got a beer-gut, red-faced, but I wasn't particularly lonely—the beer filled in the gaps when the creation wasn't working. I'd remain up each night until 3 or 4 a.m., go to sleep, rise about 2 p.m., open a beer, sit down to a typer, and repeat the process. I wrote my first novel, *Post Office*, in 29 nights. Actually I felt much like a monk working deep in a cave, unbothered.

Then I noticed that at most of the local readings in town a girl would come up afterwards and lean over the table, look at me and say, "Hi." "Hi," I'd say, and she didn't make much of an impression—I only thought, well, that's the same one. I've seen her before.

Then the girl was at my door one night. "Hi," she said, and handed me a mimeo'd sheet: it had little poems in it and rather an ingrown-ranting and love-boggling going on between certain writers in there. I read through it and thought, now what did she hand me this thing for?

A week later she was brought to my place by the owner of a local bookstore where I had given one of my readings. She ran about the room proclaiming a rather bad and rather long rhymer she had written. The bookstore owner chased her about the room. The whole process bored me and I wished they'd get out and get it on with each other. I found her name was Charlotte and after the bookstore guy left she stayed a few moments. I began, vaguely, to notice the color of her hair (and that it was long), and that there was something interesting about her nose and her mouth, and that she had an interesting behind. However, I had seen such things before. And when Charlotte left soon afterwards I didn't particularly grieve. She was 20 years younger: let some young man suffer under all that. I drank some more beer, got a good run of Bach on the radio, and forgot all about her. . . .

It was around evening the next time Charlotte rang. She had a camera and some flashbulbs. "I want to take some photos. I'd like to sculpt you, O.K.?"

"O.K.," I said, holding my bottle of beer. It was then that I noticed this long brown eye around the edge of the camera. That eye looked right into me and it seemed to be laughing and it seemed to be doing something else. A most interesting eye, I thought, look at that eye.

"You're looking silly," she said, "don't pose."

"Of course I'm looking silly," I said, "it's an old man leering at a young girl."

Then she took one of the used flashbulbs and stuck it in her mouth. "Please don't do that," I asked.

Charlotte left soon after with her photos. "I'll work off of these first, then you can come and sit."

"Why don't you stick around for a beer?"

"No, no, I've got to go."

She seemed very business-like but after she left I found myself still thinking about her. . . .

The first sitting was a week or so later at 11 a.m. at her Glendale apartment. She took me into the breakfast nook and there sat the beginning of a Bukowski head on the table. "Don't be nervous now. If I had a studio you wouldn't be nervous. Do you need a beer?"

"Yes."

Charlotte sat and sculpted me and we talked. She gave me directions on how to sit, how to turn. Those brown eyes looked at me; they were very large and warm but she still appeared business-like. What else could I expect?

"Now, get closer."

"No, closer than that."

I got closer. "You know," she said, putting those warm brown eyes on me (very strange eyes, they seemed to have no pupils). "You know," she said, "when my husband divorced me he said, 'I hope you meet a real crud.' And now I have."

I laughed. What a delightful lady.

"You've got all those scars and bumps all over your face, you really give me something to work with."

"Thank you," I answered.

"All your writings about women," she said, "when I read your writings about women I thought, now here's a man who really doesn't know anything about women."

"Oh?" I asked.

"Yes, it's true, it's quite obvious."

Charlotte had a little wooden stick with a wire loop. She shook it at me and her eyes brightened. I laughed. She was continuously waving that stick at me. Whenever she did, these waves began circling in me.

Don't be a silly old man, I thought.

"Listen, Charlotte, please don't wave that stick at me."

She laughed and desisted for a while, then shook the stick at me. She was quite good with the clay. Her works were all over her apartment and they were very realistic, amazingly human works. I held myself together through the sitting and she asked if I might come back at 11 the next morning. "Of course," I said. . . .

I don't know how many days later it was, and I was in a dream state, largely unconscious of my actions, and when she went to the refrigerator I got up and followed her. When she turned I had her in my arms, crushing her, my lips upon hers. She fought but I was too strong for her.

"Easy now," she said, "let's go easy, please."

"All right."

But when I sat down again I felt I knew her much better . . .

The days went on and the work went slowly. There were more kisses, always more and more kisses. I was an old bull heated out of his head; I had gone years without women and many more without love. But I felt that the feelings were coming mostly from me, and I wanted to be careful. She had been interested in my poems and stories and wanted to sculpture my head. There was nothing I could presume. There was little doubt that I was having love feelings of some sort. Those days in the kitchen were very magic to me. But I was just a poet, and an old one at that. I kept telling myself, Bukowski, you are supposed to know all about the world so don't bullshit yourself. . . .

I suppose I did bullshit myself a couple of days later. I picked Charlotte up and carried her to the bedroom. I got her on the bed and we kissed and clutched quite hotly for some time. But when it came to doing it Charlotte resisted. I felt that she had been teasing me, fooling me, playing high-school games. I pulled my pants up and leaped out of bed:

"Goddamn you, go to hell. Just because you're 20 years younger than me, you can't push me around!"

"And just because you've written a couple of poems you can't push me around!"

I walked out of the bedroom, across the front room, and slammed the door. I was finished. It had all been nonsense from the beginning. I got in my car and drove off. . . .

In a day or so I got a letter in the mail:

"Dear Son of a Bitch Bukowski:

I got thinking about you tonight and how smug you felt when you left my door and got so mad that I went over and put your head on the floor and I stomped on it . . . stomped, I danced. It was a terrible mess with all the black clay over my kitchen floor. I am afraid I will never get it all cleaned up. Will you come over and help me clean it up? Something. I want to put it all back together again so it is you again. What I want to know is will you make another baby with me? How could I have done it to my own flesh and blood?? Everything will be all right if you don't take this loss too hard. Darling, sweetheart, Baby, say something. Well, nothing can be done about it now. I feel just terrible . . . excuse me a minute.

I got so mad at myself I just went over and took a handful of clay . . . big black gobs and started throwing it, I threw it on the wall, on the ceiling. I went mad. My God, you Son of a Bitch, what are you doing to me? All over my white ceiling, I'm exhausted . . . it's on the stove and refrigerator; there is some even over my painting of Norman Mailer. The dog barked, the kids bawled, and then they decided it was fun and helped me throw too, it is stuck up there, it might never come down. My Christ, they are going to lock me up if anyone sees this. A big hunk of your nose right in the middle of . . . oh, oh, it just fell. It's a good thing I'm moving. I could never clean up this mess, but I feel great now. Renewed, refreshed, I can breathe deep. I just burst out of the glass bottle you put me in with little air holes. You are a madman to think you can bottle me. No games, Madman. You've met a Madwoman and I can play games too.

Charlotte . . ."

I had told Charlotte, in jest, that I would like to put her in a glass bottle with a tin lid with little air holes punched in. Or I had thought it had been in jest.

I went over the next day. Charlotte met me at the door. "I'm really sorry. I wasted a lot of your time. I'd like to do another head."

"It's all right," I said.

We walked into the kitchen. There sat the head unbroken and untouched. I started laughing. Then I kissed her. . . .

The new place she moved to had a kitchen too. It was 11 a.m. again and we sat there. The kisses and embraces and looks continued. Gradually the subject got around to going down. Don't ask me how the subject got around to going down. Charlotte seemed to move it there.

"You mean you never?" she asked.

"Never."

"And you're 50?"

"Yes."

"You never wanted to?"

"No."

"Nobody ever asked you?"

"No."

"Well, you can't teach an old dog new tricks."

"I'm a late starter. I started writing poetry at the age of 35."

"Poetry and that other thing aren't the same thing."

"I hope not."

I don't remember how we got away from the sculpture and into the bedroom. Anyhow, there we were on the blue bedspread. We kissed and fondled. All that looking into those dark brown eyes for hours, for days, for weeks. . . .

I got her panties off, then I looked at the thing.

"No, no, don't do it, you won't like it! Blood comes out of there and pee! You won't like it!"

I leaned forward and put my head down. It was hairy as a bear, matted and deranged. I plunged forward and thought of all the great men of the centuries who had died similar deaths. Little did I realize that one day I would enjoy doing it. It had a strange taste, a very strange and good taste that I recognized immediately as the taste of almonds. Almonds. I began to chew upon almonds, breaking shells, chewing, sucking . . . she quivered and twisted up above . . .

"Your first time?" she asked laying on the pillow at looking at me.

"Yes."

"You're very good; I guess it's your imagination and intensity . . ."

I put myself up against Charlotte and held her. . . .

I went home and wrote a poem about the incident. The first line began: "I have eaten your cunt like a peach. . . ." I drove over to Charlotte's, put the poem (enclosed in an envelope) in her mailbox. Then I drove back and telephoned her to look in the mailbox.

That night my phone rang about midnight: "You son of a bitch, that poem made me so hot! Goddamn you! Talk to me! Talk to me! Oh, you son of a bitch!"

I kept talking and she began making these sounds over the phone. The sounds got wilder, louder and louder. Then they reached a climax. . . .

"All right, I'm finished! I don't need you anymore!"

She hung up.

I phoned back: "Charlotte, are you all right?"

"Oh, I'm so ashamed! I'll never be able to face you again! I couldn't help it. That's the hottest poem I ever read. . . ."

"Come on now, you really didn't do it over the telephone, did you?"

She hung up again and I went back to bed. . . .

My head finally got finished and it was a sad day when that happened, and yet it wasn't so sad because I continued to see Charlotte and our relationship deepened further. Yet we fought continually. Every time we split, I'd run that head back to her place, usually along with a vile and impassioned note declaring that it was over forever. Then I'd get the head back when we got together. I lost my head again and again. I don't know how many trips that poor head has made. It's a fine work of Art and certainly a well-traveled one. After our last split she beat me to it. While I was out she broke in and stole the head back. Now I've decided to simply leave the head at her place. And when I go over there, which is often, the head sits by the back window, grinning and knowledgeable, a real crud, a beat-up old guy, but there is love coming from the eyes, love that hadn't been there for years; she caught the look of it in the clay & before it was finished, the taste of almonds.

That head is two years old now, and tonight Charlotte sits across the room from me typing. She stops, turns and asks me: "How do you spell 'schizophrenia'?" Now I wonder what the hell *she's* writing about?

Nola Express, December 8–21, 1972

Guggenheim Application: Narrative Account of Career

I began writing in my early twenties and was first published in Whit Burnett's *Story* magazine at the age of 24 and also in Caresse Crosby's *Portfolio* at about the same time. Both acceptances were short stories. At the age of 25 I had practically stopped writing and submitting except for a couple of desultory appearances around 1948 in a little magazine, *Matrix*. I began an exploration of skid row life and drifter's jobs, alcoholism and ladies of the streets which finally led me to the charity ward of the Los Angeles County General Hospital with massive hemorrhages. I was given 12 pints of blood and 12 of glucose. The priest offered me last rites which I refused, not so much because I didn't think I was going to die but I was no longer quite that type of Catholic. I came out of the hospital and got a job driving a truck, bought a typewriter and began writing again—this time almost all poetry, dozens of poems, hundreds of poems. The material was there and I seemed to be there too. Something had congealed besides my stomach. I was 35 and the work seemed to be accepted everywhere by the little magazines. As time went on editors asked if they might do books of my poetry. In one of these books, *It Catches My Heart in Its Hands: New and Selected Poems, 1955–1963*, Dr. John William Corrington, Louisiana State University, states in the introduction: "What Wordsworth claimed to have in mind, what William Carlos Williams claimed to have done, what Rimbaud actually did do in the French, Bukowski has accomplished for the American language." More poems followed, more stories, more books of poems . . . a novel. At 53 (with a typewriter that skips) and with a backlog of work behind me, I am still writing. My poems have appeared in over 200 magazines here and in Europe. I won the *New York Quarterly*'s first Lucille Medwick award for a poem "which is the best expression of the concern of our ethnic minorities—their special heritage, their unique mythology, and their desperate appeal for social justice." Awarded a grant from the National Endowment for the Arts, June 1, 1973 to May 31, 1974.

[signed] Charles Bukowski

Notes of a Dirty Old Man

"Harry," said Doug, "you sure you want to go $500 for this?"

They turned north into Hollywood Hills. Doug was driving. Harry had been drinking. "Sure, $500 is all right. You know, certain drunks in Van Nuys, Highland Park, and Compton have phoned and have been threatening me with death."

"Oh, well I've written some good things lately, too. You got the $500?"

"Yeah, I've got it. You know, if you're going to be a good artist at all, you're going to insult some people because the artist is always at least 600–700 years ahead of the masses. The people are the enemy, they are the residue of stale and common thoughts and conceptions."

It was going into evening and the road was long and winding.

"That's where Marlon Brando lives," said Doug.

"Think how difficult it is to be a writer nowadays," said Harry, "all these groups have gathered into protective camps. If you write about a woman, a black, a Chicano, a homosexual, a lesbian as not being a very good person, you are attacked right off as a pig. Yet there are women, Chicanos, blacks, and lesbians who are not very good persons. This is the Great Age of Fear."

"Harry, every time you start drinking you start talking about writing. There's not a more disgusting subject. I'm taking you up here to show you something special."

Harry didn't seem to hear. He took another nip at the pint.

"About the only person the artist can put up as evil and disgraceful is the male white. Nobody seems to care about the male white. You have to be very careful about the homosexual white."

"They don't bother me, Harry."

"Talk about prejudice. Look at *Hogan's Heroes*. The Germans are continually pictured as bungling, loud, stupid, egotistical jerks. And the Americans are so clever and humorous and nice, with such inventiveness and brain-power. One wonders how fellows like that ever managed to get into a prison camp?"

"It won't be long, we'll be there. You're really going to see something."

Doug turned left up the road and then went up a drive-way. He got out and waited for Harry, locked the doors. They walked up a pathway toward a dimly lit house. "It's the U.S. intellectual that runs the U.S. brain: a war against the Left is a useless war, a war against the Right is holy."

Doug rang the bell and they waited. "They accused Céline of being anti-Semite," Harry went on. "There was a particular passage in one of his books about 'the Jew's heavy footsteps.' And when they asked him, 'Céline, don't you like Jews?' he answered, 'I don't like people.' Then they really hated him."

The door opened. A dark-haired woman, heavily rouged, in a white gown trimmed with white fur, was at the door. A great lace of long beads dangled from her neck. The fingers of both of her hands were filled with rings with large stones. The house smelled of many scents and had exces-sively thick rugs; drapes with tassels hung upon the walls and billowed from the ceilings. The woman was about 30. "Hello, Sybil," said Doug, "this is my friend, Harry."

They followed Sybil through several rooms. They en-tered the final room. On a couch covered with the sheerest of green satin sat a girl, about nine. Sybil turned to Harry. "This, Harry, is my daughter, Pelna. Pelna, this is Harry."

"Pleased to meet you," said Harry.

"Hello," said Plena.

Plena had on a large hat of flowers with a pink ribbon that wound under her chin holding the whole affair to her. She had on the faintest tinge of lipstick and mascara. She had on a white dress that flounced outward, green short stockings, ordinary children's shoes. She was a child but something within her kept insinuating womanhood. She stuck a finger against one of her cheeks and looked up at Harry, opening her eyes quite wide.

"She's most beautiful," said Harry. "I'm afraid I can't."

"Nonsense," said Sybil. "Do you have the $500?"

"Oh yes," said Harry. He pulled out his wallet and gave Sybil five $100 bills. "Thank you," said Sybil. "I've read your books, Mr. Tallaman, and I've really adored them. Pelna has read some of your books, too. Would you gentlemen care for a drink?" The gentlemen told her yes and Sybil left the room. She soon returned with three drinks in purple glasses. "My own concoction. Good for the pecker, the heart, and the soul," she said.

"Ah, yes, quite good," said Harry, sipping at his.

"You must understand, Harry, that I must remain in the room to be sure you don't *hurt* Pelna. I'm her mother, after all. You must promise to be gentle. Doug was quite gentle."

"I really don't know if I can."

"She really doesn't mind," said Doug. "I think she rather enjoys it."

"She *does* enjoy it," said Sybil.

"But it's not proper," said Harry, "she's just a child."

"Christian morals, Harry," said Doug. "It's done all the time in India, in Mexico, in China, even in the U.S."

"You're supposed to be a writer," said Sybil, "you seek experience, don't you?"

"I can't do it," said Harry.

"I have your $500."

"Keep it. I can't do it."

"Let me have her then," said Doug.

"Come on, Harry, let's go out on the balcony. There's a lovely view."

Harry followed Sybil through two rooms and then there was a balcony. They stood there looking over the city of Los Angeles. Harry sipped at his drink. Then he finished it off.

"What do you think they're doing? Do you think he's kissing her now?"

"Isn't that an old song? It goes, 'I wonder who's kissing her now?' Feel like you're missing something, Harry?"

"Christ, what kind of mother are you?"

"Don't give me that lame shit, Harry. We all make it the best way we can. I can't write. Survival is more important than truth."

"Don't you worry about her?"

"It's *your* 500. Doug is very gentle, I trust him."

"But what about the future? What's it going to do to your child's mind, her insides, her feelings?"

"She'll probably be a hell of a lot more ready for the world than the girl who comes out of a convent."

Harry pulled out his pint and had a good one. "How long will it take? How long is it going to take him?"

"Doug likes to take his time. Sam Goldwyn Studios caught on fire yesterday. It made me very sad."

"We just stand here and wait, is that it?"

"For what?"

"Until he's done."

"Doug will let us know."

"Very funny."

"I wasn't meaning to be funny."

"What would you know about 'funny' anyhow?"

"I know what's funny out of Hollywood. To make them laugh you must state the most obvious thing and multiply by 15. Most people have a great fear of being different, so if they can laugh at a seeming truth that almost everybody recognizes, it makes them safe—it indicates that they understand the mechanism, that they understand each other, and that they are all together, laughing."

"Yes, I've heard that laughter, the laughter of the crowd together, and it's a most piteous, mewling, begging and cowardly sound."

"Let me have a bit of your drink, Harry," said Sybil. Harry passed the bottle. Sybil had a drink and passed it back. "Thurber," she said, "Thurber was a real humorist because he knew the difference between actual-subtle and unactual-obvious."

"Yeah," said Harry, "you're dragged to these parties and they tell you something about so and so, say Joe Landers, oh Joe Landers is such a *funny* guy! So you go. And there he is. He has yellow teeth and lines like spaghetti burned at the bottom of the pot. He'll point to some guy—usually me—and say something like, 'Hey, old man, I see you've been *swimming* today!' 'O.K.,' you answer, 'how did you know that I've been swimming?' 'You *must* have been! I see you left your lifebelt on under your shirt!' Then the crowd laughs."

"I'll be right back," said Sybil. "I'll get us another drink."

Harry waited, looking down over the city. Well, here he was making it as a writer. It seemed very strange. And what was more strange was how your friends attacked you, some with the oldest, rustiest saw of them all: He's too negative, he ought to be more objective. But it works that way. I dislike things too: Mailer, Capote, though I suppose it's more their affluence than their writing which disturbs me. I dislike Tolstoy, Chekhov's *Cherry Orchard*. I dislike most Russian authors who become famous and win prizes and places of exile for saying that Russia is rotten. And there's a new one every five years as soon as the preceding one has evaporated.

Harry heard the footsteps. Doug and Sybil were coming out on the balcony. Doug had one drink, Sybil two. Sybil handed one to Harry. "Harry and I have had a nice talk out here," Sybil said to Doug. "Harry likes to talk," said Doug, "I save it for the typewriter."

"Sam Goldwyn Studios caught on fire yesterday," Sybil said to Doug.

"That so? I didn't catch the papers or the news."

"I used to work there, you know," said Sybil.

"Really?"

"As Gloria Marlowe."

"Oh yes. I think I've seen you. Well, look, Sybil. . . ."

"Aren't you going to finish your drink?"

"I'll say. You make a most marvelous drink. What's in it?"

"Ta, ta. *My* witchy secret."

"Sure."

They finished their drinks and Sybil walked them to the door. Then the door was closed and they walked back toward the car.

"Gloria Marlowe," said Doug. "Yes, I remember her now. She wasn't too bad an actress."

"But she's only in her 30s."

"In Hollywood, the 30s most often means too late."

They got back into the car. Doug started it up, backed around, "Well, should I drive you home or should we stop at a bar?"

"Let's hit a bar somewhere."

"Where?"

"Anywhere. It doesn't matter."

They rolled to the right and started down out of the hills.

L.A. Free Press, May 17, 1974

Notes of a Dirty Old Man

I was too early at the airport, then the flight was set back twice. It was still before noon, and I was too sick to drink. I kept walking all about the airport, waiting. I am disgusted with most things, but I really hate airports. I finally went in and defecated. It was a strange toilet I had gotten into, with a row of bars on each side like a cage. I couldn't understand it, but I finished and got out. I walked some more, and then the flight was in and I stood with the others waiting for the passengers. There she was, smiling. I walked up to her. "Hello, Helen." "Charles," she said. She only had a flight bag, and we took the escalator down.

"Oh, I just *love* airports," she said, "the people are so well-dressed and handsome."

"I'm sick," I said.

"Oh, what is it?"

"Drinking. Last night."

We got out of the airport to the parking lot and into my car. "Listen," I said, "the racetrack's right on the way in. We might as well stop there."

The toteboard action was bad, and by the fourth race I was $40 out. "It *is* exciting," said Helen. "I won the last race."

"Good. How much did you have on it?"

"Oh, I just bet it in my head."

I won the fifth race and felt a little better. "I just love to stand in the center of the people and listen to them screaming during a race," she said.

The day wore on and by the ninth race I was $80 out. It was hot and brutal and we got caught in the jam coming out. By the time we got to my place I really needed a drink. I took a shower and came out. "Your skin is so white," she said.

"Want a drink?" I asked.

"No, thanks."

I got myself a beer and sat on the couch next to her.

"It was so great you came out just before Jim died. Robert Bly didn't look like anything reading after you did."

"Thanks."

"People are going to think Jim O.D.'ed. He didn't; he died of a heart attack."

"Yes, you wrote me."

"He wanted to *live*, he didn't want to die. We were getting divorced because I didn't want to take his trip anymore, the vomit, the shit, the hospitals. But he showed me things, he taught me many things in life. But we had to separate. I couldn't take it anymore."

"I liked his room on skid row, it had style."

"You guys were always talking about style, you were obsessed with it."

"I still am."

"Your letters to us always meant a great deal. Jim even had a novel published using your letters as dialogue."

"Yes, it was a bad novel."

"I know, he only got $1200 for it. But your letters used to make me laugh too—you were always weeping, you were always in agony, always at the edge of death. But there was humor in your letters too. I liked the humor."

"Don't you want to take a bath?"

"Oh, no. I had a bath just before I left Phoenix."

"Listen, I need more beer. Want to come along? Need some whisky, Scotch, cigarettes?"

"No, nothing. I'll come along."

I got dressed and we walked down the cement path between the courts. Helen paused at a poinsettia plant in front of the courts. She got a flower in her hand and smelled it. "Oh, aren't they *beautiful*?"

"Christ, no," I said, "they're half-dead and blackened with the smog and the heat. Come along. . . ."

When we got back I turned on the air cooler and drank more beer. We talked about Jim. "Jim and I had a lot of understanding," she said. "I remember once there was a wasp in the house and we killed it, and after we killed it we realized what we had done. We both sat down on the rug and cried."

I told her that I thought Jim was a damned fine writer and that I was going to do the foreword to one of his last books. I said I liked Jim's hard lines but that he usually

ruined a poem with the last line—going into borrowed poetics or over poetics to rather clean up or compensate for
what he had said. Take away his last lines, I said, and he'd
almost be as good as Bukowski.

We talked for some time. I wasn't hungry. She made
herself a sandwich. We undressed and went to bed. We
kissed goodnight and then slept. . . . At 6 a.m. she got up
and told me she was going to look at the sunrise.

I'd been up an hour or so, and we were talking about
Jim when Tod and Nickey came over from the court across
the way. They were in their mid-20s: Tod worked at a dirty
bookstore and Nickey danced in one of the bars. "Want
some shit?" asked Tod. "It's too early," I said.

"What'll we do?" asked Tod.

"God bless me, I don't know," I said. It was Saturday
morning.

"Let's go to Laguna Beach," said Tod. "I know where
we can get a big double at a motel for $18."

Helen leaped up and clapped her hands. "Oh, let's *do*!
Laguna Beach! I'll *even* get drunk!"

Tod walked into the bedroom, got on the phone, and
made the reservations. . . .

"This 55-mile-per-hour speed limit doesn't mean shit,"
said Tod.

Tod had it up to 80, 85, weaving in and out of heavy
traffic. Nickey smoked a cigarette and relaxed beneath her
dark shades. A joint appeared. Helen declined. It was hot
and the beer went down good. Helen crouched in the corner of the back seat watching traffic. Tod turned up the radio and we got it out of the speaker in the rear seat. I threw
my coat over it and asked them, "You ever hear about the
male frog with the three assholes?"

"No," said Nickey.

"Well," I said, "he pissed out of all three of them because his wife said she didn't want to take any more of his
crap, hahahaha!"

"Pass me a beer, will you?" asked Tod. . . .

The motel was all right, just off the ocean, bottom-floor
front. But there wasn't anything to drink.

"Where's the nearest liquor store?" I asked.

"We can all walk down there together, right along the water," said Tod.

"Right along the *water*?" asked Helen. "Oh, wonderful!" We set out.

Helen took her shoes off and walked down along the shore letting the water run over her feet. She walked along with her head down looking at the water. Then she'd turn and look at the waves. We left her down there when we got to the liquor store. Nickey needed something out of the drugstore. We waited outside. When Nickey came out I suggested that she go down and check out Helen and that we'd be along. Tod then suggested a bar on the way and we went in. There were only two seats left and they were next to a young woman. We slid in.

We ordered. The girl next to me was a strawberry blonde, young, not really a whore, not really anything, or maybe something. Just like in one of my fucking short stories. We got our drinks and I talked to Tod a moment and then I said to the girl, "Pardon me, but you are just like the girls in my short stories, and so it's funny."

"And how are the girls in your short stories?"

"Just like you, mostly like you, fair in eye and body but mostly with sensitive lips just like yours."

"Are you a writer?"

"Yes, look at my hands."

"Are you any good?"

"Oh, yes, but better in bed than at the ribbon."

"Are you better than Lawrence, better than Hemingway?"

"In or out of bed?"

She smiled. Tod nudged me with his knee: "Hey, man, you're really making it with her."

"My friend says that I am really making it with you. Is that true?"

"I'm not sure. Tell me more about the women in bars in your short stories."

"Well, like any other bar cowboy, next thing I do is to lay my leg against hers while I'm feeding her my line of

shit, but there's a way to lay a leg against a leg and a way
to feed a line of shit. Everything is a way of writing a poem
and most men can't write them. Now, here's my leg."

"I can hardly feel it."

"I know. But when I do that, anyhow, in the stories the
lady usually buys me a drink."

"Peter," said the strawberry blonde, "three drinks." She
paid. "Tell me more."

"Well, in the story I usually tell the strawberry blonde
the sad facts of my life. It's an old male ploy—looking for
sympathy, looking for mother, looking for a fuck. Get a
fuck, you score one against the female race and move on
to the next one."

"Is that what you'd like to do?"

"I'd like to, but I'm weak, sentimental—a red onion, a
piece of smitten dust—terribly weak, a crippled dog with
a red, white, and blue bunghole—brought up out of strict
parentage that never allowed emotion or love. I'm trying to
get it, finally, at this end when the gray is crawling into my
eyebrows. How'd you like that song?"

"You've got a line."

"I've got a line, but sometimes I awaken in front of a
bathroom mirror, it's like a dream, and I've got this mother butcher knife laying right across the jugular vein. So
far I have laughed, tossed the blade into the bathtub, and
poured another drink."

"You sound like a fucking mess."

"I am a fucking mess. But at the same time I am sentimental. I get attached—to dirty dishes, the sound of women
pissing, a piece of paper on the rug, even the side of a bus
passing in traffic—it seems like an old friend. I don't know
what it means, but I don't want to be cured of it."

"I'll go with you," she said, "wherever you're going."

"Oh, shit, I was afraid of that."

"What's the matter?"

"He's got a woman. I've got a woman. Mine's wandering the beach. His is watching mine. She's not even mine,
that's the sad part. We could have made it."

"I know it."

I couldn't remember my phone number but I gave her my address on a torn piece of brown paper. I knew I would never see her again and I couldn't blame her. . . . After Tod and I got out of the bar we saw her walking down the sidewalk toward the east. . . .

"Hey, there she goes," said Tod. I watched her walk away, 24 years old, red yellow hair down to her butt, revolving, moving slowly, slowly away. . . .

Back at the motel we sat and drank, all of us but Helen, she said she didn't care for any. We talked about Jim and his work, and I said that Jim's strongest poems were his poems about drugs. Helen said again that she refused to mourn Jim, and I said, that's fine, and I kept drinking, thinking of the strawberry blonde. I drank quite a bit, more than I usually drink, which is a good serving for any man. We finally all went to our beds. I remembered one of the last things Jim had told me: "She's been good to me but she doesn't need me anymore. I can't get it up."

I looked over at her in the bed. She was heavy, squat, with short fat hands, almost no nose at all. Irish?

"Why don't you turn on your fucking side?" I asked her. "You lay like a brick."

There was no sound from her bed but she was not asleep. Tod knocked on the door. "Hey, let's take a swim in the pool!"

"O.K., babe," I said. It was 12:15 a.m. and I had been drinking for hours. I didn't have any trunks, hadn't been in water for 30 years. I was in dark blue shorts, skivvies. I drank a bottle of warm beer, walked out. Tod and Nickey were already swimming, squealing, they were high on the shit. Ten p.m. was closing time for the pool. "SHIT UPON THE UNIVERSE OF LOVE!" I screamed. That awakened somebody. He came out. "I'll turn on the lights," he said, "I'll turn the heat on in the pool."

"Fine," I told him, "so long as you don't fuck with me. Just shut up and vanish."

I sat there in my skivvies, looking down at the green

water. I noticed how fat my belly was, how ugly and unpliable and graceless that flesh was, and then I noticed Helen standing behind me in a housedress.

Back inside, Helen and I went to bed again.

"You just lay there like a big box of margarine," I said.

She wouldn't converse with me.

"To live with a woman like you for nine years," I said, "no wonder your husband took the needle." Then I rolled over and slept. . . .

I awakened sick, of course. Helen had awakened me at 6 a.m. to tell me that she had wanted to walk along the shore to see the beauties of the sunrise. She came back around 9:30 and Tod awakened me to ask if I wanted to have breakfast with the three of them. I told them no and Tod came back later with a 7-UP and some Alka-Seltzer. They left. I took both, then watched a cowboy movie on TV. The girl in the movie reminded me much of the strawberry blonde, her eyes were not great but it was the lips. I got a hard-on watching her so I knew I had my strength back; I vomited and opened a beer. Then I had another. . . .

They came back at 11:15 and Helen saw me in my shorts with the beer bottle in my hand, and I was smoking a small black cigar and she said, "I think I'll sit outside and watch the last of my California sunlight." And with that she walked outside and placed herself in one of the canvas chairs about the pool. Nickey walked out and photoed her lounging in the chair. . . .

It was a long ride to the airport. Helen sat as far away from me in the back seat as she could get, she was utterly pushed against the other side of the car as if she wanted to squeeze away from me forever. I had my beer. We drove on in silence. I reached up and yanked Nickey's hair, poked my finger into her throat. She smiled back at me. I told Tod, "Please, let's turn on the radio."

The music came on through. Helen sat crouched, appearing to be viewing the landscape, then she appeared to be asleep. "She needs sleep," I said, "she got up at 6 a.m. both mornings I slept with her."

Then she leaned up, as if awake: "This is a lovely countryside."

"Look, Helen," I said, "we're going back to Los Angeles. Your flight doesn't leave until 4:30. We'll drive you back in."

"No, drive me there now."

"But it's only 12:30."

"It's all right. I'll get a chance to look at people. I'll have a drink."

"O.K.," I said.

We made International. Tod made as if to pull into a parking lot. "No," said Helen, "just leave me off in front of TWA."

"Are you sure?"

As we pulled up to the ramp area she finally looked at me. "Well, goodbye." I picked up one of her hands, kissed it, said, "Goodbye, Helen." Then she was gone into the glass doors. We drove off. I suppose the best part I remember was the dinner we had that night before in Laguna. I had threatened everybody, promised to open their ventilators, but nothing had happened—no need for me to smash glass and be belted across the back of the neck and jailed—it had come off fairly well for a change, people were laughing, even Helen laughed a little bit. The food was good—seafood mixed with steak. We ate everything, and drank—except for one of us. I liked that night.

Driving back to our court, Tod and Nickey were cooling it.

"That was a long breakfast you mothers had. I was afraid we were going to be overcharged for not making check-out time."

"She talked a long time," said Tod. "She told us a story about where her and Jim had killed a wasp one time and they sat down on their rug and cried. Then she told us the morning she got up early she went down to the shore and saved an animal, some children were trying to kill an animal and she saved it."

"It was still a long breakfast."

"I know, but she paid for it."

"It still seemed like a long breakfast."

"She said she had intended to go to Frisco to see some more poets but that after seeing you that she just didn't care to."

"My god, didn't you tell her that they weren't like me?"

"She didn't believe us. She only wanted to go back home."

We drove on in. Tod passed me a joint. "Still going to write the foreword?"

"Hell, yes."

"But she lived with him for nine years."

"She just thought she did." I passed the joint on up.

L.A. Free Press, July 12, 1974

Notes of a Dirty Old Man

They were drunk and driving along the coast near the water. Pinky, the guitar player, and his girl, Zelma, were up front. Carl and Kathy were in the back. They were on the rift.

"The time comes to finally call it," said Carl, "if you're a man of any kind at all, the time comes to finally call it."

"For Christ's sake," said Kathy, "why don't you shut up for a while?"

"The time comes," said Carl, "to discard that sound of loud ignorance that we once thought was glory. The time comes to toss that cunt into the air like a dirty napkin, the time comes, finally, to call it."

"All right," said Kathy, "we'll call it, why do you have to keep on going on and on about it?"

"Balzac had some excellent advice. He said if you got yourself a woman of 50 that the shit-level dropped way off. That was his advice, get yourself a woman of 50."

"Well, *get* yourself one then," said Kathy.

"Hey," said Pinky, "here's a place that serves food and drink. We're stopping."

Pinky drove into the parking lot and they got out. They walked in and found a table at the back.

Business was bad. There was one girl drinking at the bar and only one other table was taken. They could see the ocean from the window. They ordered drinks and sandwiches. The ocean kept breaking against the rocks but the sound seemed more neurotic than peaceful. Carl drank half of his drink. "No soup in the mainline," he said, "no heather paradise home; the whore parts her hair with a fresh yellow gladiola. . . ."

SHUT UP A WHILE!

"The asshole," said Kathy. "I caught him in the kitchen talking to this professor of French and she was asking him if he'd like to go to Paris with her, and he said, 'Sure, I'll go to Paris with you.' She's translating this poet from Algeria and Carl calls him an 'Algerian nigger' and when they go to shake hands Carl spits on his hand. You call that a great soul? He's an *asshole*."

"Yes, he is."

"I mean *you*."

"Oh."

Carl ordered another round of drinks. "Kathy likes Ransom Jepson. She says he's a strong man and that I hurt his feelings. Jepson is eternally crouched at the outer edges of art. He came over uninvited one day and crouched on the floor with his chapbook of poems that he paid to have published. And he began his funny-man routine. Unfortunately, only one or two recognize the source of his comedy: a bitchy mildewed jealousy. I got up and left and Kathy said he became very angry about that. He screamed, 'Well, we don't NEED him! We don't need him!' And he's right."

"People needn't be *invited*! *I* like people dropping by every 10 minutes! It was a hell of a lot more interesting when we were seeing people than it is now."

"Interesting for who?"

"And that house is the *perfect* house for parties! It's made for parties!"

Carl didn't answer. The sandwiches arrived. Carl ordered another drink for himself.

BALZAC

"And I'll tell you something else," said Kathy. "I've got a HELL OF A LOT MORE PO- TENTIAL THAN YOU HAVE! That's right! A HELL of a lot more! You and your stories about 10-year-old girls getting raped!"

Carl went to his new drink.

"And I'll tell you something else," she went on, "if you were as great as you think you are, you'd be a lot more tolerant toward people than you are! And you *lie* in your work! My sisters write the *truth* and I do too! We put it down as it is and you'll see, it will count for something!"

Pinky and Zelma had long ago begun a quiet conversation of their own. The sandwiches managed to get finished, and the drinks, and they paid and walked back to the car.

Carl had a few drinks left in the pint and he took one. They drove on down the coast.

"You should surround yourself with strong people," Karen went on, "all you do is surround yourself with weak people, people who agree with you, like the Mannards."

"The Mannards?"

"As it is, people wonder what the *shit* I'm doing with you anyhow!" Then Kathy settled back on the seat.

If you looked out the window, you could see that the water kept running up along the sand and then falling back. Then it tried again. Sometimes it did better, sometimes it

PEOPLE WONDER WHAT THE <u>SHIT</u>....

did worse. And up higher, perched on cliff areas, were the
expensive homes with the windows that overlooked it all,
but the homes had a sadness and a futility to them, and if
you looked carefully enough and if you caught the rays,
you could sense the agony and the argument and the uselessness that occurred inside of them. If you looked carefully enough and caught the rays, you could see that even
the cliffs were immersed in the uselessness of what was
transpiring or not transpiring. Carl caught it, the edge of it
on top of everything else. The sandwich began to come up.
He rolled the window down and stuck his head out and
vomited in the wind. Through his mind flashed the line:
bedpans as helmets out of Knoxville. Then he pulled his head
back in, rolled the window up.

Nobody said anything, not even Kathy.

L.A. Free Press, August 16, 1974

Notes of a Dirty Old Man

The Great Poet had finished his reading and was answering questions from the audience. It was apparent that the Great Poet had become intoxicated while drinking from his thermos during the reading but he continued to answer questions.

"What do you think of poetry readings?"

"I believe them to be a soul-suck but when the phone rings and the price is right I am as big a whore as the next. Next question?"

"Why don't you like readings? If you don't like them, why do you give them?"

The Great Poet lifted his thermos and tilted it. It was empty.

"Readings keep me off food stamps and ATD. A poetess I know gave 82 readings last year. She claims that if you don't like to give readings you shouldn't. 'There are other jobs, other ways of making a living,' she says. This isn't true. For some people there aren't other jobs, for some people there are no jobs at all."

"RIGHT ON, BROTHER!" screamed somebody from the audience.

"JESUS CHRIST," the Great Poet screamed back, "DOESN'T ANYBODY EVEN HAVE A BEER? MY THERMOS IS EMPTY!"

Within 120 seconds the Great Poet had a bottle of beer in his hand. "One place I read the janitor chastised me for drinking beer on campus. He called the National Guard."

"What campus was that?"

"Kent State . . . Jesus Christ, nobody's laughing! Whatsa matta with you people? People who go to poetry readings aren't interested in poetry. They want to see what you look like, they want to see you vomit, they want to see you die. They want to kiss your balls and at the same time pickle them in a glass jar. People who go to poetry readings are peep freaks. They want to fuck the poet or tame him or murder him or marry him or read to him from their own inept works. They laugh at the wrong lines, they are easy to please, and they are also vindictive and hateful. And many are nice and some are beautiful; they are bland and easy, they are soft and put to sleep by the universities. Why a poet should want to read to these outside of anything but sheer economic necessity I will never know."

"GET THE HELL DOWN FROM THERE! WE WANT TO HEAR ROBERT CREELEY!"

"YOU WANT TO HEAR YOUR OWN FARTS RINGING A COPPER BELL OUTSIDE SOME LAST SYPHILITIC JERUSALEM! JESUS, I NEED ANOTHER BEER! AND DOESN'T ANYBODY HAVE ANYTHING MORE THAN BEER?"

A young blonde girl of some beauty got up from the front row and stuck out a pint of vodka. The Great Poet accepted that, screwed off the top and drained one quarter of the bottle. "I refuse to fuck the coeds and never will. Their youth for my power is not a fair exchange. The American idea of a stud sickens me. I don't believe that a real man fucks everybody. I believe that a real man fucks somebody. The idea is not to score at random but to select with divinity." The Great Poet took another hit of the vodka, then searched the front row for the blonde. "Ah, what's your phone number, honey?"

People were beginning to walk out. The Great Poet sat watching them leave. "I fuck up at readings. Sometimes I get so drunk I can't finish. I'm an alcoholic first and a poet later. Some readings I don't remember anything about. But they remember me. They want a circus, they want a fool. I produce. But it's a fine act. It's more than the barroom drunk. They've *paid*, or the university has paid, and once you've accepted that coin, as 1918 as it sounds, it's your *duty*. One form of energy—and that's money—and as dirty as it sounds— one form of energy deserves another. You *owe* them and they know it and they're right. The only holy people are the suicides, they get on out. But if you're going to stay in the act, know the price; know you've got to get into your own ultimate high; they'll understand it one way or the other IF you get high enough. I've watched many of the poets: they just take the money and sit up there and act holy. If you're going to be a whore you might as well be a good one."

About one-half the audience remained. The Great Poet became silent and sat drinking the vodka. A very delicate boy, thin, young, stood up in the audience. "Any new books, upcoming publications, unusual adventures, dilemmas, other?" The boy appeared to be reading off a sheet of paper.

"Yes, I know a guy with warts on his dick, I have the flu, my wall heater won't light, and I have taken to masturbating against women's faces on my TV set."

The boy, still standing, read another question from his sheet of paper. "Has telling-it-like-it-is led to many censorship problems in having your work published?"

"Getting published is no problem. My editors are bigger perverts than I am."

The boy consulted his sheet again. "When did you begin to write (not literally but literarily) and why (i.e., what, if anything, do you hope to achieve in writing)?"

"*Story* magazine, 1944. What I hope to achieve in writing is never to have to go back to working for the post office again, never having to be a janitor again, never to have to travel with a railroad track gang or work a slaughterhouse or have a woman support me again. What I hope to achieve in writing is the time to love a woman properly."

"THE WAY YOU DRINK," came a voice from the audience, "YOU PROBABLY CAN'T GET IT UP!"

"I asked for questions not declarations," said the Great Poet taking another drink of vodka and chasing it with a swig from a bottle of French wine that had suddenly appeared.

The boy, standing very straight, with his tape recorder turned on, consulted his sheet. "For whom do you write (seeing as the general public, even in this liberated day, no doubt finds and has found—but perhaps will not find— your works grossly perverse and/or pornographic?"

"I write like many a good fellow, to keep from going bawdy asshole crazy. The public may or may not arrive. What counts mainly is a good smoke, a mirror to squeeze my blackheads in and, of course, unclogged bowels."

"THE ONE THING YOU DON'T HAVE," came a voice from the audience, "IS UNCLOGGED BOWELS."

"That fellow out there," said the Great Poet chasing a drink of wine with a drink of vodka, "is a plant to make me look good. I write his lines. In his spare time he teaches a private advanced poetry workshop. In the Fall he is accepting a professorship at the University of Madrid to teach the Literature of the Ages to all Spanish seamen who have caught the clap more than five times."

Still standing and still reading off of his sheet the boy continued. "What kind of mood inspires a writing session?"

"A breakup of a good love experience or a $150 loss at the track. The latter is the more formidable."

"YOU MEAN," came the voice from the audience, "THAT YOU CONSIDER LOVE WORTH LESS THAN $150?"

"Especially," said the Great Poet, finishing the vodka, "in Calcutta. The heart dies without the stomach. And whether you like it or not, bastard, the world is moving more and more toward Calcutta."

Three Women's Liberationists, four homosexuals, two lesbians, one bisexual, one Catholic priest got up and left, followed by a fellow who had one snort of *H* remaining in his apartment. That left 13.

"Notwithstanding the fundamental (and only relevant) fact that you *write*, I can't help probing your literary roots and offshoots and the rest of the peripheral lore. That brings me to queries like: 'What do you think of New Orleans?'"

"When I think of New Orleans I think of *Streetcar* and when I think of *Streetcar* I think that T. Williams is, finally, not a very good writer."

"HOW MANY PLAYS HAVE YOU HAD ON BROAD-WAY?" came the voice from the audience.

"Listen, wino, if you hook your toes over the headboard and do a deep back bend you may meet your soul in your mouth. I thought I paid you off? Why don't you go back to Bolinas and hook chestnuts into the fire with Gerard Malanga?"

The boy continued to read from his paper: "How could

you possibly have given 14 years of your wonderfully mad life to the Post Office, and, in spite of it, remained wonderfully mad?"

"I suppose that all the wonderful madmen really did wish they were wonderfully mad. But I'm not wonderfully mad. Most of the time I am very dull and I sit around waiting. Waiting is the essence. And while you're waiting anybody can come along and carry away your girl and your housecat. And if it works that way they deserve each other."

Six more of the audience left. That left seven. The Great Poet still had half a bottle of wine left. The boy read on: "This may seem too personal—but whatever possessed you to go the institutional route and get married? Are you/ were you happily so?"

"She was the first one to call me a genius. No. No."

"What's your historical perspective, i.e., do you like to picture your writings as dissertation material, as the subject of scholarly analysis, in literary anthologies, etc. or does this immortalization status matter to you at all?"

"I'm like anybody else: I guess it's better to be talked about than never mentioned at all, especially when you have to pay the rent."

The Great Poet began to sway . . . to sway and sway, back and forth on his tiny chair. He was drunk, he was tired.

"In your various claims to genius (innate) of a mythical misfit, or the literary genius (cultivated) of an original writer, or the tongue-in-cheek genius (designated) of high I.Q., prodigious inventive, and social acclaim—the term has always been fascinatingly exclusive to us—what do you mean by 'genius?'"

The Great Poet finished the bottle of wine, attempted to roll and cigarette and failed. "I don't know."

There were more questions such as, Do you feel Art (creative expression) has any function beyond itself? Were you influenced by any great writers (or ungreat writers) in particular? Do you consider anything sacred? What is your fondest hope and your greatest fear? If you had to do it over again, with a prenatal option, would you choose the life you have lived, would you choose again, in fact?

But the Great Poet was very drunk. There were two who got him off the stage both from the Department of the Humanities. One of them gave him a neat long envelope which the Great Poet placed in his inner coat pocket. He walked out of the auditorium, got lost down one hall, turned, found his way out, and walked across the campus lawn. A young girl sitting on the cement bench heard his last words: "Easy money." Then the Great Poet walked over the hill of green grass, down the other side, and was gone.

L.A. Free Press, November 22, 1974

Notes of a Dirty Old Man

H.P., New Jersey
April 3, 1975
Hello Mom:

Like I promised you that I'd write, I'm writing. This is the third letter since the new term began, and I know you're interested in how I'm doing in college but I wrote you about that in my last two letters. But I know you also want to know how I'm doing out of college. A bunch of us live together in this roominghouse. This old guy cooks for us and he stands in the kitchen cooking, dressed in these red leotards. He just keeps cooking and cooking all the time, standing in the kitchen, cooking and humming. He wears this amulet around his neck on a silver chain and it says, "I'm number one!" Bobby is his name and he has this white hair. We sit around with plates of food in the other room and somebody will say, "This food SUCKS!" Then he'll throw the plate against the wall. Nobody cleans up anything. The ants are everywhere and we've vomited in the closet and in the dresser drawers. It really stinks here, we're always vomiting, even the ants are vomiting. Bobby's specialty is meatballs and spaghetti. The other night he's standing in there humming and cooking and somebody throws a meatball against the wall in the kitchen. It hits the wall in there, breaks, and it spatters like a hand grenade, little pieces of it falling all over him. He just goes on humming and cooking, singing little words . . . "Hummmmmmmm, hummmmmm, *love* is just so *marvelous!*" And somebody says, "Jesus Christ, *look*, Bobby is wearing meatballs in his hair!" And sure enough, he is. There are these little pieces of meat hanging in his white hair. Then a guy finds this machete. He takes the machete and starts breaking up plates with it. "If we break all these plates the son of a bitch will have nothing to put his food on!" Then somebody else says, "Well, just why don't we run his ass out of here, why not run him down the street?" "All right." "All right." "All right." So we get up behind him and we break his ass out of

135

his red leotards and he's got on these black silk panties on underneath. Now, Mom, I've got nothing especially against fags and/or transvestites but those black panties have these large netted areas for the flesh to show through, but instead his balls have dropped on down through and they dangle, hanging out there. "*Awful!*" "Oh, how *awful!*" We ran him down the street, his balls flying.

This caretaker here, Al Williams, he takes care of the grounds and the plumbing, all that. He's got this strange thing about squirrels. He hates squirrels. He'll go into it about the squirrels. All kinds of things. "They chew the wires out in the attic," he says. He's always catching squirrels. He has this large cage and he baits it with food, good stuff, none of Bobby's and when he gets one he brings the cage inside, he carries it in and he says, "Looky, boys, I got me one of those rotten sons of bitches! Ha!" First time I saw him do it he sat the cage down and then came back with a can of gasoline. He poured the gas all over the squirrel. Then he lit a match and turned to us: "No energy shortage here, fellas." Then he tossed the match. The squirrel starts running and twisting, making sounds, whirling, flipping. Al watches and takes his coat off: "Hmmmm . . . gettin' kind of warm here, you noticed, fellas?"

There are dead squirrels everywhere. You go out in the yard and here's one and there's one. Here's one that's been burned, the paw twisted-up near its nose. In the wintertime he freezes them. You walk along and all of a sudden here's a squirrel. It looks up at you out of a block of ice.

But Al's funny too. This roominghouse is chopped in half by a yard in the center. We've got women on one side and men on the other. One day Al's mowing the lawn, stopping to throw dead squirrels into the rose bushes when he notices some old gal peering at him from the tiny slit under the shade. She's got this shade almost pulled down and she's watching. Al mows the lawn. She's down on her knees in her room there, peering out. He sees it. Next whirl around the lawn he whips out his dick and he lets it dangle as he walks along. She keeps looking. Too much. So he walks over and with her peering at him there on her knees he begins to whack-off. She doesn't move, her two little gnat-eyes peering. As he comes, spurting white semen into the screen at her, he screams out, "Christ died for our sins, you fucking Nazi!"

But things are happening outside of this roominghouse, too. The cops are driving me crazy. These N.J. cops aren't anything like L.A. cops. You know, L.A. cops are pretty pale boys taught to say nice polite speeches. They'll kill you if they have to but mostly they're interested in paying off homes in Altadena where they have crazy wives who keep making bed quilts by hand, one after the other, until there are so many bed quilts they stack them in the closets and in the garage and on top of the refrigerator. N.J. cops are different, though. They have guns and clubs and it makes them feel good. They do whatever they want to do and say whatever they want to say. If they have wives, their wives give them handjobs in the bathtub after work. So I'm driving along and this cop pulls me over. He walks up. None of that: "Sir, do you *realize* what you have done wrong?" "Oh no, thank you, officer, do tell me." This cop just walks up and says, "Hey, Jackoff, your turn-blinkers aren't cuttin' jackcheese on Halloween night!" "Well, look, kid," I tell him, "my mind happens to be in the variances of the monosyllable." There's this tidal wave roar and then I hear him: "Look, Jackoff, mess with me, just MESS with me, burn-out, TRY to mess with me you jackoff burn-out, I'll blow your FUCKING BALLS OFF! I'll blow 'em into jelly-slices of hot BLOODY SHIT!"

That's a N.J. cop, Mom.

So after that ticket I decide I need to hide out so I go into the first movie house I can find. The feature film's not very good, so what you do is just forget it and you start staring at the leading lady's ear. Those whirls. And down in there, most probably wax. So she's talking all this lasagna and she's got wax in the ear. Then, all of a sudden, there's another N.J. cop. He's stopped at the thick, sound doors just outside the seats. All he's got to do is to push them open and walk in. But he's standing out there and he's got his gun out and he's waving it around. "Hey! Open this place up! Open these goddamned doors and let me in! I'm the fucking heat!" I can't believe it. He keeps pounding. Some guy gets scared and lets him in. The cop swings on in. He's got one of these huge tins of popcorn and a walky-talky. He sits down in the back row. There's the walky-talky . . . . "SLeeeeech BAaar Skleetch . . ." "Hello, this is patrolman Evans reporting from the Pink Ivor Theatre . . . ." "Skee-eeeeetch SKeeeee RRrroweeweeeeeee . . ." Then he starts cracking old deaddog jokes into the walky-talky and jamming this popcorn into his mouth. It goes on like this for 15 or 20 minutes. Finally some guy asks him, "Sir, can you tell me what you're doing here?" The cop laughs and says, "Sure, I'll tell you. We got reports that a bunch of you punks are sitting around here beating your dandelions and scraping the dried snot and gum out from under the bottoms of the seats and eating it. Any more goddamned questions?" "No sir, thank you." "The tax-paying citizens of this town demand protection from you goddamned perverts! . . . Skee, SKeeeeel, Wrrrorrrr, SKEeeellllllll . . . SPITZttzzz!"

I get out of there and I get in my car and all of a sudden the steering wheel slips out of my hand and I see myself headed right at this telephone pole. I can't get out of it—I duck my head down into the wheel at the last moment and the car spins upright and stops. I pull back and look. I'm pointed toward the sky like a rocket ship and some of the wires from the telephone pole had dropped down and they are whipping against the car. The wires jump back and forth and each time one of them touches the car it shoots off like a rifle shot. I ought to be dead, I think, but I'm not. I still don't believe much in God, even then. A whole gang of people with nothing to do gather around me, not too close, but they gather around anyhow and watch these snakes of lightning flick against the car. I'm in there hooked in with the seatbelt and I'm looking at them and they're looking at me. I catch one guy grinning at me and then he reaches down and rubs his balls. Too much. I turn the key in the ignition, put the car in reverse, hit the gas and the car just climbs back down that pole and rolls back on the ground. That's it. They're still looking. I back it out a little more, shift gears, and then I gun it down the street. It feels good. Then I look into the rear view: two red lights. Two more N.J. pigs. I pull up. One cop stands back with his hand on his gun holster. The other walks up, a big one with club drawn, and he motions for my driver's license. I've lost it. I tell him so.

"Hey, hey, hey, queen of the May, he lost his *driver's* license! Ho, ho, ho!" He takes his club and he beats it across the hood of my car, making these big dents. "Hey, hey, hey!" Then he goes to work on the left front fender. He finishes that, then reaches up, and smashes my sideview mirror to bits. "And, ho, ho! He don't have a sideview mirror!"

That's about it, Mom. I'm maintaining a straight B average. The weather's so gloomy around here. We never see the sun. When I won this scholarship out here I never thought it would be quite like this. We've got a new cook and he's a little better but he's hairy-ass on garlic. He even garlics the scrambled eggs. He's one of these ultra-taste freaks. He'll walk up to you with this little bottle of imported nonpareil capers and he'll say, "*Try* some! *Try* some!" They look like little snotballs soaked in vinegar. You reach in and try some. They taste just like that. "There," he'll say, "now doesn't that make your soul *tweet*?" "Yeah, Dandy," you say, "thanks ever so much." And he wanders off, dipping his fingers in the little bottle. That's about all, Mom. I'll write again.

Love, your son,
Henry

L.A. Free Press, April 11, 1975

Notes of a Dirty Old Man

Lydia got out of bed and said, "I'm getting up, I'm tired of being in bed. I'm going to take a shower." Harry stayed in bed, thinking, well shit, five more minutes. He heard her in the shower, he let himself listen to the water without trying to think of intonations. What are you going to do when it goes but ride with it? She took a long time in there. Then she was before the mirror combing her hair. Then he heard the hairspray. Then she was getting dressed. She'd brought plenty of clothing. He waited. When she walked out he got up and went into the bathroom and took a shit. When he wiped himself the paper kept bringing back the same heavy smears of brown. He finally got it out, flushed, then walked over to the mirror and looked at his face. Well, he couldn't blame anybody. He grinned and spit in the sink. He found his clothes on the floor in the corner and began to dress. When he finished he walked down the hall to the kitchen. Lydia was doing the dishes: "Thought I might to help pay our way."

Harry walked out on the veranda and gathered up a few saucers and coffee cups and ashtrays. He brought them in to Lydia. Her face was wearing the dark cloud, and he thought, O.K., well, I'd sure like to pass this one on down to the next.

Harry went back out and got the beer bottles. He almost puked looking at the beer bottles. Why didn't people who drank beer ever finish their bottles? There was San Francisco across the way. He looked at it and was glad he wasn't bottled in with them. What was wrong with San Francisco was that it pressed people too close together, so close together that they thought love was the only way out. Whatever way was out you had to be very good at and most people weren't very good at love. Not very many people. Hardly any people.

He thought of the party. It hadn't been a bad party. Not the first party where Lydia had been the storied and excellent protagonist: " . . . when I hear MUSIC I like to

DANCE! I LIKE to be SEXY! I want men to WANT me! I
LIKE DANCING! I want men to think, why can't I have
that, how come he's getting it? I come from the COUNTRY,
we dance all the TIME! Ya gotta get them into MOTION, ya
gotta get people OFF THEIR FEET! I give LIFE to your parties! I've ENHANCED your reputation!"

Perhaps she was right. Most of his life he'd been wrong,
out of motion, driving the wrong way up one-way streets,
confused, fucked, demented. That's why he'd gone to the
poem; without love or understanding you could hide inside of a poem, maybe even score a minor victory, fool
a few. He'd always told Lydia after a reading, "Well, we
fooled them again."

The second party hadn't been bad. It had been in the
daylight and nobody had been trying to score off of anybody else. The guy in the captain's cap had been particularly good: ". . . they say when they hang a man he gets
an instant erection, ejaculates, and where the sperm drops
down on the ground, up springs a magic flower. . . ." Harry
had listened to the stories and laughed, asked for more.
Lydia had hung her head, bored. Until she found some
overhanging fruits from a tree and she kept ripping them
off and eating them, saying, "Ooo, these are good!" Then
she had seemed happier.

There were many dishes and Harry left her alone and
went back to the bedroom and stretched out. Then he heard
a gagging and spitting sound from the closet. Great Christ,
now what? He got up, walked over and opened the closet
door. There was a small brown and white kitten in there.
The kitten had swallowed a balloon and was puking, only
the neck of the balloon was stuck up inside of the throat
and the vomit just emptied into the balloon, filling it up
with varicolored and mushy objects. Then Harry puked
small driblets upon his shoes, reached down and pulled
the balloon out. He took the balloon over, pushed the glass
windows open and dropped the thing into the garden. The
kitten leaped up, showed Harry a tiny dry bunghole and
leaped down into the garden after the balloon. They were
two floors up. Harry closed the glass windows.

Then he walked into the bathroom and washed his face with soap and cold water. He dried on the same red towel Lydia had used for her shower, then he walked back out to the kitchen. "How about going out for breakfast?" he asked. She didn't answer. "We're on the 1:15 to Burbank." She still didn't answer. He walked around until he found a photo album, sat down and looked at it. He laughed a couple of times, then she was over his shoulder, looking down.

"See, there's Ferlinghetti," he said.

"Oh, yeah."

"There's Ginsberg, and Norse. . . ."

"Who's that? The black guy? Didn't we see him at the party?"

"No."

"He spoke to you."

"No."

"Who's that?"

"McClure."

Harry handed her the photo album and went over and got a beer. He opened the beer. "This is a nice place. Must run her $400 a month."

"Maybe she's fucking the guy upstairs."

"Who's that?"

"You met him yesterday. He's prettier than Joe."

"I didn't notice."

"All right," she said, folding the album, "let's go eat."

Lydia went in and combed her hair again. "Is it cold outside?"

"For you, yes."

"Should I wear my coat?"

"Yes."

They walked through the garden and then left and down toward the bay, down the long series of cement steps. As they went down the steps each of her heels hit each surface with a hard flat noise. "I can always tell when she's coming to see you in the court," a friend had told him, "it sounds like a Nazi storm trooper." But Harry still liked to be near her, he remembered all the good things she had taught him, little secrets she had helped him with, when she had met him he was almost dead of acute alcoholism, and she had loved him then, but as his luck had changed her love had changed, and the better his luck the worse her love, until it had vanished. Now they walked down the steps together. They climbed on down in silence. Harry thought about Arthur Schopenhauer; she thought, I've given him four years of my life.

It was almost noon. She wanted breakfast. Most of the places were sandwich shops. They kept walking. People with cameras walked by. Only the rich lived on such a day as Monday, or the talented, and the rich were the true lucky talented.

They finally found a place and walked in. It was empty and stank of defeat. We've found the proper place to eat in, thought Harry. Harry chose the corned beef on rye plus a side order of cole slaw. Lydia looked at the board a long time; she was competitive. She chose a plate special. Harry knew she would not be able to eat it all. But that didn't matter. He paid for the food and walked it over to the table. Harry hadn't noticed whether she had come on to the clerk or not; it had gotten wearing, those notations.

They sat down to eat. "Why don't you watch me when I dance with a guy? You say I rub against his cock. Why don't you really watch? You get drunk and you overreact. I don't give them my pussy. I give *you* the pussy. If *you* don't want the pussy, that's up to you."

But it wasn't true. She'd given the pussy to plenty. What in the hell am I doing with a woman 20 years younger than I am anyhow? I'm going to get one 30 years younger and have her Vaseline my asshole and jam a week's worth of my dirty stockings up there. "I found a kitten in the closet choking on a balloon," he said.

"What?"

"Nothing."

Harry finished his sandwich and slaw and coffee and waited. She couldn't finish her plate and passed the food over. Having been raised in poverty he finished her plate.

Plate, pussy, platitude, Plato, the words went through his mind.

They walked out and back down the runway. Same tourists, same death, same cameras, same lack of chance, of breath. For a moment he romanticized Marat in the tub with his boils, and being knifed by the high-class whore in ass-high nylons.

They walked along and Lydia said, "Wait a minute." She stopped and looked into a window. There were four or five pairs of boots twisted and drying in the sun and heat of the window and some web-like strings of ladies underthings long ago rotted with an indifference to themselves. She kept looking at them as if they contained juice and meaning and music. Harry waited, attempting to hide an irritation, then he let the irritation hit him, then he tasted it and relaxed, thinking, what the fuck, she knows the game, she expects me to be irritated. And having known that, he waited. She pulled from the window and they walked down the street together. Soon enough, she found something else. Some Dalí imitations. She sucked on them and he waited. She expects me, thought Harry, to scream at her, "For Christ's sake, stop being such a fool. I love you anyhow!" Just like when she's dancing with a Dalí imitation.

Harry waited anyhow until she got more tired with looking than he did with waiting. He'd often told her that anybody who was interested in everything could never know anything. But he'd wearied in trying to awaken her and she'd wearied in trying to awaken him in what she thought was true.

They walked along and got back up to the steps. It was a long climb. They got on up. And undressed. And got back into the bedroom. She kept kissing him and getting hot. He got down and lifted her legs, got his hands under her ass, and then she said, "Look, don't you think we better get a towel since it's their bed?" And Harry said, "Yes, let's get a towel." And she got the same red one she had showered with and spread it under herself and Harry lifted her ass again, one hand upon each mound, ducked his head in and looked, decided to do it well one more time, flicked his tongue through the hairs at first, all the time realizing that it was useless, that there was no chance, no hope, almost no feeling, he flicked his tongue down through the hairs, touched the lips, ran the tongue on up to the clit, hit it, withdrew, hit it. She farted a small fart and he went ahead.

They got the ride to the plane and on the plane, PSA, the dark cloud dropped over her face again, she felt dismal and irritated. "Well, you ought to be happy, you outdrew Ginsberg, you outdrew Ferlinghetti. Only Yevtushenko has outdrawn you in Frisco. You ought to be happy."

"Care for a drink?"

"No."

Harry ordered a vodka and 7.

"I'm going to the ladies room," she said.

When she left Harry took out the letter from Jean. "You know I've lived in this town for two months, and have carried on an inner dialogue with you most of that time. Determined not to call or write, it feels as if my own plumbing is backing up on me. Time does not work quickly enough for me, and that inevitable indifference to you stays elusive. These lines then are a therapy. Perhaps if I put them down I will give myself some peaceful time. Already I run out of things to say. Ambivalence is the problem. Each time I feel he is a destructive son of a bitch, grinning evil, a thin small voice clearly says but he can't help it, he too is programmed—I do believe you act upon people and things as you must. You are a victim, too. There is no winning for anyone except I somehow want to 'win' something. The freedom to read Orson Bean and you with the same interest is as close as I can get. To be in the same room with you and simply be affectionately interested in what you do or say is another win too. Perhaps none of the above is possible but that's the goal—I am dried out. The last year has been revealing and draining, and there never was much left to be spendthrift with. . . . I have re-learned caution and suspicion runs high. You my ex-friend can take much of the credit. So scratch your belly and have a laugh on me. . . ."

The poor girl's been drinking again, thought Harry, putting the letter back in his coat. Lydia walked back and strapped herself in. "You just don't know how to party! I can't teach you how to party! You get mad when I dance with the men, you're so jealous!"

"Most parties are a contest of minor wills . . . it's wearing."

"We never have a good time. All we do is go to the race-track and to poetry readings. We never go anywhere."

"Christ, haven't you ever realized that I'm a recluse?"

"All you do is get drunk! You don't want to *face* people!"

"Exactly."

Harry got the stewardess and got himself another vod-ka and 7. Lydia declined. The captain announced that the craft was descending and that PSA was pleased that the passengers had boarded the craft. "We hope that you'll try us again," he said. Harry got the drink down in two tries. The Hollywood-Burbank airport leaped up to meet them. There was no chance at all. The wheels were gone, the belly was gone and the heart pumped piss.

L.A. Free Press, June 13–19, 1975

Notes of a Dirty Old Man

I left L.A. International with a tremendous hangover to give a reading in Arkansas. I was lucky enough to get a seat by myself and waited on the first drink. The flight captain announced himself as Captain Winehead, which I thought fit the situation. When the stewardess came by, she asked me if I wished two drinks and I said, "Yes." She had noticed my red nose, I supposed. Airliners were more boring than riding metropolitan buses—all the men with their perfect hairdos and their Business Administration educations, glad to get away from their wives, glad to get fucked out of town, glad to see The Game of the Week at 35,000 feet. But they drank, too. We all drank. America was the land of the hustle, and if you didn't hustle, you were soon flushed away. I was going to hustle two universities for $500 plus air, food, lodging, and whatever else I could get. I was going to read them some poetry and bleed a little for them. I knew one of the stewardesses. She lived in Long Beach and I used to phone her drunk and tell her that I would eat her pussy better than it had ever been eaten by man, beast, or space creature. I had never gotten down to do it, however, and one drunken night we had both screamed at each other over the phone, and it had been over, was over. She stood up front, trying not to notice me, and I stared at her behind and her calves and thighs and her breasts like a real macho pig so that she'd have very vile things to tell her girlfriends about me—which would arouse them to buy my books. In my trade, you need talent plus an act. Talent alone won't do it. Talent alone sometimes takes a century to surface, and nobody likes to get that far behind in their rent.

We had lunch, saw The Game of the Week, somebody won, somebody lost, the after-dinner wine burned my throat, my belly, and I ordered two Bloody Marys. I drank them and went to sleep, keeping both of my feet on my portfolio of poems. . . .

I awakened as we landed and when I got off, my Long

Beach stewardess told me to have a nice day and I stuck the tip of my tongue out at her just like a carwash boy. . . .

I got onto this small two-engine job and when the propellers started to whirl, all the tin layers on the wings began to curl and slap against each other. There were no instructions. We rose and the stewardess asked if anybody wanted a drink. It seemed as if we all needed one. She bumped and weaved up and down the aisle exchanging escapism for money. Then she said (loudly): "DRINK UP FAST! WE'RE GOING TO LAND!" We drank up fast and landed. In seven minutes we were up again. The stewardess asked again if anybody wanted a drink. It seemed as if we all needed more. Then she said (loudly): "DRINK UP FAST! WE'RE GOING TO LAND!" In seven minutes—after landing—we were up again. (Repeat scene.)

When I landed in this small town in Arkansas, Professor Peter James and his wife, Selma, were there to meet me. Selma looked like a movie starlet but with much more inner class. I decided for Peter's sake (and Selma's too) not to seduce her.

"You're looking great," said Pete.

"Your wife's looking great."

"You've got two hours before the reading."

"I need some vodka and orange. I can't face those bloodsuckers straight."

"We'll fix you up."

We went to their car and Pete drove to their place. It was a nice place with rather an underground below the first floor. I was shown my bedroom, downstairs. "You wanna eat?" Pete asked. "Shit no, I feel like I'm going to vomit." We went upstairs and I worked on some beer. Pete, besides being a professor, was a pretty good poet. He'd gotten a Guggenheim when those same people had stiffed me. Many people got Guggenheims, but I felt Pete deserved one even though I thought I was a better writer. But then, I think I am better than Tolstoy, Chekhov, Auden, and T.S. Eliot. . . .

At the reading backstage, Pete got the water pitcher and emptied it and refilled it with the vodka and orange. "An 80-year-old woman runs this joint. She'd cream in her panties if she saw you drinking outright. She's a nice old girl, but she still thinks poetry is about sunsets and doves-in-flight."

"O.K., I don't want to make her cream."

"Nobody does."

"Heee, heee, heee . . . aw, Pete, you old cat's tit."

I went out and read. Same as any other place: SRO. The luck was holding. And they were like any other audience—they didn't know what to do with the good poems, and in others they laughed at the wrong lines for the wrong reason, but I kept reading and pouring from the water pitcher.

"What's that you're drinking there?"

"This," I said, "is orange juice mixed with life."

"Do you have any girlfriends?"

"I have problems meeting women, but when I do I have problems getting rid of them."

"Why did you want to become a writer?"

"Next question, please. . . ."

I read them some more and told them I had flown in with Captain Winehead and seen The Game of the Week. I told them that endurance was more important than truth and that when I was in good spiritual shape, I only ate off of one dish and washed that immediately, but most of the time I was unable to do that. I read some more poems. I read poems until the water pitcher was empty, then I told them that the reading was over. There was a bit of autographing, then we got out and went to the party at the professor's house. . . .

I got drunk and did my Indian dance, my belly dance and my broken-ass-in-the-wind dance. Then I came back to where the drinks were. It's hard to drink when you dance. Pete knew what he was doing. He had couches and chairs to separate the dancers from the drinkers; each went about their own art without conflicting with the other.

I got my drink and Pete walked up. He looked around the room. "Which one do you want?"

"Is it that easy?"

"It's true Southern hospitality."

"Pete, I hope you get another Guggenheim."

"It was a good reading. But one thing you've got to realize now, you're an entertainer."

"Ah, Pete, you're two old cat's tits. . . ."

There was one I had noticed, she was older than the others and had protruding teeth, but her teeth protruded perfectly—pushing the lips always outward into this open passionate flower-shape. I wanted my mouth on that mouth. It looked like the entrance to Nirvana. She wore a short skirt and her pantyhose were pulled tight around good legs that kept crossing and uncrossing as she laughed and drank and tugged at her skirt which would just not go down. I sat down next to her as the guy on the other side of her vanished. "I'm . . . ," I started.

"I know who you are. I was at your reading."

"I'll eat your pussy. I'll drive you crazy."

"Really?"

"Umm hum."

"What do you think of Allen Ginsberg?"

"Look, don't mislead me. I want your mouth, your legs; I want to stick your fingers up my ass."

"All right."

"Remain about, I've got a bedroom downstairs. Servant's quarters."

I got up and got another drink. Some guy seven feet tall walked up to me. "Look, Chinaski, I don't believe all that shit about you living in skidrow Hollywood and knowing all the dope dealers, pimps, whores, junkies, horseplayers, drunks . . . all that."

"It's mostly true."

"What do you mean?"

"I mean, I write poems, stories, novels. The poems are basically true, the rest is truth mixed with fiction. Do you know what fiction is?"

"No."

"Fiction is an improvement on life." Having destroyed Mr. 7 by nothing, I spun for another drink. There was this blonde, about 19, with rimless glasses and a smile. The smile never left. "I want to fuck you," she said, "it's your face, I want to destroy your face with my cunt."

"That's been tried before."

"I can do it."

"What do you do, stack Gillettes in there?"

"I can do it."

"Listen, I know that any woman can destroy any man she chooses to destroy. The graveyards of America are littered with broken cocks and tongues. Women have always controlled the destiny of men and man. All this female liberation bullshit means is that women want control of the whole ballgame instead of three-fourths of it."

"You're funny."

"So was Christ. Look, I'm fucking that old one over there with the lips and the legs."

"You're having *me . . .* I *insist.*"

I walked back to the couch and started playing with the legs of the one with the short skirt and flower lips whose name was Lillian, of all things, Lilly. Whoever thought (it went through my mind) as I squeezed her knees and reached upwards that writing down one little word after another would ever lead to such generous and miraculous endearments?

The party ended and I went downstairs with Lilly. We undressed and sat against the pillows drinking vodka and vodka mix. There was a radio with a bad tenor sending his Sears-Roebuck soul into the room. Lilly told me that she had worked for years helping her husband through school, and when he had gotten his professorship he divorced her. "That's rough," I said. "You been married?" she asked. "Yes." "What happened?" "She divorced me when she found I couldn't cure her of her nymphomania."

Then I kissed Lilly. It was as good as I had imagined. That flower mouth was open. We rocked and I sucked on her teeth. We broke.

"I consider you," she said, "one of the two or three best living writers of today."

"You can do better than that," I said and switched off

the bed lamp. I kissed her some more, played with her breasts and body, then went down there. I was fairly drunk but I did all right. But after I did that to her, I couldn't do her the other way. I got up and rode and rode. I was hard but I couldn't climax. I rolled off and went to sleep. . . .

In the morning, Lilly was flat on her back, snoring. I went to the bathroom, pissed, brushed my teeth and washed my face. Then I went back to bed. I turned her toward me and started playing with her parts. I was always very horny with hangovers, not horny to eat but horny to blast—fucking was the best cure for hangovers, it got all the parts ticking again. Her breath was bad so I couldn't use the flower mouth. I mounted. She groaned. It was very good. I don't think I gave her more than 11 strokes before I climaxed and rolled off. I heard her get up and go to the bathroom. When she came back I pretended to be sleepy. When she got in I turned her back to me and decided on another three hours of sleep. After 15 minutes she got out of bed. She began to dress.

"I gotta get outta here. I gotta take my kids to school."

"Oh, I'm sorry, kid."

"Don't call me *kid*!"

"Oh. Do you still consider me one of the two or three best writers in the world?"

"No."

"All right."

"I gotta go."

She closed the door and walked up the stairway. I poured a vodka into a drinking glass, walked to the bathroom, mixed it with water, drank it down, puked it right up. . . .

L.A. Free Press, February 13–19, 1976
and Feb. 20–26, 1976

Politics and Love

Paul Caval was dubbed by his enemies as "the playboy butcher." He had overthrown that South American nation with, as he said, "Seven bullets. One which missed and a half dozen which found their proper places in the proper bodies." He also said, "You either make history or history makes you. I liken myself to the Maker." He was short, he was fat, he had little chubby fists, and he had a habit of laughing at the oddest times. That habit had often gotten him into trouble. Now, he made the trouble. The people weren't behind him but the Army was, and since the Army was the people with the guns as opposed to the larger group of people without guns, that margin was sufficient.

Now Paul Caval was behind his desk, he was fairly drunk, and he said, "Come on, Mr. Brodsky, join me in another drink! What the hell, you've arrived at one of the Thresholds of History!"

"I'd rather not, Mr. President."

"We tend to dislike Americans, Mr. Brodsky, they have bad manners. In my country, one never refuses a drink."

"Well, it is an excellent wine," said the interviewer, Mark Brodsky from the magazine *World View*. Paul Caval had never been interviewed before and he already had one hour of Paul Caval on tape. And none of it was dull; it was erratic, maybe insane, but not dull at all. The man was a monster power with a grand stage presence. The interview would make both of them famous.

Paul's wife, Monica, who had sat with them through the interview, got up and did the honors, pouring Mark Brodsky a new drink. She was a handsome young woman, although she did look a little stark as if she had seen too many things too fast. She complimented Paul Caval. They were rather like a pair in a circus cage controlling the lions and the tigers together, doing it all with an offhand grace.

"Thank you, Mrs. Caval," Mark Brodsky said. Then he looked at Paul Caval. "Now you were saying that a true democracy can't work because the vote of the average man is the vote of an idiot. . . ."

At that moment the tape recorder clicked off.

"Pardon me," Mark said, taking out the tape and replacing it with a new one.

Paul Caval drained his drink and Monica got up and refilled his glass. She moved with short steps under her long bright red gown but under that gown was a figure that any Miss World might accept. She refilled her own drink and sat back down.

Then the tape recorder was going again.

"Now," said Mark Brodsky, "what do you consider. . . ."

Paul Caval belched.

"I'm tired of talking about that crap."

He took a drain of his drink. Just a half-glass.

"By the way, American, have you met my wife?"

My, he's really getting drunk, thought Mark. Caval must have drunk at least two bottles.

"Yes, sir, I've met Monica, she's very charming. . . ."

"No, Mr. Brodsky, I meant my first wife, Andrea."

"Andrea?"

"Yeah, yeah. . . ."

"No, Mr. President, according to my notes your first wife died seven years ago . . . I never had the pleasure of meeting her."

"Well, now you will. . . ."

"Mr. President, your first wife is. . . ."

"Look buddy, Mr. President is so stuffy! Besides, I'm a dictator. Just call me Paul."

"Yes, Paul. . . ."

"Drink up, drink up! I want ya to meet my first wife."

Mark Brodsky took a drink.

"It's all right, sir. I needn't meet her. . . ."

"She's very nice," said Monica, "you'll like her."

"Damn tootin'," said Paul Caval. He had read up on old American colloquialisms.

He pressed a button on his desk, spoke into the intercom, "Maria, will you have Andrea brought down here? Now . . . And thank you. . . ."

The tape recorder spun on. Mark thought it might be a good time to continue.

"Now, Mr. President, I mean, Paul, how does your administration differ from the preceding one?"

"It doesn't."

"What?"

"We're just as ruthless and corrupt, maybe more so. . . ."

"You want us to publish that?"

"Sure, I don't give a damn," Paul Caval laughed, "what the hell can anybody do about it?"

"You've got a great sense of humor, sir."

"I'm not trying to be funny, Mr. Brodsky."

"He's funny when he's serious," said Monica, "and he's serious all the time."

Then the doors swung open and two guards entered carrying Andrea, followed by Maria, the maid, who walked a little bit behind the group.

"Put her in the chair, gentlemen, thank you. . . ."

The two guards sat Andrea in the overstuffed chair, then left. Maria bent over Andrea, applied a touch of lipstick, brushed a few strands of hair into place, and left.

Andrea was dressed in a mini-skirt, blouse, high heels, pantyhose. She had on large green earrings and she stared straight ahead. Monica was beautiful but Andrea was more so.

"Brodsky, this is Andrea, Andrea, this is Mark Brodsky, American journalist."

Mark Brodsky looked at Paul Caval.

"I'm pleased to meet her, sir."

"Don't tell me, tell *her*!"

Mark Brodsky looked at Andrea.

"Pleased to meet you, Mrs. Caval."

Mrs. Caval didn't respond.

Paul Caval smiled proudly.

"Look at her! Outside of a few cracks, she's just as good as new. We had her hair done today."

"Yes, she looks quite *real*, sir."

"What do you mean, *looks* real? She *is* real!"

"Of course, sir."

"He is very serious, Mr. Brodsky," said Monica, wife #2.

"Fill all the glasses, Monica!"

"Oh, yes!"

Monica had opened a new bottle and was ready. She did the refills and sat back down.

"A drink to Andrea, my most beautiful Andrea!"

He lifted his glass. Mark and Monica lifted their glasses. Then they all drank to Andrea.

Monica refilled their glasses.

"Now, sir," said Mark, "I'd like to continue with the interview. . . ."

"Don't you want to take some photographs of Andrea? Perhaps one for the cover of your magazine?"

"I don't know, sir."

"He's very serious, Mr. Brodsky," said Monica, wife #2.

Paul Caval got up from his desk, walked around to the overstuffed chair where Andrea sat. He reached down and pulled back her skirt.

"Look at *that*, man! You *ever* seen legs on a woman like that? *Look* at those legs!"

"They are quite beautiful, sir."

"I'm jealous," said Monica.

"Just think, Brodsky, put those legs on the cover of *World View* and think how many copies you'd sell!"

Paul Caval walked around and sat behind his desk again. He sighed contentedly.

"I sometimes take Andrea to public functions, the opera, the sporting events, to cabinet meetings. . . ."

"It's a great love you have for her, sir. . . ."

"A great *fucking* love," said Paul Caval.

Then nobody spoke for some minutes. Mark thought he might try it again. The recorder was still on.

"What do you do, sir, about pressures from Russia and the United States?"

"I tell them to go fuck themselves."

"He really does," said Monica.

Paul Caval took another drink.

"We got enough oil, enough natural resources to more

than sustain ourselves. We don't need to be freed from anything."

"Self-sustaining, that's fine, sir."

"Shit, we could make it on our cocaine exports alone, Brodsky."

"Your government has a hand in that?"

"My boy, the government *is* the hand! By the way, why don't you tell your people that Reagan dyes his hair?"

Mark felt that was a long shot but he ignored it by asking another question.

"Is your government doing anything for the poor, sir?"

"The poor? The poor are meant to be poor. That's what they are there for. That's their function. That's what they are best at. If they didn't really want to be poor they'd figure a way."

"Maybe there isn't a way, sir?"

"I was poor."

"But maybe the other poor aren't like you."

"That's just what I was telling you."

"But don't you have any compassion?"

"Hell yes!"

He looked over at Andrea whose skirt was still flipped back.

"*Look* at that! Doesn't that give you the rocks?"

"She's very beautiful, sir."

Paul Caval seemed to be making some motions beneath his desk. Then he stood up. He looked down just below his belt and laughed.

"Look at *that!*"

"I'm jealous," said Monica.

"Don't worry, baby, there's plenty for you."

He sat back down and made some more motions beneath his desk. Then he looked up at Mark Brodsky.

"Bet you'd like to fuck my wife."

"What, sir? And *who*, sir?

"Bet you'd like to fuck *Andrea!*"

"I'd like to proceed, sir."

"Great, go ahead."

"Well, after Hernandez was assassinated, what. . . ."

"I meant: go ahead, fuck her."

Paul Caval appeared to have a glazed look to his face. He picked up his glass, drained it, said "shit," softly, then hurled his glass against the wall. The glass shattered like a shot.

"She was always a whore!"

The door crashed open and two guards rushed in. Their guns were drawn.

Paul Caval laughed.

"It's all right, fellas, go back to your posts."

They both glared at Mark, then exited.

Monica went to a cabinet, took out another wine glass, placed it on Caval's desk, refilled it. Caval took out a cigar, bit off the end and Monica lit it. He looked up at her.

"You love me, don't ya, baby?"

"Of course, Paul."

"And you ain't no whore."

"No way, Paul."

"Good girl!"

He reached around and grabbed her ass, gave it a good squeeze. Then she went back and sat down, appearing not to be as jealous.

The recorder was still rolling.

"Sir," Mark asked, "is your name really Caval?"

"No, it's Mendez. I changed it to Caval a long time ago. It was my first step to get away from where I was. I got class so I gave myself a class name."

"I see."

"You see nothing. You need a name to fit you. I'm going to name you 'Dog.' Hey, Dog, I'd bet you'd even like to fuck Monica?"

Monica giggled.

"Sir," Mark suggested, "you've been drinking a great deal. I'm sure you don't mean what you say."

"I always mean what I say."

"He does," said Monica.

"I'd like to continue the interview."

"You do? Well, Dog, *I* feel like PARTYING! I get *tired* of running this government! LET'S PARTY!"

"Sir?"

"WHAT?"

"I feel that I have enough material for the interview. With your permission, I'll take my leave now."

"You'll take nothing, Dog!"

"Sir . . ."

"WE'RE GONNA PARTY!"

Caval got up and came around to where Mark Brodsky was sitting. He pulled out a coin.

"Now, you call it! If you call heads and it comes up heads you fuck Andrea. If you call tails and it comes up heads you fuck Andrea. If you call tails and it comes up tails you fuck Monica. If anything else happens, I'll fuck you, got it?"

"This is ridiculous, sir. As a visiting American journalist, I have rights."

"In my country, you're a Dog and dogs have no rights."

"That's right," said Monica.

"I refuse."

"Where do you want your body shipped, Mr. Brodsky?"

"My body?"

"Yes, some address . . . a mother, a father, a wife, some relatives?"

"You mean?"

"He means," said Monica.

"I can't believe this."

"Believe it," said Caval, "here goes!"

He flipped the coin high into the air.

"CALL IT!" screamed Paul Caval, "HEADS OR TAILS!"

"Tails," Mark called weakly.

The coin fell to the floor. Caval bent over it, peering drunkenly. Then he got down on his knees and looked very closely.

It had landed heads.

"You lucky dog," said Paul Caval, "you get to fuck Andrea."

Paul Caval got off the floor, went back behind his desk. He liked it behind his desk. Desks were symbols of power. He liked symbols of power. He looked at Mark Brodsky of *World View* magazine.

"Well? . . ."

Mark was still not sure that things were occurring as they were. Then he looked at Caval's face, at his eyes: the man was insane.

"I don't know how to begin, sir. . . ."

"Just get the fuck going. . . ."

"You're not joking, sir?

"He's not," said Monica.

"Get on with it," said Caval, "don't try my patience. I don't have much of it."

Mark walked over and stood in front of Andrea. It was senseless. She might have been any object, a dishpan, a vacuum cleaner, a hair dryer. He didn't know what to do . . . He touched her arm . . . hard as rock. He looked at her face, it was only a carved photograph of something long ago that had been real. The dead are to be buried, not caressed. He reached down and touched her left leg. It was too hard, ungiving. It was like trying to love death and he had never been suicidal. Everything was *hard* but. . . .

He turned away from Andrea and looked at Caval.

"Sir, this woman is dead, she's been dead for seven years! I can't make love to this woman!"

Caval pulled the luger out of the desk drawer. He pointed it at Brodsky.

"I *told* you! You try my patience! Now, get on with it!"

Mark leaned forward and placed his lips upon Andrea's lips. The lips were cold. Cold as the dead. He placed his hand upon one of her breasts. It was large, full, well shaped but again like cement. Mark wondered what the *other* PART would be like. He ran his hand upward, kissed her behind the ear.

Then he heard the laughter of Paul Caval. Then Caval's laughter was joined by Monica's laughter.

Mark turned and looked at them. Paul Caval was bent over his desk laughing and Monica was laughing so hard she was beginning to cry.

Mark left off of his love affair and waited upon them.

Monica stopped laughing first. Then Paul Caval stopped. He sighted Mark.

"Get out of here, American."

Mark walked over to the table where his tape recorder and the tape cassettes were. He opened his briefcase to put the stuff in there.

"Leave that crap here, Doggie," said Paul Caval, aka: Mendez.

"All right," said Mark.

"You sure you didn't get a hard-on?"

"I'm quite sure," Mark answered.

"You can take these," said Caval, "if you wish. . . ."

He tossed a two-headed coin, heads upon both sides upon the table, plus a dildo.

Mark Brodsky left coin and dildo and found himself escorted out of there, through those doors by a very large and impassive guard. The elevator wasn't far off and as they stood there Mark wasn't sure but it seemed as if he heard that laughter again, Caval's quite loud and obtrusive, Monica's more like a shimmering razor blade against a nightmare mind; his: he had really wanted to fuck Monica.

The elevator doors swung open.

Oui, May 1984

Dildo Man

don't get on me about how it came about, I hardly remember, I think he got me into this court, nice place, and he also might have fixed me up with a piece of ass, anyhow, I got to know this fellow, Dave, although I really didn't like him too much, he was a rather mellow, rested sort, really had very little originality and he dealt a little bit in drugs and he kept opening new Adult Bookstores, I mean, he would run them for a while and then close them down and then he would open another one, and in each place he positioned himself higher and higher on this elevated platform, "I can see 'em all stealing . . ." and he had the cash register high up there and people would have to reach way up and hand him the money and he would reach down with the change if needed, and all around and below the elevated platform were these glass cases full of dildoes, awful looking things . . . and when somebody wanted a dildo, Dave would have to climb down this red ladder full of paste-ups of angels with erections or with wet pussies and he would unlock the glass case and ask, "which one?"

all of his places were just about the same: a number of dirty mags and books and a couple of machines in back where you slipped in the coins and watched the action. well, I happened to be in Dave's place one night, the newest place, although I can't remember what for and Dave said, "you know, I can fix it so you can give a poetry reading here."

"here?" I asked.

"yes, here."

"not much room, Dave, I mean all these dildoes and things about. . . ."

"I can make room, I can swing things around, I can bring in some chairs, get in about 30 or 40 people."

"I'll think about it, Dave."

"we'll split it right down the middle," he said.

it was about this time that I decided not to give any more poetry readings, then I got a letter from Dave, he had moved to Vermont or was it New Hampshire? he stated that our friendship had been so great and now he was in Vermont or New Hampshire and he was back with Jan again, it was very strange, they just met on the street one day, anyhow, Dave said he wanted to renew our friendship but I never answered his letter because I didn't want to tell him, no, Dave, we never really had a friendship even though it had been nice of him to line me up with that ass and that place in that court, and also that I had been honored that he had offered to let me read in his bookstore, but like I said, I never answered and Dave probably thinks I've gotten the fathead and think that I am hot shit because I've gotten a few books published and maybe it's true, I only hope not.

Bombay Gin, Summer 1990

INTRODUCTIONS
AND CRITICISM

Editors (and Others) Write

Anyone can be an editor, but not everyone should be. The least these fly-by-nighters, who mostly have money dreams and dreams of under-the-counter recognition by fellow(?) editors, could do is to return submissions. You list them in *Trace*, and we send—many of us not egotistical enough to keep carbons. Or energetic enough. How cold can a man or woman be, simply to wastebasket poetry sent in good faith, with return postage and envelope? And this is not an ordinary occurrence, it is a continuous one.

Furthermore, many of the editors of so-called avant-gardes, besides racking one with delays of years in actual publication or, finally, no publication at all, except (during this yawn of nothingness) an exchange of correspondence and ideas and general b.s.,—and often, when not coinciding with their thought-patterns, a return of accepted material ensues.

I have often taken the isolationist stand that all that matters is the creation of the poem, the pure art form. What my character is or how many jails I have lounged in, or wards or walls or wassails, how many lonely-heart poetry readings I have dodged—all this is beside the point. A man's soul or lack of it will be evident with what he can (or can't) carve upon a white sheet of paper. And if I can see more poetry in the Santa Anita stretch or drunk under the banana tree than in a smoky room of lavender rhyming, that is up to me; and only time will judge which climate was proper.—not some jackass second-rate editor afraid of a printer's bill and trying to ham it on subscriptions and coddling contributors. If the boys are trying to make a million, there's always the market, the lonely widows, or the John Dillinger approach.

Let's not find out some day that Dillinger's poetry was better than ours and that the *Kenyon Review* was right. Right now, under the banana tree, I'm beginning to see sparrows where I once saw hawks; and their song is not too bitter for me.

Little Magazines in America: Conclusion of Symposium

It might be a little too late to hear about the "littles" from me, and also the horses walked over me today, so all in bad shape, so, hell, fine, I'll tell you all that I know about the "little" magazines. They are a scurvy lot, most of them, run by homosexuals, madmen, posers, people with acne, fast-buckers, snivelers, religious old ladies, whippers of hounds, and so forth. Mail out a selection of poetry and chances are:

1. you won't get it back.
2. you'll get it back with a promise of publication but it will never be published.
3. your work will be returned, after some years, without either a rejection slip or a note.
4. they will think you a genius and they will come to your door to look at you and drink your beer and talk.
5. you will get semi-literary letters from divorced ladies with children or from ladies with various maladies such as:
   6. missing leg.
   7. overfat butt
   8. a love for Henry James
   9. a stock of old poems about the sea and the moon.

Many of these magazines are started by young people without drive or followthrough, imbued with the first flush of life without mama, tangled with tapes, gin, easy lore, unrealistic romanticism, manes, scandals, accents, politics, the front-lawn love of dogs, familiarity with jazz and a touch of pot, and god knows what else and God doesn't damn well care and neither do I, except they waste our time, my time, and I'm an old bear and I have some talent but not much time, and if I am going to waste it myself and not have it done for me by a group of amateurs who believe the

Literary Life is something they've read somewhere instead of being New when our blood can hardly bear the world, and the only honor is carving what we can before they find us dead in some alley and our canned heat and our pale purple rejects from *Poetry Chicago*.

We are at the mercy of these people, these fakirs, because the way we write can only be sent, with our liquored grief of homage, to small publications that will not be seen laying around on chairs in the barbershop or on Aunt Emma's frontporch swing or down with her bloomers in the bottom drawer either. We've got to take the gamble and hope it's better than betting the horses; but the horses have been g.d. better and the whores, and the rats too. I've lost over 200 poems into the space of literary amateurism and fakism and soft-ass-ism. I do not keep carbons. Why not? you ask. That's a thing in the mind that tells me that if I keep carbons, I too am a posturer looking for gravy and easy light. Hell, you say, haven't you any respect for your work? No, no, I don't. Not *after* it's written. Then, it's dead. Who wants Christmas trees in April? And yet I bitch because these poems (and stories) have been destroyed or asswiped, I bitch not out of personal loss of a creation of Art (?) but from the fact that they will not face up, these putrid overnight editors; they hide, destroy, malface, eradicate, pollute, damage, piss-on, masturbate away the little hope I have of honor between men and women and g.d. trees and silence and a rose whacking it up in a glass of liquor.

I shoot these things out on a thin stem to these people because when I get drunk I write a good deal and I am drunk a good deal of the time and I get embarrassed sending poems to the same places especially when these places tend to accept my work. It is like going to the same whore two nights in a row; it just isn't done. If the thing is still working you got to stick it someplace else.

Little magazines (and I wish to god they wouldn't call themselves "little" but literary; it is a mind state that builds smallness—let's use the good words) tend to start well if they are going to start at all, but it is not long before they begin to be formed by pressures, the pressures of opinions and other editors, critics, readers, writers, printers, street car conductors, lady friends, university libraries, eunuchs, soothsayers, subscribers, punks, dilettantes, clowns, fame-seekers, and the steam and stench and grip and strappado of going down to the heavy Voice of the Thing Outside telling us what to do. Eventually the average literary magazine becomes the front room of one group of tea drinkers. This ravage of reality and wideness is most common and those who break bread together also toss the worn ribbons of their Underwoods into the same shrine and praise and comradey, ejaculating warm literary handshakes across the same worn table. Shit, this does not make ART! I would rather run in the forest with ten dogs looking for some poor stick of meat than have hand in their photo-snapping, all-engulfing GROUPS: BLACK MOUNTAIN; BIG TABLE; GINSBERG; CORSO, BURROUGHS, WHAT THE HELL else group the mountain-sheep watchers and so forth. And Martinelli writes me that old man Pound knew what he was doing and that the Communists are XXXXXX. I agree that old man Pound *sometimes* knew what he was doing but I will not admit that the Communists are XXXXXX. I would rather admit to the obvious: that mankind, given the soul and the opportunity of the history of centuries of Art and History and what else, turns it down for a can of beans and a light in the mirror that makes monkeys, I will only admit that Mankind is (or are) XXXXXX.

What I am getting at with all this slaver is that you don't have to be a XXXXX to use one. Nor do you have to use one to be one. The little magazines, on the whole are a XXXXX mess. You wouldn't catch me at the nearest bar with one, or any other place where I have to, or hope to, hold my head high for a little while.

And when we are all dead, and the small weeping ceases and the grass grows on the countryside and the rabbit comes out and stares stupidly at the sunshine, then, I guess, baby, it will be clean for a while—for a while—for a while—you can't have it all—you can't have it all—we don't have it g.d. now!

Ah, I know the subject was the Little Magazine. What a

subject. Let's talk about the use of the 4-edged screwdriver. I'm out of beer. I have four dollars left which will buy me 12 good bottles plus a pack of cigarettes. The whiskey makes blood. Met a guy on the corner today, black beard, asked me for 50 cents. Glad I didn't give it to him. Might have been a little magazine editor.

Mainstream, Vol. 16, No. 6, June 1963

Introduction to John William Corrington, *Mr. Clean and Other Poems*

I am not saying that you cannot find a better poet if you look hard enough; there are enough of them blowing and mewing, god knows. But William Corrington's oblique and viscid honings recommend a little more than burial in the slush pile.

I remember, upon reading the early works of Hemingway and Sherwood Anderson, I had the feeling of the words themselves digging into the page, gripping, or being like rocks at the bottom of a clear river. This is an essence that cannot be garnered by trickery.

Corrington, although he is a poet, is also a shaper of the word that cannot be brushed away. There is this curious digging in. And I'll be damned if I can ignore it. I have tried.

John William Corrington, *Mr. Clean and Other Poems*,
San Francisco: Amber House, 1964

The Corybant of Wit:
Review of Irving Layton,
The Laughing Rooster

Here I am in Los Angeles, California, eating an apple, drinking coffee, and talking about a "legend." The back cover calls Irving Layton a legend and I do suppose it's true, especially down here where most of us don't buy his books and his poems have filtered down through reviews, quotations, over drinks, and in letters. Now, at last, I have gotten hold of his latest book and it sits here with me in this breakfastnook like a beautiful drunken whore. These are the latest poems except for four which were pulled out of fading yellow newspapers by one George Edelstein and which our rooster says, ". . . gave the first signs of my impending genius. . . ."

The apple and the coffee are finished. Let's get into some white meat and maybe a drumstick. Irving Layton resides astride the back of a rooster upon the front cover. They both look pretty cocky, having a way with the hens.

Layton begins with a preface, which takes some doing. When Loujon Press asked me to do a preface to my coming collection of poems *Crucifix in a Deathhand* I found I could not do it. I found I got to talking about the night I slept on a park bench in El Paso, Texas, and then went into the library hungry and read *Notes from Underground* by one Fyodor Mikhailovich Dostoevsky (1821–1881). The idea was to tell them something of the poet's life (mine) but most of us have lived rotten lives and I decided why drag them through all the drunks, whorehouses, factories, jails, roominghouses, hospitals? The poems, in one way or another, do that. So I spat it out and told them to get another boy for that sort of thing. There's nothing more deadly than talking about your own poetry; the gods make it this way, and if you haven't been fattened or sugared too much, you listen to the gods. Layton dives in. "Can anyone really explain what happens in the writing of a poem?" he asks. He notes that Freud has tried and Dr. Northrop Frye, and mentions Plato's assurance that "the poet is an inspired dunce." For those of you not familiar with the passage it is where Socrates speaks to Ion:

> In fact, all the good poets who make epic poems
> use no art at all, but they are inspired and pos-
> sessed when they utter all these beautiful poems,
> and so are the good lyric poets: these are not in
> their right minds when they make their beautiful
> songs, but they are like Corybants out of their wits
> dancing about.

(Corybants were priests of Cybele who celebrated like hell about the mysterious things they were not quite sure of.)

I.L. says he will try to throw some light on the creative process more by description than explanation; not "why" but "how" the poems came about. This is what I tried to do when writing about my park bench in El Paso. It is much safer than dancing with the thick-tongued, well-read, well-bred, and dull critics as to mechanics and ultimate concern of verse. So Layton will go into how it happened like a bowel movement say or like lightning which struck a tree. All right. One day he took his wife to the beach at Caughnawaga and stayed all morning and part of the afternoon. This seems to me to be a fine thing to do. How many poets take their wives anywhere? How many poets even want wives? Anyhow, he finally took her home and went out for a walk alone. He went down St. Catherine Street (I take it he was re-gathering thinned out wits that had been pummeled at the beach) and turned into a restaurant for a cup of coffee. He had no sooner sat down than the whole thing came: turds and wings and shaft-eyed screaming, and luckily he had a pencil and "Nothing existed for me at the time except the words I saw forming on the napkin: an irregular black stain whose magical growth gave me a sensation of almost unbearable ecstasy and release." Of course, the waitress probably thought he was crazy, but who ever heard of an immortal waitress? One of his poems,

"The Bull Calf" (See *A Red Carpet for the Sun*, Toronto: Mc-Clelland & Steward Ltd., 1959), was written in less than ten minutes while he was enjoying some afternoon sunlight. "Whatever else Poetry is Freedom" was put into his mind, he says, while walking along the road that led away from his summer cottage in St. Marguerite. Another time he was awakened from a deep sleep by the line: "Lie down in my ghostly mental bed," which is a pretty good line, you'll have to admit. But he sat there waiting more than an hour but nothing else arrived. You'll also have to admit that this is real dedication to poetry, especially on a cold night. "El Gusano" was written in a field in Denia, Spain. Not everybody gets to Spain: some industrialists, some actors, some bullfighters, but few poets. "Women of Rome" (see *The Swinging Flesh*, Toronto: McClelland & Stewart, 1961), was written in Rome. Layton has "respect for good workmanship and painful revision." I do not. "Think of Swinburne's last inglorious years," he asks, "or recall Rilke's decade of painful sterility." I'd rather not; I'd rather drink a beer. Yeats, I'm told, ran dry for two years, "No ferment, no poetry: that's the long and short of it!" Well, poetry is a dangerous game, no doubt. I lay drunk in the alleys until I was 35 and then I began writing poetry. Now I come inside to get drunk. Layton is properly worried: reputation is dangerous and praiseology is deadening—they and the fawning ladies with big asses and the professors and the free whisky ripped Dylan Thomas apart like a cheap toy. A man can go to bed being a carpenter and awaken still a carpenter, but a man can go to bed being a poet and awaken and be nothing at all. We turn to the first poem:

I stand on a hill;
my mind reels in terraces
and I'm sucked into a whirlpool
of earth.
As evening wind rattles the almond trees.
In the hushed arena of the sky
the bloodied bull sinks down
with infinite majesty:

the stanchless blood fills the sea.
Triumphant matador, night
flings his black cape across the sky.

I'm afraid that this poem could have been written by any high-school girl with a bad case of acne who had missed the Senior Dance and was sorry for herself and creating a seemingly beautiful escapism. Am I being too hard? Yet I feel that this is the type of poetry (poem) that drives the few and almost real people away.

"In Canada we have no tradition of brawling, irreverent poets, no Villons and Rimbauds. Only a bunch of squares. We need wild-eyed poets . . ." says our rooster.

Then, Irving, stop writing square poetry!!!

In "El Caudillo" we are told that Franco hardly exists in Spain although the people know he is very much there. It is a good poem, not a bad line, and close to the best Layton genius. But being in Spain is strange to Layton; he expects much dust and hollering, perhaps butterflies dreaming of Lorca. But things are much the same anywhere. Life takes hold; motorbikes go by; young ladies on bus benches are often good and careless enough to show us much wondrous and fascinating leg; there is toothache and rain and comic strips. Our leaders, our masters, are there somewhere . . . up in a tree branch, behind a steeple, a paper face on the editorial page, a foggy thought over a martini until the taxes get too high or they are assassinated or until we see them riding through our town peering at us with human eyes from under a mass-manufactured hat. God save us from everything! Let us eat an orange.

"Stone-splitters in Alicante": the worms are underground in Alicante, the ringing blows on rock startle them as Spain sleeps so beautifully in the evening sun. We are all Romantics!—a hell of a fix!

"The Cactus" is modern enough. A little Auden, a little Eliot, a little Jeffers, a little Layton. . . .

From this odious ramshackle affair
of pulp-ponderous roots and shoots

will the airman finally appear,
his face torn under a comic crown
of spiky, fat-fingered polyps;
his bleeding feet, ah, shod
in the sandalshaped leaves of the cactus?
But where . . . where will he go?

I don't know. I'm told Christ #1 got rather roughed-up.
"Fornalutx" is Layton taut and good, the "spiegeleisen":

Light? O no! More like dark perhaps.
But that too is not quite accurate:
I mean about the dark. The sun smoked.
That's the nearest I can come to it.
And no air stirred, and we almost choked.

He's the same in "Encounter":

Is it because
I really wish to kill him,
to pierce him with a nail
and mess up this trim armorial?
Is that the reason why?
Is that it?
Go away, lizard, go away.
There are tears in my eyes.
It is dangerous for you to stay.

All right, each of us kills the thing he loves, eh Oscar?
Some think of doing it with a nail. This is not bad poetry, and
the lizards are often more beautiful than the blondes. And
although rhyme frightens me, many things do, and many
things are not against the rules. "At the Pier in Denia":

Such hair, such necks
for stroking;
such bosoms, which seen,
starving men might turn from melons;
eyes, *ojos*, that when raised

from the books they're reading
are clouded with love.
They sigh, reading *True Romance*
—Spanish version—
but ignore the suntanned caballeros
that squat behind them:
three stunned bulls.

You can't write much better than this. It is the genius,
finally, come out to play, without tricks.

Now he's coming on. The better poems are reserved for
book center and further on. My God, yes!!!!: "Portrait of a
Genius":

My friend Leonardo
gives himself real scars
with imaginary razors
that he tests on the pubic hairs
of his old nurse.
When the storewindows of the supermarkets
are unwilling to listen
he shows me his scars
and we use them to play Noughts and Crosses,
taking turns winning.
Nevertheless he's always one game ahead of me.

"Vigil," one of the early poems dug out of old newspapers, shows that most of us have a chance to finally write
very well (or some of us, anyhow) if we once wrote badly,
depending upon the traffic of the living and the luck.

But you just can't get too critical of Layton when he
starts laying it down, the preface and all that be damned!
He gets you sliding up and down the emotional ladder like
a drunk searching for his lost cigarettes. You are just going
to have to buy or borrow *The Laughing Rooster* in order to
read "I saw a Faun." I'm not even going to quote it in part
as I did a few of the others. It's a damned good poem. Get
the money out! We poets have lived too long in narrow and
smoke-dimmed rooms nursing that last drink.

For those who like the wild-eyed poet, here's something for you: "The Maddened Lover":

> With no words
> terrible enough
> to carry my loathing
> I grab
> the doting, bejeweled wife
> of the eloquent banker
> and screw her in the bathroom

Layton knows his women, knows them well. "Coal." So true, yes. Then "Release":

> I shall rejoice when you are cold, dead clay;
> Nor shall my hate be cheated by the dust
> That fills your eyeless bones or cools your lust
> With passionate embrace of quick decay.

And "Lust":

> Desire
> without reverence
> is lust
> I know that
> by the way
> my phallus stands up
> at sight of you.

There are more poems on women, on sex, on love . . . swift, carved, exact, delightful . . . Layton is best here. He knows plenty and writes it down very well in play, in dread, in wonder and it remains as Art, capital A. Aviva is his love and he has much heart and that is why you can listen to him. I'd listen to him without Aviva but those who head college English courses might feel safer this way.

I began writing this review while the sun was up, have smoked half a dozen cigarettes, repaired my typewriter, which stopped spacing, drunk a pot of coffee but no beer or wine yet, and it is dark now, there is gloomy classical music on the radio and I have gone through *The Laughing Rooster* slowly while telling you about parts of it, and this re-reading was better than the first reading, and Layton gradually takes one in, and there is no reluctance—when he is good he is as good as anybody else and when he is great he is as great as anybody and when he occasionally gets bad, I forgive him. We must go out and get some dinner. Apples are not enough. The book goes into the bookcase alongside *Poems for all the Annettes*, by that other fine Canadian writer, Al Purdy. It has been a real afternoon for me, at least one glowing number painted in the rather foggy days of my life.

The world is full of fish; there are few real writers around. Irving Layton is one of these writers. That I found trouble with the preface is minor. That I found trouble here and there is minor. That I found Irving Layton is important. Mr. Layton? Ah ah ahh!

I think I'll go out and mail this somewhere.

Evidence No. 9, 1965

Introduction to Jory Sherman,
My Face in Wax

One must be careful with introductions. Very careful. There is a tendency to oversell your product. And as I sit here listening to the music of Samuel Barber and drinking my ever-present beer and writing this thing, I think of a book I received in the mail in February 1962, signed and with a few words from the author. Two weeks earlier a fine woman I had known for 14 years had died, and this was my first return to writing or things of writing. It was a sign that I might make it after all. I opened the book of poems and noticed an introduction by a famous modern poet, and this must have been quite a thing for this almost unknown poet, to have this contemporary half-immortal poet and editor of a university magazine introduce him. That they both taught at universities, I suppose, gave them some relationship. Well, I read the introduction. Among the phrases was this one: "He uses American as it strikes him—as it probably is—with a rich baroque guttural, learned or New York-ese, bombastic or tender, with the full gamut of the comedy of our unbelievable, impossible heritage." Now after reading this, I expected some sort of steel god from the gutters saying it red the way it is red and smoke where the fire is, mixed in with barren mad speech of our brothers and along with this any soul or Art the author had retained. What did I get? Carefully conceived, pale and ineffectual poetry? Hell, yes. You guess it. And then I threw the book across the room. That was the comedy, full gamut, and the guttural, the three or four words, were mine.

Now this is no introduction to Jory Sherman. Yet. There's time for that. There's time for everything. The bomb. Another bottle of beer. Wait a minute.

Down to ten bottles. Perhaps an afternoon. But, going back, now when I think of this famous poet, who has really written twenty or three poems that will be hanging around streetcorners long after I am gone, I only think of him as the guy who messed up an introduction. Through friendship, through kindness, out of the best and worst motivations, he stumbled. It is all right to say good morning to the mailman, but whenever a man sits down to a typewriter, poem or not, his soul is on the line. And the toteboard blinks. And I don't like to lose.

Sherman and I are friends but not in the University fashion. We have crossed overhand rights on dark nights when the only way to know blood is to see it. This may not be too holy but it clears the air.

I first came across Jory Sherman in the Winter 1959 *Epos*, which is not too long ago, as time goes. There were three poems, of which two are included in this book. "Reflections in a Bitter Eye" and "Perhaps Fear in a Rainynight." These poems struck me as damned odd and damned original (although the first title rings of Carson McCullers's title), and there is something of the poetic in them, and usually I do not go for the poetic (I use a hammer myself) but something caught here:

> grief, we must gnaw grief as grey
> grease grief
> is absolute . . . :
>
> My innocent vein rippling foamblue
> opened eager to the stab . . .

I remembered putting the magazine down with a great sense of shock. After all, who expects to read anything in a poem, a magazine of poems? Poems are generally slippery things, onion-skin things, that say things in a rather refined and poetic fashion and then slip away to be forgotten. I can pick up any issue of *Poetry* (Chicago) and the pages are oiled and smooth. The intent is not to disturb and to have as little to do with life as possible. It is no wonder the poets starve. And the editors wail that there is no culture in the land. Even Whitman said, and a poetry magazine long carried it on its cover: "To have great poets we must have great audiences too . . ." This is the worst kind of rot. Give us the great poet and the great audience will follow.

The crowd comes to see the performer. Mantle. The crowd came to see Manolete. Franky Roosevelt held them in his palm. The crowd is usually wrong until greatness becomes so great that it becomes truth and myth and explosion and everything. Christ walking the earth again, tossing dice with the boys in the crapper, fire and death and the word. Manolete. Jeffers. Lorca. I shiver and the chills run up and down my arms.

When I run my hand across a page of poetry, I do not want oil and onionskin. I do not want slick bullshit; I want my hand to come away with blood on it. And goddamn you if you are otherwise.

Anyway, getting back to earth, getting back to Sherman, when I read these first three poems, I knew that something was happening. I do not say Manolete. I do not say *Guys and Dolls*. I do not say Mickey Walker, the toy bulldog. I do not say anything except that these poems have a wonderful sound of quite not being before, anywhere. This is important enough. I do not like all these poems. I do not like all of anything. But I think for the relationship and the feel of the goddamned thing, you ought to read them all. Maybe you'll think a little of Keats and a little of Lorca, but something else had come in too. The song and dance of J.S. and I don't mean Bach and the crowd is looking on.

All right, wise guy, asks a voice, you know so much— what makes a good poem?

I call many of these good poems and if you'll sit down, punk, I'll put you straight. Words are colors. We each have all the colors at our disposal. Most of us go fruit and mad and drunk. Have you seen a child with a box of crayons? He'll use them all. Most of us never grow up. I don't care for rules but I'd say the inexorable rule is this: words must be lived down through before you can use them. This is the secret. I have little doubt that old lady Stein told Ernie this, and also Picasso, for the color of color and the color of the word, all Art is similar. The old lady knew the secret but she was unable to live down through the word, so she passed the palm on to stronger people. All the old lady could say was a rose is a rose is a rose, because she was unable to live well. Ernie said a little more and Pablo, stronger than any of them, said plenty. People thought Hem's clipped style was formula, but it was only the result of saying just what he had truly lived out. Later in life he began to say more than he felt. People think he did it because he did not want to be spoon-fed through a lingering illness. I know why he did it.

I say that many of the poems in this book are good because they have been lived down through; the "Shermanese," the occasional clumsiness are necessary. I am very suspicious of any man who waltzes on through.

The introduction is much longer that I had intended, but in fairness to Sherman and myself I could not make it shorter, without leaving out items that made it important in the final way. The poems are the thing. But I keep thinking of the famous poet who stumbled and fell flat on his cazazza trying to do what I am doing here, and I do not like to fall on my cazazza, or as I said earlier, I do not like to lose.

And as long as I have burned up all this paper, I might as well go on a little longer. There is a certain night I remember. I drove all the way to San Berdoo from L.A. (60 miles they lie to me, seems longer between drinks) and Jory had given me an apartment number and an address. But like all people involved with tinkering with things he did not tell me much else. I found the place and started looking for the numbers. There was nothing of such a number in the main building and nobody around and I was carrying two tall six-packs of beer and a bottle of sauterne wine and the stuff was getting heavy and I was getting thirsty. By God, I thought, maybe this kid is living in the garage. Poets have lived worse. Out back the ground was full of holes and it was dark, not dark as hell, but dark as the way down. There was a building in back and I went staggering looking for the number. The numbers were hard to see. I vented a bit of the guttural Bukowskese upon Sherman. Nothing downstairs. I went upstairs and there weren't any numbers at all. Just a rickety balcony thing that reminded me of New Orleans and death and rats and Mickey Cohen, slugged for income tax. I had to peek through the windows. There was a passionate love scene upon a couch. People lived in Berdoo.

Well, I walked down the stairs, leaving them at it. I said to hell with it. I am going back to L.A. and drink this stuff myself. I walked back through the yard. Then I heard it. "Tat a tat a tat a tat a tat tat tat." There was a small court over to the east that I had not seen. "Tat tat tat a tat." I walked up to the door without looking in. And banged it. "Let me in, you bastard."

"It's open," he said.

It was. I walked in.

"Hello, friend," he said.

"Hello, poet," I said.

It was summer and he had his shirt off and the walls were green and every now and then a train came by on the overhead and everything shook. This is no university. This was no easy way. This was it. Doing it now. And now Faulkner's dead. And soon all of us.

Jory opened a couple of beers. "Good to see you," he said.

"Likewise," I said.

Like I said; you've got to live through it.

And this is the only kind of introduction I could write

Enter reader, as the worms pant over the bones of Manolete.

Jory Sherman, *My Face in Wax*
Chicago: Windfall Press, 1965

Lightning in a Dry Summer: Review of John William Corrington, *The Anatomy of Love and Other Poems*

For those of us who learn towards the poem as life slowly pulls us apart, there are long areas—years, years—when nobody comes along and it seems as if nobody ever will, and we have to be content with the occasional poem we may find among the hundreds of ½ poems, fakirs, misfits, and lepers which appear with irregular regularity in the "littles," meanwhile thinking of the giants who once appeared with force and then seemingly dissolved very quickly as if the game were too much for them—Spender, Eliot, Auden; and e.e. cummings who was good when his style did not entirely mutilate his content; Shapiro who was good early and then forgot how to write; Jeffers who never forgot but he died on us; Pound who simply does not like to be played with has withdrawn to a kind of semi-immortality while still alive. . . .

And with the arrival of *The Anatomy of Love and Other Poems* we have, at last, the stirring of a possible new giant, a man who strangely has put his chips on the most horrible of the intellectual monsters—the novel. "I feel that poetry is the outpost where men learn the trade of words, and the novel is where they make it count. I like poetry; I love prose." I have read Corrington's first novel (*And Wait for the Night*) and while it is good, it has all the hamperings of the novel and all the hamperings of the novel and the novel-mind. The poetry is his Art. And now he has begun a second novel. I can see the novelist consuming the poet, and in a book-of-the-month-club Hollywood TV world where people would rather fall asleep under a lamp reading about the Civil War than stare at a slim boned-down poem, it figures. The real trouble is that after the novelist consumes the poet the novelist goes on to consume the novelist and then we have nothing left. But to hell with the future—right now *The Anatomy of Love* is one of the finest collections of poetry to appear in the past five years or in a possible decade. The only other collection being equal or close to it is *Poems for all the Annettes* by Alfred Purdy.

The forward by Richard Whittington to *The Anatomy* is confusing because it is intellectual, sand-dry, and is written in the old textbook style which slugs the senses. He *does* make some points, if you want to be stabbed and bled along the way. You listen to me now; Corrington is obsessed with the cruelty, the drone, the almost meaninglessness of life; he is obsessed with the men who conquer, quite no matter how they do it. He is obsessed with the going-on, the beaten, the raised, the disabled; he is obsessed with the stumbling and the shots of sunlight, and broken words from broken mouths, and the going-on. The going-on . . .

> angels with copper eyes
> and feathered parachute,
> asking:
> —*Who Blew Up The Road?*
> ("Algerian Reveur")

Corrington gives us the clean line, the clean word clear, hung there, saying it:

> and from behind him an
> iron factory of smoke
> and the odor
> of birds on fire ("On Earth As It Is")

Corrington's obsessions, and they become purified through the Art of the poem like a man beating a donkey with a stick and crying, can be seen in his titles: "Lucifer Means Light," "Note From a Dead City," "Metaphysician at Huntsville (The Texas State Penitentiary)," "Trust Me Just This Once."

That Corrington came from the University, taught at the University and did not become the University, tells us that there is still a chance; that all men will not sell out up the river, and, if as they say, any man can be bought for a price, it appears for some of us they have not yet thought up the proper coin.

> should I sell short
> is there a balm in gilead
> do you think it will rain
> ("Prayers for a Mass in the Vernacular")

Corrington knows that they will eventually get us—the ideal, the gut, the nerve will wilt finally. The Jeffers, the Gandhis, the Pounds in life are really more gods than men and they must also have a little luck—and say in the case of Gandhi it might have run short, depending upon how you view the table manners of death. Yet some of us go on, we all don't jump overboard like Crane in his pajamas with hangover and needing shave and going to propeller and/ or shark.

> grace
> has lighted our faltering
> way
> through grim ages
>
> *darius for his*
> *humanity*
> *caesar for his*
> *joke about the turnip*
> *napoleon for his*
> *modesty*
> *julian for his*
> *love of the old ways*
> *bismarck for his*
> *kultur*
> *alexander for his*
> *pointed way with friends*
> ("Prayers for a Mass in the Vernacular")

I would like to justify my greed for the poem, and in this case Corrington's poetry, by hoping the good reader who reads this will contact Fort Lauderdale and buy a copy of *Anatomy*. It would be nice to use *their* money to prove our point; but there's really not much use: bad novels will always outsell great poetry, and this, in a way, proves our point too: that we have no point to prove. Mozart starved, Wolf went mad; Frank Sinatra boards a ship for Europe. We'll let them have most of the world. Just leave us enough to stay alive, an occasional beer and a book of poems like *The Anatomy of Love* every decade. Surely at our final death we will be able to smile at some of the good things that *did* happen.

Ferment No. 6, June 1965

Another Burial of a Once Talent: Review of John William Corrington's *Lines to the South and Other Poems*

"fear that Sartre's asleep, fear that Genet is kidding
Fear that there isn't anybody here"
>—Charles Bukowski
>From *Crucifix in a Deathhand*

John William Corrington, *Lines to the South and Other Poems*.
Louisiana State University Press, $3.50.

This latest hardcover of Corrington's poems contains seven poems (including the title poem) from his two earlier books. This, of course, is the tip-off. The book is neither a selection nor a collection and since there are but 61 pages of short work, we can see that some padding was needed. Since I reviewed most of these poems in a recent issue of *Ferment*, I see little use of re-reviewing old work, except to tell you that the old work was best and that I praised it with open heart and feeling and asked the reader to take a chance. Now I must advise the reader to take it easy. $3.50 can buy you a pint of very good stuff or a quart of not so good or it could buy you *Lines to the South*. I would suggest the pint. Having met Corrington personally and having once held a long correspondence with him does not free me from the truth. I can lie to a hot blonde but not to history or the invisible reader.

The dust jacket warns us (in part) before entering: this work "represents an important direction in American poetry."—Peter Michelson, former editor of *Chicago Review*. "Corrington is regarded throughout the country as one of the best young poets writing today. . . ."—Roy Miller, editor, *San Francisco Review*. "Corrington is a live and important talent. This volume proves that he has moved beyond

promise and found his own voice. He has courage, inde-
pendence, a good eye and a fine ear, all the craft and art of
a true poet. *Lines to the South* is a distinguished collection."
—George Garrett.

Well, then, let's see if we can find what these fine fellows are talking about. Corrington now has his doctorate,
is a prof at L.S.U., and has written two novels and three
books of poesy. I also ate some food with him in a Chinese
café in New Orleans' skid row and he is a handsome devil
and a fine talker. But I don't know how he got people to say
such things about this book of poems. Let's open the book
anywhere. On page 26 we find:

> Who sorrows interment or dashes in bits
>   The plenary serpent's tail?
> Who shudders the crush of ordnance wheels,
>   or takes up the orphan's wail?
> across the sky in a swatch of mist
>   when green night clings like a pug,
> pearlyskinned lovers ogle the stars
>   with a pinch, a sigh and a hug.

Who the hell does he think he is kidding, Dr. Benjamin
Spock? This is schoolgirl poetry of the first water, or the
second, at least. I'd flunk anybody out of Creative Writing
class for writing one like that but luckily for a lot of little
dolls I do not teach Creative Writing. I write it.

"that messianic sun" he says on page 2. I tried to get
him to strike out that line when he sent me the poem sometime back. "twofaced sun" we have on page 40. On page 32
we have "under a mercenary sun." Other suns may occur
in here, most of them being described with "m-," but I do
not intend to continue to search. Perhaps it is that a writer
writes for a while and then he gets careless or begins to
believe in himself or in what he can get away with. There is
much poetic-meaningless poetry here, done perhaps in the
manner of a garage mechanic turning the same bolt under
his moaning sun. Some of the worst phrases are as follows:
"our brief staccato lives" (page 5). "the static lie" (5). "Their

chary love/impoverishes the heart" (page 6). "mimes of passion" (6). "immured in/memory" (6). "the strum of lost evening" (6). "tepid years" (page 7). "a dark calligraphy of tooth and nail" (7). "sob chill rumor of your sinking flesh" (7). "endless as our love" (7). In fact, you may think me a Hitler but I'd say the whole poem, pages 6 and 7 ("A Memo from Lilith"), should be burned.

On page 8 we have "his eyes like cloudy topaz." Page 9, "his mind like a scavenger." Page 10, well, on page 10 we have "a tumescent cloud." On page 11 is a very good poem: "Who Do You Think You Are?" How did this get in here? Since you probably think me quite the hatchet-wielding bastard by now, I'll quote the whole poem:

> this guy in the cozy grille
> was telling me
> how rubber looks like milk
> straight from the tree
> and at the bar
> a woman with dirty heels
> coughed consumptive ballades
> and watched her empty eyes
> all orphanannielike
> in a dark mirror
> framed with rye
> someone screamed
> —hash
> while in the booth behind
> dr Jekyll solemnly shook hands
> with mr hyde
> and i
> believing only
> what i choose to believe
> lifted the top of my hamburger
>
> fearing cheese

On page 14 we have "high as silver verity"—which would be a good line in relation to a common drunk but is only artificial poetry in relation to the zeppelin "Hindenburg." Page 20: "succinctly arrived."

But before I continue perhaps I had better clarify the issue. I say this is bad poetry, these bits I quote, and I do not know if these terms have been used before but they could have been. What I mean is, it is a circus act because it does not come out of *essence* but out of *instrument*. The whore is selling you dead pussy, and only we who write continually and know the game can spot the rot. When a poet uses these dead and false terms he is thinking "I am a poet" but he is not, in any sense, actually *creating*. He is jollying us, he is shoving it to us. Right off the mark allow me to make up a few. Look here:

> *A gratitude of treasures*

> or: *A hoopla inferno*

> or: *The bandaged sun*

I could go on and on like this and I am not as talented as some. But this stuff, this bullshit, this fakery runs throughout American poetry and non-American poetry too. I am not saying that I am a genius and that I want to form a new school. I travel alone, but I get tired of being robbed by these guys when I am awake. And it is usually when a man assumes a position of culture, say teaching at a university or cutting into a man's guts with a knife, that he finds it easy to *turn it on* and get away with it because here in the United States we over-respect education, the doctor, the lawyer, the professor—and we allow them to shit all over us while we smile. But a diploma is not a soul and I have met whores in Philadelphia and New Jersey who knew more than any of them and didn't bother to lie about it.

Page 20: "time of gratuities is ending." Page 23: "calls to mind the irony of shutters." "would spring have been the same," same page.

"A Trip to Omaha," page 24, is a very good poem.

Page 26: "a lucky moon." And 27: "and tomorrow must sullen come." Shakespeare watered with D. Thomas.

"The Portable Goya," page 30, is a damned good poem. Maybe you ought to buy the book after all? Page 33, "The Mystic," is also a good poem although Corrington once again insists on ending with talking about "what he suffered every spring." It's the easy way out, of course, and standard, but we all get tired.

"Where impatient lovers grope" (page 36). Eliot, of course.

On page 40, "Surreal for Lorca" I would say is a truly beautiful poem only I don't like the world "beautiful." And, besides, there is probably a line stolen from Charles Bukowski: "and God, no taller than a landlady," from "The Sunday Artist," has been changed by Corrington into:

> while
> god
> no taller than a scream

But that's all right, and besides, it's not the *same*. Besides, it's nice to be an influence. Besides, besides, besides.

Page 45: "Thus we sat dissecting silence." Bad writing? Of course. Even you won't argue that with me. When I was editor of *Harlequin*, under the hammer of my first wife's money, I rejected 20 rather well-traveled poems from a seemingly famous poet. "We all write badly at times," he wrote back. Of course. But why send it to me or ask $3.50? See your priest or rabbi or preacher for your sins. I don't have time to play around.

Hang in. Only 15 pages to go. Then you can catch that drink or make the maid when your wife goes to her bridge party. In fact, you can have the drink right now. I've been having them as I go along.

"A Man of Terrible Integrity (Considers Himself at Morning)" seems quite similar to a Bukowski poem called "Face While Shaving." Probably untrue, of course. The terrible problem always being that I write the poem first. Like I said, it's nice to be an *influence*. Look at the way they build bridges and houses and bombs. Somebody *had to* be there first. I was reading library books long before I ever owned a typewriter, and although most of them put me to sleep I do not deny moments of light for Camus, Dostoyevsky, Blake, Jeffers—even from Conrad Aiken.

My God, the treachery of Man. Here I've drunk with this man, have spoken with him—and yet an editor sent me this book for review, and what would *you* do . . . saying the poems seemed bad to you? Would you lie around the corners, play the game in order to get a favor in return? What would you do, friend? Pity me as well. I am not a natural born killer. But Art is all that is left for many of us. I mean, Art makes Life. They are the same. I am on the hot spot. Would you choose that I kill myself? I will probably do it, finally, so don't get nervous.

Page 54: "grief stands like a squad of riflemen,/where time must bandage the eyes." This is truly bad writing, of course, and I needn't even bother to explain.

Yet the dust jacket still talks to me. The cover falls back and I hear further from Peter Michelson: "Corrington's work synthesizes the intellection of a Wallace Stevens and the wit of a Ferlinghetti. The result is both intellectual substance and emotional excitement." Are these people reading the same poems that I am talking to you about? Where *is* the TREACHERY?? Am I, truly, the traitor?

Page 55: "and an ending that plunders all." No kidding? I didn't know that. Maybe I shudda gone ta collitch?

Page 56: "Faith is a cunning vise/to pinch our freedom into useful paths." It sounds good, doesn't it? But it could only be a tin of sardines, a slur of words, or too much Jeffers. I don't want to go into the old hack, the tiring bit of "define faith." But poetic license too often turns into a carney show, and if I pay $3.50 to get in I want to see if that son-of-a-bitch has been really buried in the ground for 60 days, what he does with his piss and his shit, and what he does for nooky.

Poetry, most of it, has always been a glass house. It has little reference to the average man or to myself or to slipping in the bathtub or catching the siff, to sleeping night after night with a wife who has lost everything but her tenaciousness or to 22 monkeys on a football field really wanting to reach up into the sky and find a Face. It has nothing to do with waking in a drunk-tank with some idiot who has never read Rimbaud, some diddling idiot vomiting into your face. Poetry is faker than hell although it is always talking about hell and pain and love and man and earth and Spring and Summer and Winter and Autumn—o o o, Autumn. And poetry seldom reaches most men because most men are almost dead, of course, but also because most of the men who write poetry are almost dead. I can't see all the shining flaking glass and the mirrors and tricks of the men who write it. I see only their fear of saying ANYTHING—especially anything that can be understood, even by themselves. Men only seem to rise to temporary courage or love or Art through war or poverty or an unlasting madness or having their arms cut off or finding their prostitutes asleep with men of greater dicks and greater lines—to the south, to the north, to anywhere at all. I can only see a general slime and a sinking and a formula for lying. Almost all the poetry of centuries has been wasted, and it has been wasted because the children do not sing it in the streets; it has been wasted because I do not think of it before I attempt to sleep or when I crawl out of a car shattered of glass, and me . . . one ball dangling . . . a bull without a heart or a way. Christ, when are we going to BEGIN?

I am tired and ashamed of the sham.

And besides, and besides.

Let us take the next to last poem in the book. It is proficient, it is almost good, you know. Really. But, but, but??? Is this what I have lain drunk in skid row alleys for years for, small children poking sticks into my back at high noon? In that "messianic sun"?

Here it is:

       THE LATE LATE SHOW
       (Ripeness is all)

       The number of my purchases
          declines; night is for sleeping

and the pleasures of silk; a
   flank of polished oak replaces
green excursions.
   These latter days revolve
like a charger's bloody eye
   and friends steeped in shadow
fall away, leaves of a shrinking tree
   Athwart the coolness of this age,
within my shabbing flesh,
   there chronicles no prickly
need; these veins are full
   of tea.

Each dawn is a surprising wine;
twilight thunders its obvious line

and Venus returns, cursing, to the sea.

Now do you understand a bit of what I mean? Dr. Corrington gives himself away, unknowingly: "within my shabbing flesh . . . no prickly need. . . ."

And so, this is a review of John William Corrington's 3rd book of poems.

I now need to piss some more, drink some more, and sleep.

Steppenwolf No. 1, Winter 1965–66

Foreword to Steve Richmond,
Hitler Painted Roses

It is a sweet goddamned pleasure to write a foreword to these poems. Yet this foreword, like the poems, is going to bring the enemy out from under the rock. Well, at least we will be able to look at him and vomit.

This is Steve Richmond's 2nd collection of poems. The first was called simply "poems" and was issued in 1964. Steve has come a long way since then—whether he has changed his liquor or his women or his diet, I don't know. Yet I suppose it's mostly a solidifying, a gathering of intent, more cement in each line. The words are harder now and clearer now and gripping and racking more on that slippery and goofy belly of Truth.

To those of you used to the comfortable screams of the Dickeys, James and William, to Mott and Moss and Morse and Morris and Mason, to Sarton and Scannell and Sexton and Stafford and Stanford, and Wagoner and Wilbur and Witt, to the play-patterns of Creeley drawing dull and accepted zeroes; to those of you used to the lies of your presidents, your girlfriends, your wives; to those of you used to the lies of the centuries, the lies of the Art of our centuries . . . these poems aren't going to be much good to you—unless you have a miraculous reserve tank of recovery.

It is not difficult for a man to figure he is pretty well fucked upon the earth. A good turn around any city street can tell you this. Yet the game goes on: frenzied and insane men run in and out of buildings, their breathing choked by neckties, their faces slaughtered and hanging in the air like turds. Even their children, by the age of three, begin to look like butchers. The women are only beautiful in body for a short while, and never with faces, always the paper-blank face. Everywhere everywhere is the stink of death—in the churches, in the museums (of course), in the Art galleries, in the libraries, in the parks, at the symphonies, at the play-houses, everything stinks of death and is death and nothing is said. WHERE IN THE HELL ARE THE POETS? WHAT

THE HELL *IS* THIS CON GAME? You scream and there isn't any answer. The people go insane. They kill themselves. They kill each other. But the troops of society straighten out the kinks—they build more jails, madhouses, graveyards, and the rest of the game goes on. Richmond's poems are the feel and scream of a living man immersed in this death-shit and not wanting to go down into it. The comfortable poems of the well-known poets aren't any good to him. The time is raw and the time is NOW. He has to write his own poems from the kitchen light. From the curbing. From the sink where he heaved. From where his dinner went. From his balls. From his belly. From the area where he'd like to cry from but doesn't quite know how. What a fix. Millions of men born and walking around as if everything were all right. Centuries of poetry and literature with no more meaning than a man snoring. The Lost Generation . . . the Atomic Generation . . . the Fucked Generation. Richmond's poems are about a man reaching only for what he can see, and he hardly trusts that, but it beats reaching for what *they* tell you to reach for—judging by the looks of them. I am sympathetic with Richmond's poetry because here, a good 20 years older, I feel much the same way. And about here, I must enter another word, for protection from another type of death. About here, upon reading, say, Richmond's poetry or some of mine, the World Savers LEAP in. "Ah ha!" they say, "yes, very powerful poetry! You know the world is fucked-up! Fine! You are aware! Now, look, all ya gotta do is this. . . ." To them, all we need is a better form of government. Everything else will take care of itself. The eyes will come back into people's heads. Their backs will straighten. Their walks will not be wooden. Their voices again will have a decent tonality. The World Savers are con-stantly upon us with their literature and their pleas. The World Savers love to rub together like chickens on a cold day; they huddle in their houses, meet once, two, three times a week . . . they cannot meet enough, they just cannot meet *enough* to cold-cock their insecurity. They continually make little light bright jokes to each other and giggle and argue and agree with each other and make each other. The only trouble is that they are a sickly lot, unable to create, and I look upon them and I see that I was wrong: no, they are *not* sickly, they are simply dead. And the dead will not like these poems because they will feel that there isn't any "social message."

What they forget is that a man must be *alive* in order to be saved. And that the way to stay alive is not to memorize Karl Marx and play a guitar and march in Peace Marches and Freedom Marches. The way to stay alive is inch by inch; horrible, pewking, praying, cussing, fingernail-breaking, blood-red inch by inch. There *aren't* any formulas. There aren't any pot-luck lunches. There aren't any poetry work-shops. There aren't any tea-meetings, cookie-meetings, cocktail meetings. There is none of this weak pansy cock-sucking bullshit.

There is just one man thrown upon the earth, belly-naked, and seeing with his eye. Yes, I said "eye." Most of us are born poets. It is only when our elders get to us and be-gin to teach us what they teach us that the poet dies. Rich-mond has not been "gotten to" yet. Maybe they will get to him. But, as yet, these poems are memorable bellows and wailings and cussings. These poems are the living work of a living man. These poems are *Art*. Be glad you are here to read them.

Richmond has been to college. He is not a rag-picker. But if he were a rag-picker *and* Richmond, he would still write, essentially, the same way. And don't argue with me. I am tired of you rule-believers and book-noses. You, locked into your compartments of this-is-good, this-is-evil; right-wing, left-wing, center-of-the-road; pro-war, anti-war; pro-God, anti-God, and on and on . . . Ah, you icecream dandies! Ah, you 18th-century versifiers dressed in 20th-century clothing!

The cusswords that the church-pewkers and rhymers will object to, the cusswords are both a frustration and a joy and a non-trust of the language and the life by a man who senses the stockpiles and deadmen everywhere. A man who can feel his balls and know that they are there, that man is alive. Our poets and statesmen, our loves have left us very little that we can trust. We begin at beginnings so that we may not end. Each of these poems is, in a sense, a demon turned loose, looking for light. Each night is one more night and each day is unbelievable. Dramatic? Sure, like a knife going in. That's our culture, don't kid yourself. You can forget your courses in Appreciation of English Literature. That's just dried skin glued to a corpse. But if you don't understand something of what I have said up to now, there's no use reading these poems. Just throw the book away or give it to the first person who passes.

Do you realize that there will even be people who will object to the title? More loss. Again divisions. Good and bad. Good wars, bad wars; good men, bad men; good nations, bad nations. (A bad nation is one that loses a war.) There are monsters and heroes. Men are different and their difference terrifies us. It may please you if I tell you that I didn't care any more for Hitler than I did for Gandhi. You will say, that guy is really nuts, and then you will feel better. Fine. I want you to feel better. But, you will insist on asking (still in your cubicle of division), how could Hitler have painted roses? Then let me ask you: have *you* ever painted roses?

But enough, enough. I have certainly written enough here. I feel that these poems can now take care of themselves, or perhaps would have been better off without me. I will get some agreement here, I am sure. It is a Tuesday in March, mid-March in Los Angeles. The year is 1966. And my radio gives me Mozart. One of the few who forgot how to lie. The pay was poor if you want to count it as money or the way he went. Anyhow, Richmond's poems here, now . . . a young man bringing it to you through the fire of the bombarded graveyard. Here they are.

Begin.

Steve Richmond, *Hitler Painted Roses*
Santa Monica, CA: Earth Books and Gallery, 1966.

Essay on Nothing for Your Mother-Nothingness

Literary magazines are like a can of tuna fish, cheap, if you can ever get through it you forget all about it. Most of them are brought out by distraught young boys or old lesbians and what do these know about the Arts? Exactly. Nothing. They are pushing their own tin-can agony upon us in fancy dress—that is: bad poetry. The short story. Forget it. The last man who remembered what a short story was was Edward O'Brien who died too many years ago. And artwork? They think artwork is something that *looks* like artwork just as they think poetry is something that *looks* like poetry. The fish is dead. Poetry doesn't look like poetry, poetry is, just like a whore is or a drunktank or a cancer is. The "littles" are a mess begging for an audience. The audience is a mess begging for a soul. In between these two messes you have four or five men who can lay down a decent line of poetry or a decent flow of paint, and, of the four or five, one is going to commit suicide and the other one or two are going mad or thinking about suicide. Outside of that you have nothing but towers, green fields, bums, presidents, bombs, beetles, tits, textbooks, and the pulling of teeth and other various time-triflers.

It is hardly worth a damn to go on. Just a peek of leg, a little free ass now and then. The timeclock. The butcher-shop. The flushing of a toilet. The car that won't start. The ugly face on the street.

So, another magazine? The editor asked me to write something about another magazine. What can I say? Will there be another Ezra? Will Ernie H. chase another lion through our minds? I think that we are a little harder to fool nowadays. The bombs are stacked everywhere and we are ready to die whether we want to or not.

I just don't know anything, I just don't know what to say, so wherever you are, in a bar or in a jail or in a bar-bershop or in a library, and you pick up this magazine and begin to read it, I hope you do find something in it, even if it is only this bit that I have just written. I am not trying to be tricky; I am through with tricks—I only wish the rest of the world were the same way.

Spectroscope, Vol. 1, No. 1, April 1966

Who's Big in the "Littles"

I'd have to place them this way: 1. *Ole*; 2. *Wormwood Review*; 3. *The Outsider*. And, I might say, the real pros are Jon and Lou Webb (*Outsider*), who often put in an eighteen-hour day on their magazine or Loujon Press books, selecting the material and printing it on their own press, without any income except returns through the mail in book sales or subscriptions. This, at an age when most people are thinking of retiring to some sort of jaded safety. All three mentioned magazines print a living and electric literature.

The "Mimeo Revolution" is sometimes more revolting than revolutionary—printing hasty faded careless and misspelled poems and stories. Yet I do suppose that the very lack of pressure and expense *does* create a freedom from which arises some good hotbed literature. Some of the more interesting of these rags are: *The Marrahwannah Quarterly*, *Wild Dog*, *Kauri*, *Blitz*, *Simbolica*.

Snob publications that print an icy and glass-spun, unreal type of work are *Evergreen Review*, *Poetry* (Chicago), *Trace*, *The Sewanee Review*, *The Kenyon Review*, *Contact*, *The Antioch Review*.

Of course, if you want to join the sewing circle there is always *The American Poet*, *Bardic Echoes*, *Jean's Journal of Poems*, *Merlin's Magic*, *The Promethean Lamp*, *South and West*, *World Poetry Day Magazine*. Many others.

El Corno Emplumado continues from its Mexican base with Meg and Sergio Mondragón pumping out the magazine and books (and babies) with a free and beautiful intensity. *Evidence* staggers on, somehow, bringing us good work from Canada and also some U.S. writers. *Vagabond* leaps up from Munich, Germany, promising a gutty and searing work. *Earth* is being printed in a small bookshop in Santa Monica run by a mad poet (Steve Richmond) who carries only "little" magazines and books of poetry upon his shelves. The *Steppenwolf* shakes its fist from Omaha. *Spero*, Flint, Michigan, lives on pennies and still comes out in letterpress. *Notes from Underground* has vanished again along with slippery John Bryan, but he can't quit the game and he'll be back with another of his wild and flaming issues of hot truth.

The "little" mag world goes on and on, stronger now than ever, more living now than any time since its birth. There are more magazines and more writers, more writers and better writers—that some of them will go the way of *Esquire*, *The New Yorker*, *The Atlantic*, the novel, this sort of death, is true. But to assume that the "littles" are only the proving ground for young writers is untrue. Many of us are no longer so young and we continue to submit and get published in the best of the "littles" because they are the only remaining platforms of truth and good art in a very frightened and sick Age. Many of us would not consider wasting a stamp on *The New Yorker*, not because we write too badly but because we write too well.

We continue to hope through the machinegun fire.

We continue to hope along well-worn typewriter ribbons.

We continue to hope while starving.

We continue to hope in the libraries.

We continue to hope in the factories.

That our small words, printed in issues of 150/200, will be read and saved and heeded.

Did you ever see a man with a bookcaseful of old *Atlantic Monthlies*? Of course, not; they would laugh him out of town. The "littles" are big enough to live. Believe it, baby.

Literary Times, Vol. 4, No. 5, Winter 1966

The Deliberate Mashing of the Sun
(d.a. levy)

It is not just levy, it is all of us, it is not just poets or spiders
or fleas or corncobs, it is all of us, it is the deliberate mash-
ing of the sun. sometimes you don't have to wait upon History to find good from evil. sometimes acts are so vile, so
contraband, so clearly snakes eating eyes out of skulls, that
any unbiased study is something akin to studying a turd to
see if it will ever grow into a flower. the roust of levy is such
a stale turkeydeath badbreath smeartit deal that i imagine
even the police treat it as a playact, a movement, a practice
workout, a pinch to pinch something they figure can't bite
back. what did levy say? what were the words that bothered them?: shit? fuck? cunt? DIRTY WORDS? OBSCENE?
I am more afraid that they have been used and overused
and could only bore the most ivorytower old maid. DOES
LEVY USE THESE WORDS IN ATTEMPT TO SOMEHOW
MAKE 89 cents a day? my ass! does levy uses these words
as a dirty little boy? ah, he does? does he paste them on
the side of his new Cadillac? does he put them on a big
sign in front of his $60,000 home in suburbia? my ass! does
he scratch them into doorbells of the people who set him
out a plate of food, does he work them in with a pin while
looking over his shoulder? your ass. DOES HE PUT THESE
WORDS INTO HIS BEST-SELLING NOVEL? does he run
around hissing them out of the side of his mouth at little
girls aged 4,5,6,7? who in the hell *is* crazy in CLEVELAND?
in the UNIVERSE? what bothers them then? you guessed
it: POETRY. one of the last untrammeled fortresses where a
good man can work out, holy and free and burning. WHAT
BOTHERS THEM IS THAT WHEN A REAL ARTIST USES
THE WORD "SHIT" IN POETRY THEY CAN SMELL IT,
and they don't want to smell it: the shit of their lives or the
shit of their shit. poets are not very careful—they are only
interested in the dirtiest of words: TRUTH. corncob, sure.
corny, sure. hardly pays a damn thing, BUT THE REAL
WORKERS IN POETRY WOULD PAY TO BE ABLE TO

WRITE POETRY. i mean in dollars if they had them. NOW THEY ARE BEING MADE TO PAY IN ANOTHER WAY. all these bookstore raids, the pinching of poets that has come very close together these past few months, it is like a friend said to me in a very weary and sad voice, wondrous voice too in that he felt that nothing at all had been gained: "It's just HOWL all over again." "yeah," i said. meanwhile, the true users of FILTH FOR PROFIT know all the boundaries. what CAN BE SHOWN IN A PHOTO, what can or can't be suggested. what words you never use. what words you use to get around words. the BIG BUSINESS OF FILTH KNOWS ITS BUSINESS. the psychopathic homicide maniacs this business causes to bust loose in the back alleys and streets of cities are vast and numerically hideous. almost everybody likes a good piece of ass but what these uncontrollable smut nudey mags cause in borderline cases would be obvious to a psychiatrist or just even an average thinking human being. but to pinch a starving poet for 34 or 50 pure poems, and even the PURE BAD ONES SAY AS ART THEY ARE STILL ART, WHY SAY EVEN HERE IT IS LIKE TRYING TO PINCH THE SUN FOR GIVING YOU A SUNBURN, IT IS LIKE TRYING TO PINCH THE SEA FOR DROWNING A MAN, IT IS LIKE TO PINCH BEETHOVENS 9th BECAUSE A BRAIN DAMAGE CASE CANNOT UNDERSTAND IT.

because what happened to levy could happen to me. i earn about 30 cents a day writing poetry. think of it. them busting down my door and ripping a poem from the typewriter and taking me in and setting a bail i couldn't pay. i've been pinched for drunk, for drunkdriving, and once for causing a traffic jam in the city of INGLEWOOD, i believe. i think i was in Inglewood. anyhow I went to a Culver City court. i had stretched out on the top step of a very well-lit mortuary at 2:30 a.m. in the morning upon one of the main streets. i was charged among other things with "blocking traffic." i took all this with a kind of fear and yet a good-humored resignation. but think of them busting in here on top of my poems? "Bukowski?" "yeah?" "come with us." SOUNDS LUDICROUS LIKE A KID OF KATZENJAMMER

NAZI MOVIE SCENE. yet if you try to run away they'll club you with a stick or shoot you in the back. when it happens to somebody else it is kind of mathematic, kind of a mistake, but when it happens to you it is very damn real VERY FUCKING REAL, and you leave that place, your typewriter sitting there, one bottle of beer in the refrigerator some old clothes on the floor, 3 days left on the rent, and you walk along between them and wonder what it is, you even make up vague things of safety for the puzzled mind: JUSTICE PREVAILS; THIS IS AMERICA; I'VE DONE NOTHING. only the last two thoughts are true, and then you get it—the thing, all the things going on, the neat little brutalities, the sluggings in dungeons, the internment camps. . . . where? somewhere in Oregon? in Arizona? no need to get dramatic only Hitler shines an apple in Argentina and smiles. you walk down the stairs between them, trying to look like a young George Raft, a living H. Bogart. you already feel guilty and you are guilty BECAUSE THEY CARRY THE GUNS. WHERE IS THE JUDGE WHO WILL MAKE THEM GUILTY? WHEN WILL HE SHOW?

obscenity? god, you should see what they do to their wives! these big fat clean-clothes boys i walk between.

what else can I say? where are we? levy, i once wrote a little book you published called THE GENIUS OF THE CROWD. I'd like to read it at your trial, but never mind, I'll probably read it at mine. —if they let me.

from *D.A. Levy: A Tribute to the Man, an Anthology of His Poetry* (Cleveland, OH: Ghost Press, 1967).

Charles Bukowski on Willie: Introduction to *The Cockroach Hotel* by Willie [William Hageman]

Willie is a guy you can't hate. Willie is having a look around. He's no phony hippy, he's no phony anything. Willie is all the way there. How long he will stay there, I do not know. But I am very happy that you are doing a book on Willie, I mean a book of Willie's poems, which is the same thing.

A lot of these guys come off the road with a chip-on-the-shoulder I know it all bit. I've made the road and I know that there's not that much to learn out there. It's death and a drag and hot and cold weather and not feeling so good, but nobody comes in with a new concept of human values. I didn't. Willie doesn't pretend to. He drinks his beer and scratches himself. And not saying it, he says it more than ever. Willie's got a book coming. Willie is a miracle in a time of very little miracles. When the damn thing comes out bill me for a copy, and feel that we will both collect.

—Buk

Los Angeles, Aug. 12, 1967

Willie, *The Cockroach Hotel*
San Francisco: Black Rabbit Press, 1968

Introduction to Doug Blazek's
Skull Juices

It is not easy to realize that you are dying in your twenties. It is much easier not to know that you are dying in your twenties as is the case with most young men, almost all young men, their faces already oaken slabs, shined puke. They only imagine that death might happen in some jungle war of nobody's business. Blazek can see death and life in a shabby piece of curling wallpaper, in a roach wandering through the beercans of a tired and sad and rented kitchen. Blazek, although he would be the last to realize it and is not conscious of it at all, is one of the leading, most mangling, most lovely (yes, I said, "lovely"!) sledges of the new way— The Poetic Revolution. It is difficult to say exactly when the Revolution began, but roughly I'd judge about 1955, which is more than ten years, and the effect of it has reached into and over the sacred ivy walls and even out into the streets of Man. Poetry has turned from a diffuse and careful voice of formula and studied ineffectiveness to a voice of clarity and burnt toast and spilled olives and me and you and the spider in the corner. By this, I mean the most living poetry; there will always be the other kind.

The Poetic Revolution has also passed the Muse down to the dishwasher, the carwasher, the farmer, the x-con, the grape picker, the drifter, the factory worker. The safe and sterile college professors have begun to look more like their poems, and their poems, more like them. They have been found out and even now their plan is an attempt to understand on the one hand and to degrade on the other. These gentlemen have much more leisure time than we (thrice, four times ours) but they have no heart to sort out the minutes. Their work reaches no one but themselves. Allow me to enter with a short and recent personal experience: This last week I received a letter from Germany from a streetsweeper who had seen a poem of mine in an English-printed magazine in Germany and he showed the poem to a postcard seller in the streets, and the postcard seller read

the poem to a group of young people he had been convers-
ing with, translating as he went along, *there*, in the city of
Munich. I hope it doesn't sound too thick or romantic to
you, but this means that, at last, poetry has grown up, has
become a force, a tool, a thing of love and wonder, an explosive concept of Art, instead of a quiet dull little boy in
the corner, told to come out and do the tricks for mamma's
friends and then go to bed and never be heard from again.
That day is over; the little boy is now a man and is done
with jumping through hoops. If you are a lady, he'd just as
soon run his hand up your skirt, and if you are a man, he'll
take you out in the alley if necessary. This does not perforce
mean hardness; this merely means an end to nonsense.

Douglas Blazek, poet, worked in a foundry anywhere
from 8 to 12 hours a day or night, depending upon the
whims of business and his bosses. Any man who has faced
the continual grind for years of going to a dull job day after day, watching the hands of the clock curl in like knives,
each minute shot, each hour mutilated beyond all reason,
each year, each day, each moment, shit upon as if it didn't
count at all, any man who has faced this knows how it goes,
how many of us there are, little Christs nailed forever to
their goddamned cross and with no way to let go (almost)—
choosing between this and suicide and madness or starving
in the streets or watching your children starve. Any choice
you make will be a wrong one. And how many of the workers *do* go mad! Actually. They hit the clock and go on in, but
they are deliriously mad, insane, insane . . . they jest with
each other throughout their work—dirty mean little shit-
dog jests, and they laugh; their laughter is mad and unreal
and vicious, depraved, gone, poor devils! And *sports*! What
SPORT-FREAKS they are! They'll argue baseball down into
fits of actual anger. And what *lovers*! God, they get fucked
night and day. They get fucked, all right.

And coming home from a 10-hour shift, there it is again.
Your body and mind *kaput*, hardly able to drive on in, she
is in front of the TV, and the kids are whirling, balling it
up, yeah, and they are innocent, the whole batch, you need
them, their eyes and bodies are yet living. But you see, there

had been no space between the factory-factory and the home-factory and it's dinner and bath, the baseball scores, and bed, trying to sleep through muscles and nerves that dart like arrows of fire, and the faces still there, the laughter, the hatred—the bodies gone mad and striding cruelly. Everything stinks and hangs and the whole city sleeps except you; and then up and at it, again.

Can you expect us to fuck with polished verse and rhyming couplets?

Can you expect us to be interested in the history of the Peloponnesian Wars?

Can you expect us to get excited over Yeats?

Do you wonder why the educated critics call us "savage"?

Do you wonder why we often have to drink ourselves to sleep?

> Trapped into combat
> like a cork in a tank muzzle
> I drag my James Cagney
> tommy-gunned body
> out to the car—
> on the way to work
> I pass a thousand convertibles
> while a hunched seed of bitterness
> grows along the stubble of my wings—

Blazek's writing is cleaned and cleared by an almost uselessness of experience that only shows him more of the same death, not only a death that claims him but which claims a whole goddamned nation which doesn't have guts enough to admit it.

> my feet lift out of the Chevy
> as I groan a little
> dying from old age in my twenties.
> claimed by the nightshift
> & when the back finally
> breaks I'll know

it wasn't from straw, but
from answers.

There may be some gentle weeping here but no self-pity, no denunciation of some Enemy somewhere. The fact, the poem, is stated and let go. Such men are very hard to kill, even in foundries. Such men have the touch of the bull-fighter or the game little bantamweight fighter I saw the other night. Such men have the touch of the gypsy. Such men can make you feel good when you watch them walk across the room or light a cigarette. Such men are poets, like Blazek, and there aren't very many of them. Such men are caught between the razor blade, a bloody rotting bit of dead meat on the half-clean sheets; such men are caught between this and an impossible love for life. Not a glowing hot-shot and ridiculous shouting of Life—Yeah! but small things, miracles, like a can of beer at midnight, sitting in a kitchen alone, smoking cigars, watching the smoke. The Blazeks are not bitter or vindictive, just the unholy sadness, present agony, the pitch of the electric light, the love of a woman who is wise enough not to hate you.

For instance, Blazek speaks of an old love couch that must be thrown into the basement:

Such a couch!
I love it so entirely
That sometimes
I don't know whether I'm loving
You anymore
Or perhaps this couch
Is you
With crumpled haunches,
A swayed back
& breasts like a laundry bag stuffed full.
I love it
The way things
Are always loved: the way a beggar
Drinks a cup of hot coffee
At the Salvation Army,

The way a teaspoon
Floats thru cereal in the morning—

There can be no greater affirmation of life, sweetheart,
than love for a broken-down couch.

There's love and madness and a going-on, temporarily
anyway:

the trees are hot
the grass is hot
the kids are hot
& screaming like hideous nightmares
riding their tricycles
up & down your sagging spine . . .

or:

The garbage men came
today
even tho I didn't go to work

Magic lines because they are magically true, and simply
and beautifully true. Perfect art is the Perfect Truity of the
Moment that has never been quite spoken or noticed in that
way before. These lines are recognizable as such, and their
easy-seemingness is the essence of their miracle. It was not
so long ago that I stayed home from work for a couple of
days and like Blazek says, sure enough, here they came.
They had on yellow steel hats and they dumped their cans
into the mouth of the truck while I peered at them from
behind my kitchen window. What boys they were, too!
Marble tombstones they were. Neither of them pulled out
a knife and killed himself before my eyes; the flies, and the
garbage crawling the streets. Hell, no, they dumped the
garbage, got on the truck, and drove to the next stop. The
garbage men will keep coming as we ponder our futility
and our love.

Our being here:

did you ever
run your fingers along your arm
feeling all the hairs
like threads on an old dishcloth . . .
if it wasn't
for hairy arms
we wouldn't
know
we were alive . . .

There are some lines that the college professors will never be able to write. The nature of their small agony is so comfortable that they haven't a chance.

When I read Blazek, one word comes to my mind: WARM. Blazek is the warmest poet that I have read. He states simply and clearly and without fear, exactly the love, the thing, the part that gurgles him, makes him see the wall, the heater, his children, his woman, his pants, the milk cartons, his dog, his turds, the shades on his windows,

poetry is useless
unless we try to capture
every second of our existence
like wild buffaloes, like hummingbirds . . .

And his use of words is exactly what the moment obviously states instead of some fancy and brightly-polished literary trick sword that will someday rust:

a 'good' poem is written
with No Control
the way a 'good' woman is loved
& afterwards, throw away the word 'good.'

Perhaps the best thing that has happened to Blazek and the few other young poets of The Poetic Revolution is that they have not been charmed and recognized by the large circulation magazines or even the fancy small-circulation and fancy but snob-literary hound dogs. They are allowed to go on working freely—freely, haha, on coffee breaks, say, scribbling a line on the inside of a matchbox or on the back of an inventory sheet when the high priest of a foreman turns his back, or in that space when the wife goes to sleep, snoring perhaps, and you go to the chair in the front room (if you have a front room) and write it naked across your belly as a million people sleep dreaming of atom bombs and jelly sandwiches. This type never gets a special Grant or any sort of Guggenheim or anything of that sort. In fact, this type doesn't even know where to apply for a thing of this sort, and if they did, they wouldn't. Guggenheims are for people who don't know how to write or for people who have made a racket, a con-game out of writing.

> no matter what
> we do
> it seems pretty silly
> & the sea
> doesn't have enuf sense
> to open up.

Meanwhile Blazek goes on:

> I didn't want to be a clown or
> be drunk, I simply wanted to drink this woman
> slowly, all night, like a bottle of wine
> that I keep snug between my legs.

Perhaps at the age of 46 I grow sentimental, but I can't help wishing we had a whole society composed of such men of warm and easy clarity, and yes, with agony thrown in. You can't help thinking when reading this stuff of, say, a cold strawberry icecream cone at the Fair Grounds when the heat is 98 degrees and everything has stopped except the sound and the color and the sun and your heart like a pet chameleon wriggling under your shirt.

You can't help thinking, say, of a singer dropping dead on the stage while singing in an opera, there on the floor in his wild costume. We ridiculous clowns that must crap and piss and sing and poem and kill each other and cry at night. You can't help thinking of a man driving in after 12 hours in a factory, barely able to maintain a straight course on the road, yet breathing in the air from the window, feeling the night all about him like a wonderful whore—seeing the pulled-down shades, the lights, the liquor stores, the wounded and beaten and mad city. You can't help thinking of dirty undershirts, unwashed water glasses, lions sitting in cages at the zoo, unable to sleep. The courage of us all. If we could only stretch out. If we could only cut across our shame and our pride. Meanwhile, Blazek goes on:

> I know only too well
> how records spin
> how fingernail clippers
> lie like silver fish
> in the ancient swamp
> of a brokendown bed,
> how walls sag when old
> like wet shoeboxes . . .

It is difficult to stop writing about Blazek and his poems.

> I know only too well
> the uselessness of memory—
> brief moments reappearing
> out of lazy summers
> romantic as legends of Tennyson.
> Memories, formless junk
> In the museum of life.

You couldn't mount a machinegun in the forest and punch down a dirty army any better that this. I don't know what will happen to Blazek, how much longer he can go on, but he has left us a very special poetry already. When he walked back into his foundry, he would just be the pipe inspector or the janitor or whatever he did and nobody would know, but *this* is what he does best, so very well:

> I will have to start charting things
> a bit rougher
> so when a poem gets published
> I will have to *feel* to make sure no bones are missing."

The possibility of this young man's death, in any manner, should be enough to make the world weep together, at last, and forever. It won't, of course. That's the way it works, and the kid wouldn't care for it either. Let's just say, then, that here are some poems that I think wouldn't hurt you to read.

It's night now and very quiet and I am finished with this.

Doug Blazek, *Skull Juices*
San Francisco: Twowindows Press, 1970

The Impotence of Being Ernest: Review of Hemingway's *Islands in the Stream*

This book does not make it. I wanted this book to make it. I have been pulling for Hemingway to hit one out of the lot for a long time now. I wanted another novel like *The Sun Also Rises*, *A Farewell to Arms*, or *To Have and Have Not*. I've been waiting a long time. *For Whom the Bell Tolls* was mediocre (comparing Hemingway to Hemingway) and *Across the River and Into the Trees* was worse. Our hero had let us down. The big man had struck out with the bags loaded. *The Old Man and the Sea*, while it fooled many of the critics and prizegivers, did not fool the serious reader or writer or Hemingway maniac.

So here, in *Islands in the Stream*, is his last at bat. From beyond the grave. What a chance for drama! But Mr. Hemingway took a called third strike, lying down. Well, he has done enough and he's about as embedded in American literature, and in us, as anybody can get. He quit with a high lifetime average; let's give him that.

All right, the main character is Thomas Hudson, a "good painter." At least, he survives on his paintings. He's in Bimini in a house that faces the ocean. It's dull for the reader as Thomas Hudson lounges about thinking about "discipline," how he has learned discipline, while his houseboy insists that he (Thomas) should take a drink. Of course, you and I know that discipline is something old men claim they've learned after they've lost the strength of non-discipline. Meanwhile, his three sons are coming to see him the next day. That night Hudson does manage to get out on the docks somewhere and there's a hell of a lot of drinking. In fact—"hell, hell, hell," that word is used very extensively throughout the first part of the novel. When I was a little boy, that used to be a bad word, now it's a yawn; it has passed from the tough boys to the effete.

All right, there's the secondary character, Roger. He's

Thomas's best friend. Roger wants to write a novel. He hasn't done so. Everybody's on the docks. Some drunk in a boat throws Roger some verbal swill, the drunk's main word being "swine." The drunk is objecting because another drunk with a signal pistol is trying to set the town on fire and blow up some drums of gasoline. But instead of calling the man with the signal pistol a swine he calls Roger a swine and Roger is just sitting there, you know. So a fight begins. And it's all Roger's. The fight scene is in the best Hemingway tradition, written as the master used to write. . . . Well, the next day the three sons arrive and it gets dull again. They are some sons. They all talk like very sagacious philosophers; in fact, almost all of Hemingway's characters do. Hell, yes. And there's talk of Paris and Mr. Joyce and it all wheezes on. A day or two wheeze by and then a sagacious and beautiful lady gets off a rich man's boat and the next thing you know, bing, she's out swimming with Roger and the three sons while Hudson paints, and then Roger runs right off the pages somewhere with the sagacious, beautiful lady and we lose our secondary character and wonder if the novel ever gets written. This one doesn't.

O, wait. Before Roger runs off, the boys and a drunken boatman and Roger and Thomas Hudson go on a fishing run. It's the worst part of the book. The young boy, Dave, hooks a big one, the biggest one they've *ever* seen, and they strap him in a chair and let him go to hell while giving all sorts of Big Man advice. It drags and drags and drags, page after page after page. And finally they get the thing close enough to gaff, it's about finished, and you guessed it, it slips off and sinks down into the sea. *The Young Man and the Sea.*

Then that's over and Thomas Hudson is on a boat going somewhere (a big one, not his) and the lady is honorable and has a husband and there's much sagacious talk between them, and the lady is lovely but she does object to most of the places Thomas Hudson wants to take her in order to make love. She's a fine lady. Finally, I believe, they make it standing up on the deck with something wrapped around them.

"Now are you ashamed of me?" she asked.
"No. I love you very much."

Next, Hudson is in Cuba and he has trouble with one of his houseboys but the other houseboy knows how to pimp Hudson up, make him the fool, and Hudson likes him. Hudson also has trouble with his chauffeur. A surly chauffeur, worried because his family was almost starving to death. Hudson sits in the back with a cork-lined drink and straightens him out. It's a good big drink. Fresh green lime juice mixed with cocoanut water and Gordon's gin, and also tautened by bitters. Thomas H. ends up in a bar with an old whore named Honest Lil and a few other horny characters. The wind's blowing too damned hard, Hudson figures, to chase Germans through the ocean. Time out for the War.

Hemingway knows his drinks and his drunks and the bar scene is good and the conversation is a little bit on-stage but not bad. You can get thirsty reading this part. I didn't. I drank all through the book. And I drank everywhere I read it. I read it in the bathtub, on the crapper, in the bed, on the couch, in the breakfastnook, and so on. But here it came again—a woman gets out of a car and comes into the bar. Another very sagacious and lovely female. They embrace. It's one of his x-wives. They run back to his place, pack into bed, make it, then argue a bit, just like old times. But their arguments aren't like other people's arguments. They have this deep wisdom. Then Thomas packs off to sea. In the wind. Orders.

It's quite a ship. Everybody drinks and talks that talk. Sassy. A few "shits" enter and a great many "hells." But, for it all, this is the best part of the book. There's a movie in this part, and a good one. A German sub has been sunk and part of the crew is on the run. The Germans have knocked off some people on an island and gotten themselves a boat. Hudson and his sassy drunken crew must catch the Hun and give him Justice. By the way, all through the book there is a great deal of talk about what a "rummy" is and who is a "rummy." Actually, they're all rummies. The chase is a good one and the writing and the conversation is early Hemingway—crisp and fine and interesting. It felt wonderful to see the old boy back in shape. There is an encounter with one German and then another with the main group. Hemingway knows his warfare, large or small. He writes of it with accuracy and brilliance.

Like the old-time reviewers, I will not give you the ending. Maybe you can guess.

All in all, Hemingway knows his men and his war and his food and his drinks and the wind and the sea and the birds, and how to boat, and he knows his crabs and his wild boars and his dogs and his insects, and he knows his death is coming. He's weak on his women but most of us are, and his conversations aren't quite real; they are Hemingway conversations, but once you realize this you can accept them. And there's free knowledge in the book on all sorts of little things besides making good drinks. Although I don't care too much for his peanut butter with raw onion sandwiches. Or hanging up a slightly demobilized bird in the kitchen with a piece of string by one leg and finding out later that the big cat got it. 466 pages are many pages and maybe that's why it's ten dollars or maybe it's because it's the last of Hemingway. I suppose it matters how you feel about Hemingway and how much money you have, or both. No, the book doesn't make it. Few do. I'd say buy it just to know which way things went. They went that way. And he's gone now. You know how. And, without lying, let's not try to be too unkind.

Coast FM and Fine Arts, November 1970

An Introduction to These Poems: Al Masarik, *Invitation to a Dying*

This old man has been reading poetry for some years, mostly with a feeling of disgust, futility, and frustration (plus anger, boredom, seasickness, so forth). Much of this poetry I was forced to read, having once been editor of the little magazine *Laugh Literary and Man the Humping Guns*. If you believe that *printed* poetry is bad, you ought to read some of the things that arrive in the mailbox. My problem is that not only does little mag underground poetry displease me, but also the sterling accepted stuff of a more holy and rarefied air (no need to name names). But it does seem to be a bloodless, cloudy gang full of tricks and niceties.

I feel that the breakoff of real poetic talent began with World War II and that it never returned. What the causes were (are) I don't know. But from the beginning of World War II and up to 1971 it has been a very barren time for poetic production, not only that form of production but, I feel, creation in other art forms & originality outside of the art forms. Even our clothing styles must revert to past eras. It is as if we simply lack the energy and the initiative to break into new molds. Poetry, in particular, has remained without movement, stale. (Concrete poetry? Please, my friends!) Jon Webb, editor of *The Outsider*, told me not too long before his death, "Bukowski, it's a bad time for poetry, it's a very bad time, very little is being done." Jon was forced to read many more manuscripts than I. Each morning at the p.o. box there was a bucketful of mail, a bucketful of shit.

Al Masarik arrived one morning in my mailbox and I listlessly extracted him along with the others. I had an Alka-Seltzer, a beer, and two hard-boiled eggs and decided to knock off the dead. Neeli Cherry, my co-editor, lives in San Berdoo, and I was the official reader. I always tried to say something kind and amusing even if the poetry was bad. You can destroy a man or a woman for a week with a nastyass rejection. But then if you write too generous a reject they'll be back with more bad poetry. You have to know how to kindly murder. I kindly murdered some of the dead. Then I opened another envelope—from one Al Masarik—and began to read. The first few lines drew me in. You just don't know what it is to discover a new poem, a new talent. It's a once upon a time experience for most. I thought of Whit Burnett when William Saroyan came along one day in yellow second sheets single-spaced. I thought quietly, this man can write. And I've been thinking that ever since . . . when I see a poem of Masarik's in the magazines. The man *can* write, and I welcome him to the club. To my mind there are only four or five writers writing poetry in the U.S. today, and I probably can't name those unless I am goaded to do so.

Whereas World War II killed most poets and poets-to-be, I have the feeling that the Korean War awakened Masarik. Not that this makes the Korean War noble or that Korean Wars are necessary to create Masariks. But it did take him from the hard and plastic American dream and set him in a landscape of uncovered and real lives, and deaths. His Korean poems about the whores, about the boy taking a shit, all the Korean poems have that simple picture quality that says it with such an easy totality. The sign of a good artist is his ability to say or create or re-create a real thing in a simple way. By simple I mean without accoutrements that will weight it down later as a display or a trick. To be simple, to be basic is a thing that most artists simply cannot do. Ah, to get down to the bone, to cut away the swill. Masarik does this. He does it with an almost unbelievable easiness. I mean, the writing seems easy; the price is probably something else.

When you read Masarik, you might feel like eating an apple or drinking a beer. All the good writers make me hungry for food. It's like the writing comes in with warm light, it enters you; you simply feel like jamming more substance in. Céline gave me many a bellyache. I used to read Céline in bed, laughing and eating *Ritz* crackers. I was in a trance, reading, and slamming crackers into my mouth. Soon the whole box would be gone and then I'd get up and drink water, and then, jesus christ . . . what a gutache. Céline, you son of a bitch: Masarik, too, makes me hungry.

When I'd see my few friends I'd tell them, "There's a

new guy around, Al Masarik. He can write." Then I'd show them a poem. "Hmmm, yes," they'd say.

I've written three or four forewords for some other young men, all of them showing some original blaze. I meant what I wrote. The fact is that those I wrote about have not advanced in their writing. In fact, they have gone backwards. Something in life has gotten them. For this, I can't be responsible. I don't have time to go around pointing out the traps to young genius. Masarik has gotten off well. Not only in the Korean poems here but the others. "Autographed Baseball": check those last three lines. "Marilyn Monroe" poems, we're all guilty of them. I wrote one myself. This Masarik one is as good as any. "Mentally Retarded" is Masarik at his best. Focusing. Check the last five lines. If there are surprises, they are surprises of truth. I rather think of most of Masarik's poems—although some of the Korean whore poems are love poems—as photographs from hell. An almost lovable but still worldly hell. See, he says, it's like this and here are the words.

I feel that Masarik will go on. He has style but I don't think he will be confined by his style. Let's hope not. I see him going on, his style altering ever so imperceptibly, his photographs changing as his life changes. This selection, along with his earlier work, is one grand foundation. It has been quite some time since a vigorous, plain-talking new blood has entered the scene. This is a victory for all of us. It shows us that *new* men can do fine things. We had almost forgotten. We had almost lost hope. Masarik, you son of a bitch. Come on in. It's been a long drought. Those scarecrows out there. I thought they had us. We've fooled the killers again. Sit down and have a beer, Al. On the house . . . . . .

Al Masarik, *Invitation to a Dying*
Redwood City, CA: Vagabond Press, 1972

Foreword: Steve Richmond, _Earth Rose_

These are poems written by a human being. These are poems written by a man who sees demons and lives alone in a shack by the ocean. These are the poems of a loner and the loner is, finally, the only true creator. These are the poems of a loner who is capable of love but who has trouble—like the non-loners—in finding it. These are lines put down true, and like lines put down true can make one feel so good one can laugh at times. Truth is jolly, truth is the sun of laughter. These are poems like warm butter, sex on a stick, and the laughter of the mad. Richmond has broken through the wall. He lays it on down. It's there. It's a gift, a curse, and a signal. Steel in motion. Flash of night on rubber tires. The workings.

These are poems written by a human being. I have met many writers, mostly poets, and while some of their work was very fine, upon meeting the actual creators I became sickened by their rays, their voices, their manners. How clannish and bitchy they are. They eat together, sleep together, talk together, party together, plan together, breed together. They have no chance in the final arena of creation because they weaken each other with their agreements. The creator must finally be the loner. Richmond is almost always alone. You'll find no stereo going full blast at his place among the beerbottles and the gossipers and the wife-pinchers. There'll be an occasional woman bringing him a plate of meatballs and spaghetti, but the next time around she'll be gone.

I like writers who are strong as their work. That is the final test. I don't believe you can separate the man and his work. I don't believe that if the work is strong and the man is weak that the work is all that matters. The strong man with the strong work will endure. No publishers have come to Richmond. The publishers are wrong. This work will endure. The poems you read here will endure. Not all of them but many of them.

These are the poems of a human being, these are the poems of a loner, of a man with a face, of a man who can laugh, of a man who can walk across a room with easiness. These are the poems of a man who gives off good rays, strong rays. These are the poems of a man who deserves a good woman and has not found one yet. No matter. He'll go on. Someday he'll be found, some day he'll be discovered, the universities and the groupies and the parasites will embrace him. At the moment he's safe working. The longer he's ignored the better the poems will be. I wish him a long period underground. Meanwhile, to those of you who have fallen across this book, this is the gift to you, these poems. Take them, taste them, button them onto your shirts, glue them on the shithouse walls, mail them to your aunt in Des Moines, feel good, these are the poems of a human being, he's got it, and now you've got it. You're early and the power runs ripe. Amen.

Steve Richmond, *Earth Rose*
Santa Monica, CA: Earth Books, 1974

A Note on These Poems: Appreciation to Al Purdy's *At Marsport Drugstore*

All right. I corresponded with Al Purdy for years, and then as such things go, we stopped. At the time he was in splendid shape—had a house and a woman in it who treated him well, and best of all—he made his own wine.

I don't know how he's doing now—outside of the poem—but looking at these I know that he hasn't lost his magic. Whatever the *viewpoint* of the love poems, it's still Purdy writing them. And that means a Purdy full of sorrow and grace and humor and lines that roll across the page and wash back and roll forth again.

The proper authority for lovers is pain

How many of us have doubled up in our rooms alone, holding both hands to the gut, verily chopped in half?

Most of us have been in love.

These poems are recordings of that almost impossible way.

Nov. 24, 1976

Al Purdy, *At Marsport Drugstore*
Sutton West, ON: Paget Press, 1977

About "Aftermath"

Whit Burnett's *Story* had discovered William Saroyan and many others and although they only paid $25 per story there was something about getting into *Story* which was much better than getting into the *Atlantic* or *Harper's* or *The New Yorker*.

I wrote two or three short stories a week and sent them all to *Story*. I even liked their standard rejection slip which began: "This, alas, is a rejection slip. . . ."

I drank, starved, moved from city to city and kept writing two or three stories a week and mailing them to *Story*. My typer was in and out of hock, and then finally I couldn't get it out. I hand-printed my stories in ink. I hand-printed so many stories that I was able to print faster than I could write in the standard manner. It was stamps before food, envelopes, paper before food. But not before drink.

Each time I moved to a new city I had dozens and dozens of rejected stories which I boosted into roominghouse trash cans. I only had one suitcase and when you fit in the radio, the extra pair of work shoes, shirts, underwear, shorts, stockings, bathroom stuff, towels, and the like, there wasn't much room for unwanted pages.

There were new cities and new hand-printed stories. And Whit Burnett was no snob. He read them. And often there was a personally typed note: "This one almost made it. Please send us more. . . ."

Any typed reject was an immense miracle for me. I think I continued writing just for typed rejects. . . .

It was a night in St. Louis. I had been working overtime as a packer in the cellar of a ladies' dress shop. As I was leaving, the boss called me into his office. He sat behind his desk smoking a cigar and a friend sat in an overstuffed chair near him. They both looked very fat and healthy, rather imperial, almost intelligent.

"I want you to meet a friend of mine," my boss said, "he's a writer too."

"Hello," I said.

We didn't shake hands. He just sat in his overstuffed chair. Both of them sat smoking expensive cigars. They were totally relaxed. My whole day and evening had been eaten away uselessly for a pittance, for the barest of a survival, never enough money to escape, let alone endure. Slavery had not been abolished, it had been extended and enhanced to include the black and the white and any other usable color.

My boss exhaled a wondrous plume of rich smoke, leaned back a bit in his leather chair, and said, "My friend has had many books published, he makes much money writing . . ."

I ha.d put down on my application form: Writer. Mainly as an excuse to cover my long gaps of unemployment.

I stood there. There was nothing I could say. I finally asked my boss if I might leave. He told me that it would be all right. . . .

I always walked home to my room and it was Autumn and the trees had no leaves, just dozens of bare branches sticking out, and it was dark already. My feet hurt, my back hurt, my eyes felt sucked dry. My clothing was cheap and rumpled, there was a button missing from my shirt down near the waist, the front pulled open revealing a dirty undershirt. I was 24 years old and already three-quarters murdered but still dedicated to the short story.

As I walked along, my mind changed. It was easy, it just went the other way:

I thought, I'm going to go out and get it. I may not have a dime now but somehow I'll get money. I'll hire and fire men just for my own entertainment, I'll buy furs and autos for women and toss them aside when the first wrinkle appears. I'll re-invent the word "ruthless." I'll become colder than the coldest cold and I'll love it! And if I can't rule factories, I'll hold up banks, I'll set fire to half the universe! I'm tired, I'm tired, let all this writing be damned!

I walked along, found my roominghouse, went up the stairway, opened the door to my room and there on the rug, via the courtesy of my landlady, was the same old manila envelope. It was fat, a returned story.

I opened the window, took the bottle of chilled wine from the sill, opened that, poured one. The cold St. Louis Autumn air chilled my wine perfectly. I took a hit, sat down, lit a smoke. I sat on the edge of my bed and undid the clasp, as per custom, slid the pages out.

At least it was a typed reject.

"Dear Mr. Bukowski:

"We are sorry but this one didn't quite do. But we very much liked 'Aftermath of a Lengthy Rejection Slip' and we will run it in our March–April issue. We have been much interested in your work and we are happy to. . . ."

Signed, "Whit Burnett."

I walked over and put the note on the dresser top. Then I had a good drink. I sat on the bed looking at the walls. I took my shoes off and threw them across the room. I looked at my shoes. I looked at the dresser. I noticed each knob on the dresser drawers. I poured another drink. I drank that. Then I got up, walked to the dresser, picked up the note and read it again. Then I put the note in a dresser drawer and went back to bed and drank some more. Then I got up, opened the drawer, and read the note again.

Whit Burnett, he had class.

I finished the bottle of wine, found my spare in the closet, open that, drank that . . . listening to my one Mozart album on my record player a couple of times. . . .

In the morning I awakened without a hangover, found the note, and read it all over again.

Charles Bukowski, *Aftermath of a Lengthy Rejection Slip*
N.P.: Blackrose Editions, 1983

Preface: *The Bukowski/Purdy Letters 1964–1974*

Getting a letter from Purdy always got my day up off the floor. I found my life more than unappealing and his letters lent a steadiness, some hope, and some hard-rock wisdom.

I wrote letters to many in those days, it was rather my way of screaming from my cage. It helped, that and the gambling, the drinking, the paintings, the poems and the short stories. *When* I did all this, I'm not sure. The night job was truly killing me—eleven and one-half hour nights as a routine for eleven and one-half years. And receiving a Purdy letter was like hearing from another world, indeed. I think he sensed he had a rather mad creature at this end and he kindly nursed me along. And his poems read bright in my darkness.

And here I am, still not cured, and I never thought I would *ever* be 63 years old. There are some differences now: I buy my wine by the case and play the horses a little bit better than I used to. And I recently received an inscribed book by Purdy: *Birdwatching at the Equator*. And he hasn't lost a step. It's still all there, fame has not blemished him. The most human endure in this way because it's the most natural thing to do, and he is naturally one of the most human.

Thank you, Al. Much.

yrs,

Buk

Charles Bukowski and Al Purdy, *The Bukowski/
Purdy Letters 1964-–74: A Decade of Dialogue*
Sutton West, ON: Paget Press, 1983

Introduction to *Horsemeat*

Well now, why do I need the racetrack? Hemingway liked the bullfights, right? He saw the life-death factors out there. He saw men reacting to these factors with style—or the other way. Dostoevsky needed the roulette wheel even though it always took his meager royalties and he ended up subsisting on milk.

I need the racetrack. If I stay away from the track for a while, I can't type. Something about betting the horses makes this machine jump for me. That, and a couple of bottles of wine.

So, you might say the horses have written my stuff for me and my critics will agree. "Sure, that's where all the horseshit comes from." My critics don't know an exacta from a mud-mark. They also don't know about the trick which touches and churns the gut, so I'll forgive them.

The racetrack is far from nirvana. There are some things which I resent about the racetrack. One of my main resentments is being made to wait 30 minutes between races. This is a sacrilege against life. One doesn't need all that time to make a selection. But the track needs that time to wait for the last sucker to come in over the hill, needs that time to sell food and drink.

So they lay that 30 minutes upon one. I've taken a small notebook out there and attempted to write. No go. I've attempted to think of plots for dirty stories for the girly magazines. No go. Creativity doesn't occur *at* the track. I buy the daily paper and read almost every page. I read Ann Landers, the financial section, sports; the murders, the wars, the rapes; show biz; and even the comic section. I am up to date on all the crap in the world.

Lately I've taken to strolling about looking at the people. This is odd for me because long I ago I decided what the people were and that looking at them was meaningless. But then, with 30 minutes to kill. . . .

Sometimes it's rewarding to look at the women. I look

at this one and think, I'm glad I don't have to live with her. And then I look at another and I think, I'm glad I don't have to live with that one. I keep looking and thinking the same thing over and over again.

Please don't misunderstand me; I'm not a misogynist, just a realist.

Anyhow, I come back to the action feeling pretty lucky. The horses are coming out on the track and I'm about ready to bet. . . .

Another thing I dislike about the track is their "give-aways." About every two or three weeks, to reel the suckers back in, the track gives away some item. Each time, it's different. Sometimes they give away tote bags; other times, caps with the track's name inscribed upon them; or T-shirts, likewise inscribed with advertising; or a horseshoe pin; or half-price on beer and hot dogs; or a free meal—which at least *is* something most of the players need. The mob pours in on "giveaway day"; the poor working people and the unemployed come and they get their trinket and/or their bite to eat and then lose their few dollars.

There is nothing generous about the racetrack. It is not a place to go to jump up and down and holler and drink beer and take your girlfriend. It is a life-death game and unless you apply yourself with some expertise, you are going to get killed.

Can you imagine people going to the stock exchange for a day of fun?

Yet let me admit that for all the negative factors the track did give me hope when I was working in the factories and at the post office. Hope is damned important when you're on the cross. Hope, you know, even if there isn't much, can keep you going. Just that small *maybe*. It made me feel as if my slavery might not be a forever thing. Throw in the bottle and a few bad women and you had something else to consume you besides the impossible job. . . .

But I wouldn't advise the racetrack for everybody. When I quit my last job eleven years ago at the age of 50, some cracker asked me as I walked off, "What ya gonna do, Hank, play the horses?"

"Any damn fool can go to the track and most of them do," I told him. . . .

I have many sayings about the racetrack. One I have often repeated while looking around: "Those who bet the horses are the lowest of the breed."

Often when I was unfortunate enough to have one of my ladies with me she would ask, "What are *we* doing here?"

Another of my sayings is: "Show me a man who can beat the horses and I'll show you a man who can do anything he makes up his mind to do."

This is true. The concentration, the dedication, the necessary insight would create a winner in any other non-physical endeavor.

But let me warn you: the track does *not* create great lovers. The track is a mighty destroyer of energy. And many an evening I have come home to one of my ladies and heard the same thing, as if they were all of one voice:

"For Christ's sake, look at you! Your ass is dragging from that goddamned racetrack! What good are you going to be in bed?"

"Now, baby, I'll just have a few drinks and I'll be as good as new. . . ."

"Yeah, I *know*! You'll just end up playing with your typewriter! *That typewriter is your woman!*"

. . . I had a buddy once, he has since vanished somewhere, but I met him at the track this particular day and he told me, "Well, Hank, my wife laid it down for me. She said, 'Listen, this is it: you're going to have to *choose* between the *horses* and *me!*' Well, baby, I told her. . . ."

So? Another of my sayings is: "Time is made to be wasted." I might even alter that to: "Time *must* be wasted."

People are just not constructed to function at 100 percent all the time. I consider it better if I choose how to waste my time rather than somebody else choosing for me. So, we have the racetrack.

Now, for the uninitiated, let me give you a few basic facts. Out of each dollar wagered the track takes between 15 and 16 cents. This "take" is divided almost equally between the track and the state (in this case California). The track doesn't care which horse wins. The track and the state share the "take" no matter whether a 50-to-one shot wins or if a one-to-two shot wins. The larger the mutual (money bet) the more the track and the state "win." Roughly speaking, you give the track a dollar and they give you back 84 cents, to bet with. (In exacta wagering, the most popular public form of wagering, the track takes 20 cents and gives you back 80.)

Yet most people lose much *more* than 16 percent of their money. They lose all of it. I'd say that only the few professional bettors (about 1.8 percent of the crowd) regularly take their cut along with the track and the state.

Some mathematicians claim that the "take" is more than 16 percent. Their view is that a 16 percent "take" on 9 races adds up to a 144% "take" on the money wagered. Which proves why almost everybody loses. I'm no math freak but I still feel all you have to beat is 16 percent. I mean, you give them a dollar, right? They give you back 84 cents on the next race and they take 16 percent of that. And so on down the line. Yes, much money is lost to the "take" but much is also lost because of stupid betting.

There are many sad and depressed faces each day at the track—jobs, homes, lives down the old drain. I've seen people with their heads buried in their laps, not moving, sitting on benches and in corners. I've seen tears of agony and disbelief.

I've seen and felt the anger and madness of the people

driving out of the parking lot after the last race. They drive viciously and in ugly fashion as if the bad bets they made were the fault of some cruel universe. It hurts when the dream is gone.

And it's a long drive back in to what's left.

I often wonder if on my deathbed (if I'm lucky enough to die in one) I'll be wishing for one of those 30-minute delays, those waits between races?

Meanwhile, after decades of horseplaying I'm only about $10,000 in the hole, which ain't bad. I mean, I'm getting *better*. Maybe by deathbed time I'll get even.

The track has given me many sad and magic moments, tragic moments. I've seen many unhappy racing accidents for both man and horse. I've witnessed the death of a jockey.

I once caught a horse that paid $225 and change. And during one very strange period I won 23 races in a row and none of the horses were favorites. I remember that time. I walked around feeling very much like god. My voice became rich and beautiful, my eyes brilliant. Everything was clear. I was sure of everything. I walked up to the most beautiful lady at the track, took her by the arm, walked her to my car, drove to my motel, and made love to her.

After that I plunged into a losing streak and quickly became humble again. Sometimes I think there are forces that lift us up for a while in order to see how vain and foolish we can become in victory.

"To consume and be consumed," I wrote long ago in an old poem.

That is what has happened to me at Santa Anita, Hollywood Park, Los Alamitos, Del Mar, Turf Paradise, Caliente and at the dog races at some track whose name I have forgotten just outside Phoenix. The dogs are great, I have never lost at the dogs but since this book is about horses, forget it.

Many of my hours, days, weeks, years have been swallowed by the racetrack. Think of all the time I could have spent weeding the garden, mastering chess, karate, the dance; maybe I could have become a great chef, a pool player, a pianist or an acceptable mystic. I might even have been a policeman in a patrol car.

But it's like my buddy said to his wife, "Baby, I'll take the horses."

He vanished, poor fellow, but I have a new buddy who says to me, "I can't talk to anybody but a gambler."

This limited edition book is for them—the gamblers—even though it will fall mostly into the hands of collectors who won't care what I'm talking about. Michael takes great photos and when we sit down with our copies of this book we'll probably get good and drunk together, and that is how this particular introduction will finally end.

5/7/82
(after another winning day at
the track, drinking 1978
Mirassou Gamay Beaujolais)

Charles Bukowski and Michael Montfort, *Horsemeat*
Santa Barbara, CA: Black Sparrow Press, 1982

Foreword: Douglas Goodwin, *Half Memory of a Distant Life*

There is a curious thing about good and original and fresh poetry: it makes you laugh a little bit inside, it connects the edges, it eases off the meanness of some of the living, it helps you to continue flushing toilets, opening doors, sleeping, eating, breathing, looking, walking, it helps you continue all the sundry acts on your way through your life and towards your death.

Brothers and sisters, good and original and fresh poetry helps much; the trouble being, there is so little of it.

When I first read the poetry of Douglas Goodwin, I was immediately taken. The stuff boiled with the agony of life, and the daring to go on with it anyhow. Courage is infective. So is wild, raging humor. Goodwin has these things. And he lays the lines down clear and clean; there is no posing, no posturing, no poetic gimmickry.

That's all. And that's enough. Plenty enough.

Welcome to a new voice. The ranks have been thin for some long time.

It's better now. We can laugh, again, a little bit, inside.
7-2-87

Douglas Goodwin, *Half Memory of a Distant Life*
Storrs, CT: Clock Radio Press, 1987

Foreword: Macdonald Carey, *Beyond That Further Hill*

I first came across the work of Macdonald Carey in the pages of the *New York Quarterly*. I was taken at once by the ease and humor and warmth of the writing. Here was feeling that was not afraid of feeling, here was feeling that was not afraid to laugh at itself.

Yet these were but a few poems. Most poets can be good once or twice or maybe once more but not too many held up over the long course.

Upon reading these, I am happy to report that Macdonald Carey has. And you will soon realize this too.

That Mac has spent almost an entire lifetime as a Hollywood actor and yet is still able to write these delicious poems, well, that's quite some miracle. Hollywood is the killer of souls. How this man ever retained his sensibilities and probably even enhanced them is beyond me.

But welcome, anyhow, to this Daring Old Man on the Flying Trapeze.

To this wonderful and original show.

[signed] Bukowski

December 12, 1988

Macdonald Carey, *Beyond That Further Hill*
Columbia: University of South Carolina, 1989

Further Musings

1.
the sound of one life scraping
against another.
2.
life's sensible repetitions are
galling.
3.
once I phoned somebody to
bail me out of jail and his
answer was, "I can't, I'm
entertaining somebody from
Spain."
I'd just as soon he had told me
to go fuck myself.
4.
once while reading D.H. Lawrence
on a train I decided that I'd like to
drink wine with him.
then I decided it would be better to
drink wine alone because
we would not like each other and,
besides, he was dead.
5.
the worst people are not those that
you've already met.
6.
hell is where you are now, even
when you are laughing.
7.
I told her that I had a great
time that day by cleaning out my
desk and finding all sorts of odd
and forgotten things.
this immediately made her angry:
"That's what you old guys do!

That's what old farts do!"
A week later she tried to run me
over with her car.
things had not been going well
for some time.
8.
as a boy I often pretended that
I had important things to do with
my time.
now, nearing 73, I find myself
still doing the same
thing.
9.
I often can't tell if people are at
peace or just being
dull.
10.
"Who?" asked the owl, "is going
to die next?"
never guessing.
11.
why are novelists so boring?
is it because so many of them
write about their own
lives?
12.
I'm not certain of what I am
doing, are you?
think of how impossible it would
be
if we did.
13.
a wise man knows when to step
backwards.
14.
the bell only tolls for itself.
listen.

15.
that curious thought I had about
3 a.m. last night
would have fit nicely
here.

Half-Truth, Nov./Dec. 1993

INTERVIEWS

MAILER IS A JOURNALIST.

Stonecloud Interview

Interview by Phil Taylor

STONECLOUD: You don't give too many poetry readings, do you?

BUKOWSKI: No, but you know, of all the readings I gave, the one I gave at USC was really the deadest. Something about the audience or the campus, I don't know. A lady wrote me and asked if I would read. I was working in the post office, and I was very anti-reading at the time because I had a job, a little money in my pocket, and I was saving my soul. I wrote her a two- or three-page letter and said, "Happily I'll go to my grave without ever giving a poetry reading." Now I've given about twenty or twenty-five.

STONECLOUD: How many of them did you enjoy giving, or how many came off well?

BUKOWSKI: Out of all of them, maybe four or five good ones. It's really a drag though, hard work like being in a ditch. I'm not an actor; I do it for the money, strictly a poetry whore. For the time, giving all these readings at colleges around California, I'm living off the poetry fat of the land.

STONECLOUD: Are you publishing any more issues of *Laugh Literary and Man the Humping Guns*?

BUKOWSKI: As Linda likes to say, "woman the humping guns." Women's lib, you know. No, I've turned it over: got so much bad material. We really didn't publish anything good except our own.

. . .

STONECLOUD: Are you glad that you've had as much or as little money as you've had?

BUKOWSKI: I'll go back to the corny concept of the "starving writer" days. Especially when you're young. You don't know where your next meal is coming from, you don't know if you're going to be able to get the rent up, and the landlady's footsteps are going by. When it isn't terrifying, it's kind of interesting. The good old early days, it's kind of romantic. When you're young you have these ideals, you're going to be a writer, it's kind of romantic. It carries you through. It felt good; I didn't mind starving. As long as you're young you say "Shit, I can do it; I can always straighten out and become a damned fool or an industrialist or something. I've got these years to really burn in glory." But when you get older, you're starving in a room at the age of fifty-two, you're trying to be a writer. . . .

STONECLOUD: It doesn't seem so romantic anymore.

BUKOWSKI: Hell, no.

STONECLOUD: Do you have any regrets? Would you change anything in your past?

BUKOWSKI: No, especially the way I live. It's been pretty damn good, a wide-open gamble. I gave up writing for ten years and I did that ten hard years of living; drinking, hospitals, jails, women, bad jobs, madness. Even now, I think of a night that happened, write a poem, a short story. I can draw into that even now. I don't see how guys still in their twenties can hardly write.

STONECLOUD: You mean because they haven't experienced anything?

BUKOWSKI: You can't reach in and get it. When I was twenty I was writing like mad too. I think you write the way you feel when you're young, more than your experiences. I think it's better to be old, though, and reach back.

STONECLOUD: When you talk about style, in terms of clarity, or freedom from excess baggage, or naturalness, what are you thinking of?

BUKOWSKI: I'm really an "essentialist." Maybe reading so much poetry that seems to me devious and secretive, people who have little secrets with their friends, you know. A game, a code that no one else quite understands. I try to break it down and make it just as simple as possible, just say what I'm thinking. That doesn't sound like much, but I think it's important. Like I'm talking to you now, I say, "My elbow itches," something like that. Of course if you write down "My elbow itches," not many people are going to take to that. You know what I'm trying to say.

STONECLOUD: Just let it come natural.

BUKOWSKI: Yeah, naturalness.

STONECLOUD: Certain poets demand of you knowledge of all sorts of myths, legends, historical facts, etc. But whatever poetry you're writing, it seems you always expect your audience to have a certain amount of knowledge, about life and certain feelings of the times you're writing in.

BUKOWSKI: Well, I don't know. In the old poetry they refer to mythology, the gods. . . .

STONECLOUD: I'm thinking of twentieth-century poets like Yeats and Eliot and Pound. Where do you stand there?

BUKOWSKI: Well, you especially have to know your Chinese. All this stuff, reference to mythology and so on, is dropping out. It's been so standard, you're supposed to know the gods, etc., etc.

STONECLOUD: It seems like baroque embellishment for its own sake, have you ever used a god in one of your poems?

BUKOWSKI: Not knowingly. I've said my poetry could be understood by an East Kansas City whore or even a college professor.

STONECLOUD: Don't those people, whores and such, bring to your poetry a knowledge of life that is in its own way just as complex and deep, though not as well versed in the arts?

BUKOWSKI: Yeah, I just don't do that kind of academic thing. I don't have any excuses.

STONECLOUD: Have you ever tried like Charles Olson

to construct theories about the way you write poetry? Line breaks, form, rhythm, etc.?

BUKOWSKI: I stay away from these Olson essays and all that. I think I've broken through more or less to the common language. But we don't want to make it too common. I think the mistake that some of the black writers are making is—oh Christ-y, this'll probably be construed as anti-black, but it isn't—the mistake is that the language is too common, like "Hey baby, big train. . . ."

STONECLOUD: You mean because their language belongs to everybody, and therefore to no one poet?

BUKOWSKI: It's kind of like flaunting the street language, instead of using it. I think they gotta calm down a little before they get to it. They've missed the mark there so far. What you end up with is a lot of clichés and platitudes posing as wisdom. If you use the common language, you've still got to stay away from the cliché and the platitude. I think that's where they make their mistake.

STONECLOUD: Which of the poets writing today or, say, after World War II, do you like?

BUKOWSKI: That's a tough one. I don't read anymore, I don't even read newspapers. I've gotten so locked up in myself. You can call it ego, or whatever, Jeffers is dead. I can't think of anybody, frankly, who has really stirred me. This is a very bad time for me to look around and say that this man's good, or that one's bad. I really can't say.

STONECLOUD: Is that simply because you don't follow what's being written?

BUKOWSKI: I don't think it's that. I drop on a few lines but I'm so turned off by what I read I just say I can't waste any more time on them. It's an instinctive turn-off. I used to like Karl Shapiro, something called "V Letter," which he wrote in World War II, very clear, simple. Then he became editor of *Poetry* and *Prairie Schooner*. Like others, he was good just in the beginning.

STONECLOUD: What's your feeling about experimental forms like concrete poetry?

BUKOWSKI: Concrete poetry? It's just a cute trick.

STONECLOUD: It does seem that there's no way concrete poetry can contain any real feeling.

BUKOWSKI: There's not enough meat in it. I tried something more profound. Write a line of poetry that comes to mind; say the first word has five letters, the second three, the third seven, etc. Under that line, you have to follow with one that makes sense with the top line but yet has the same number of words, with each word containing the exact number of letters as its corresponding word in the previous line. Kind of a stylized vision. It'll be like a set of columns finally. It's a good exercise to make it make sense.

STONECLOUD: Have you ever tried sestinas or. . . . ?

BUKOWSKI: I don't even know what those mean. I don't tie myself up with all of that, rondeaus or any of those things. I took a poetry class one time. I looked around and said, "Shit, look at this." I decided not to learn what they were learning.

STONECLOUD: You've read a lot of stuff from the past, but as a whole you're not thoroughly schooled in the history or the craft of poetry?

BUKOWSKI: I wouldn't say I could hold a conversation with Olson—of course he's dead anyway, so I couldn't hold a conversation with him—or Creeley, for example. Breath pauses and all that. If I'd bogged myself down with all that, I wouldn't have had time to live. I put my stress elsewhere.

STONECLOUD: There are only a few works of literature, past or present, that really move you, is that it?

BUKOWSKI: Yeah. I get more out of the *Racing Form*.

STONECLOUD: Have you ever gotten a kick out of Roethke, for example?

BUKOWSKI: Oh, no. I read him. Everybody talks about

him. He's too comfortable. I don't believe him. They build him up so much, but he's so comfortable. He was out of San Diego or somewhere, wasn't he?

STONECLOUD: I think he used to teach at the University of Washington. Do you mean he was too comfortable in his approach to poetry?

BUKOWSKI: Yeah. I've never met him in person.

STONECLOUD: He died eight or nine years ago. He was a very heavy drinker. He lived pretty hard too.

BUKOWSKI: Well, you can be a heavy drinker, but that doesn't mean you're a creative writer. Somebody sent me this book [holds up a book by Blaise Cendrars, the French poet and journalist, whose photograph is on the cover] and I said if this man writes like his face, I might as well give up writing. I thought I'm really going to read something here, and I opened it up and ... nothing. Well, I still have a chance. But he has got quite a mug on him. If he could write like his face; he probably could if he could get the right mirror turned on him or something. Once people sit down at that machine they tie up. They can't be themselves.

STONECLOUD: Have you read anything of Sylvia Plath's?

BUKOWSKI: Yeah, she did the thing, didn't she? And she didn't get famous until after she did it. I never read too much of her stuff.

STONECLOUD: Have you ever written a poem about suicide?

BUKOWSKI: Yeah, there's a poem I did call "The Last Days of the Suicide Kid." Well, actually it's about old age. The only good woman writer I know is Carson McCullers. She wrote *The Heart Is a Lonely Hunter*. She drank herself to death, and she might have been not quite a woman. Some people say she was a dyke. She was really good, though. I said to myself "A woman wrote this?" A powerful writer. I almost cried. She died on a ship somewhere, in a wheelchair, drinking. She was on her way to Europe when she died. Men can't ever write the way she did.

STONECLOUD: It seems that the easiest thing to do is to learn how not to write bad poetry, to become a competent technician. I gather you're sort of down on things like teaching positions, fellowships, prizes. . . .

BUKOWSKI: I'll take them all! I have nothing against money that allows me time to write, but I've never applied. I was sitting around with some professors one night. Miller Williams and two others, and one of these guys gets a scholarship every year. He goes to a little island. He's a nice guy—a fair poet—maybe he deserves it. I'm sitting there drinking and I say "OK, goddamn you bastards, you get these things; all I want to ask is where do I get the form to fill out, at the corner drugstore, or where you buy a *Racing Form*? Where do you guys get these papers?" I really got in a fury, and they wouldn't answer me, they all looked at me. Then I said "Tell me, goddammit Where do I get a paper to fill out?"

STONECLOUD: Well, you've got to have a Ph.D. or at least a master's degree.

BUKOWSKI: Oh shit, no wonder they wouldn't say! They were trying not to hurt my feelings.

STONECLOUD: Write to the Ford Foundation. Tell 'em you drive a Ford loyally, you've owned one for years.

BUKOWSKI: I know a guy up in Canada, he was just awarded $40,000. He filled out a paper. I don't know if he has a Ph.D., but he does teach.

STONECLOUD: There are prizes, though, like the *Atlantic Monthly* has.

BUKOWSKI: The odds against that are so high. It's usually somebody's sister's brother who wins it. Those name magazines like *Playboy*, *Esquire*, etc., there's a lot of politics in getting published in them. If you know someone, a cousin, or a brother-in-law, it helps.

. . .

STONECLOUD: I read your novel *Post Office*, and the aspect that interested me most is how you got by from day to day. You had to put up with a lot of shit.

BUKOWSKI: Listen, I had to quit or go crazy. They really have some creatures there. I think the supervisors are picked not for their mentality but for their brutality. They go by the book, just like in the Army, though I've never been in the Army. "These are the rules." I wrote *Post Office* in twenty drunken nights. When I was young I said I'll have to be fifty years old to write a novel, and now I'm fifty and I've written it, right after quitting the post office. I'd come here each night, have a pint of whiskey, some beer, three or four cigars, and turn on some symphony music. I'd say I'm going to type at least ten pages as a quota, and if I run over, fine. So I drank and I typed, my music going on, and never remembered going to bed, and I'd get up in the morning. First thing I'd do is go in there and take two Alka-Seltzer, and I'd come out to see how many pages I'd done. I'd find maybe seventeen, eighteen pages spread out on the couch and say, "My God, that was a good night." I finished in twenty days. It's not immortal, but it's OK.

STONECLOUD: It seems to me that the individual sections stand better by themselves than as parts of a whole.

BUKOWSKI: I know. This is deliberate. I'm so bored with novels that I made each chapter like machine gun bullets, fast and short. I've tried so many great novels, like *War and Peace*, and you've got to climb through so many mountains of shit to get to where it's going. I thought I'd make each chapter a short story by itself, each relating to the central theme. So I wasn't bored writing it. My theory is that if you get bored writing it, the reader's going to get bored reading it. As I re-read it one time, I saw it could be a hell of a lot better.

STONECLOUD: It's got a real strong character. The central autobiographical character is the strongest point. It makes the book stand by itself.

BUKOWSKI: At least I hope it keeps a lot of people out of the post office.

STONECLOUD: What are some jobs you'd particularly like to forget?

BUKOWSKI: I've had about a hundred jobs. The novel I'm working on now is called *Factotum*, which means a "man of many trades." I'm coming upon all my hundred jobs, one by one, and when I think of them I ask myself, "Did I really do that? Was it that bad?" Dog biscuit factory, slaughterhouse, railroad track gang, stock boy at Sears Roebuck, gas station attendant. I don't even think I've lived that long. I used to gather bottles of blood for the Red Cross; janitor, shipping clerk, it's all so drab. I burned up the years, and now I'm crying in your beer.

STONECLOUD: That's your beer.

BUKOWSKI: Then I'm crying in my beer. I wish I could just leap up and say something astounding. I really can't.

STONECLOUD: What would strike you as startling or astounding?

BUKOWSKI: Oh, something like, say, if Artaud were here, he'd leap up and say something like "I hate people with feet on their feet." Something really wonderful. What was that he said one time, "I hate well people, they're disgusting," something like that. When he wasn't quite mad he'd come up with—but he's right, by God. There's something about healthy people. It's obscene to be healthy, it's unreal.

. . .

Confessions of a Badass Poet

Interview by Loren Means
(Linda King is present)

BUK: What's this, *Open City*?

LM: That's John Bryan's paper. He calls it *Open City* on the inside and *Phoenix* on the outside.

BUK: Old John puts out the most lively paper there is. At least he used to. He's always up to something—he's too much.

LM: You did some writing for John, didn't you?

BUK: Yeah, when *Open City* first started down here, he said, "Why don't you do us a column?" and I said, "Hell, we'll call it 'Notes of a Dirty Old Man,' we'll see what happens." So it's turned into two or three books—it was lucky. It was a nice paper—we sat around and drank beer, it wasn't formal at all. It was real loose—it never did tighten up.

LM: What ever happened to the paper?

BUK: He got busted twice. You know, lawyers' fees—he just had to leave town. So the paper folded, and I wrote for *Nola Express* for a while, then the *Free Press* picked me up. So I still do a column a week, whether I feel like it or not. Some of it's bad, some of it's good, some of it's in the middle.

LM: You miss a deadline now and then?

BUK: Once in a while. Get drunked up. . . .

LM: Didn't you quit writing for a while?

BUK: Ten years. Concentrated on the bottle. We had a romance going. Still married. It was a pretty rough trip. Park benches . . . odd jobs, here and there, most of the time I wasn't working—I don't know how I made it. I was always drawing unemployment insurance—I really got the last ounce out of that system. It's nice to get fired. But I missed a lot of meals. Got pretty thin. I hit L.A. one time, and I was down to one hundred and thirty-one pounds . . . usually weigh around two hundred. I was down to nothing. If you don't eat, you melt away. It's that simple.

LM: When did you go back to writing?

BUK: I started writing again when I was thirty-five. I'm fifty-three now, That's eighteen years.

LM: Where were you publishing?

BUK: Just in little magazines. That's my stuff behind you there—most of it's poetry. So you get published in those things, then somebody picks you up, they read your stuff and ask if you want to do a book. Jon and Lou Webb did some of the first ones, and they're really nicely done. Like this job here—paper's supposed to last two thousand years.

LINDA: Doesn't look like it's holding up too well. . . .

BUK: It's got stuff all over it. They did nice work. That was my first big break. Amazing people. They starved in order to publish.

LM: *Crucifix in a Dead Hand.* . . .

BUK: *Deathhand* . . . I didn't like that title. I had other titles, but he insisted on that title which I don't like at all—it's too staid, too dramatic. It's the title of one of the poems and he claims it highlights the book. . . .

LM: Had you written any fiction when you started writing for John Bryan?

BUK: Yeah, I'd written a couple of short stories that were published in this magazine *Story* when I was twenty-four years old. That was the big magazine at the time—they discovered William Saroyan and lots of guys. Then I hit in *Portfolio*—in there with Henry Miller, Jean-Paul Sartre, everybody was in there. So I did score a couple of times, but then I went on the drinking thing when I was about twenty-five. I just gave up writing and hung around bars—I don't know, I just gave up. Then along came the hospital, and all that, and after that, I got out, got a typewriter, bought a couple of sixpacks, and started typing all over again. Had a long rest—lots of material stored up. I don't know the reason for it—I just took ten years off.

LM: Does that *Free Press* deadline help you get work done?

BUK: Sure it does. But of course, I wrote more than the column, I write poems and I'm into my second novel. It's called *Factotum*, and it's about my ten years on the bum. I read *Down and Out in Paris and London* by George Orwell, and it's a pretty good book, but I said, "This guy hasn't been through anything—I can play the piano better than that, as far as experience goes." He had some rough trips but he didn't have as many as I did. So, it'll be an interesting book, I think. We'll see. So I've been making it on my writing the last three years, since I quit the Post Office. It's all right, I can't complain. Little checks come in, royalties . . . I'm a professional writer, man, get up at noon, get up at six, get up at three, hell, my life's my own. But that can get rough too, you know, you have to face yourself, it's all sitting on you. But it's lively.

LM: What's the relationship between Bukowski and your hero, Henry Chinaski?

BUK: Same guy. Most of it's true—there is a little fiction in there. It's a beef stew, but most of the meat is true meat. Like Chinaski, my shorts were hanging down in the rain, I screamed at old women, I was a mess out there.

LM: I keep hearing you called a male chauvinist pig. . . .

BUK: No truth in that at all . . . I used to like to play the old game, you know, the story opens up, "I walked into a bar, there was a blonde sitting on the end stool, I bought her a drink, she had nice legs. . . ." It's not so much my attitude's changed, I just get tired of writing that kind of thing; I'm going into another area. But I don't know if I'm a male chauvinist pig. . . .

LM: Linda thinks you are. . . .

BUK: Linda says I am—she ought to know, hell. . . .

LM: But your latest piece in the *Free Press* is about three women raping a guy . . .

BUK: Well, actually that was just comedy. I was neither sympathetic toward the women or the guy, I just put a twist on it. Women are always getting raped, so I had the guy get raped. The reason I wrote that, one time a guy was walking down the street and some women tried to force him into the car, so I took it from there. Of course, I had the women talking like men, talking about the Lakers, how many points, you know, it was just a comedy . . . I don't know what it meant. Just an idea you write about.

LM: Then there's a recent one about a poet being interviewed by some guy. . . .

BUK: By me. That's all fiction. . . .

LM: And you asked him his advice to a young poet, which I suppose people ask you all the time. . . .

BUK: Oh, yeah. . . .

LM: But I figured it would be more appropriate to ask your advice to an old wino.

BUK: I don't have any advice for old winos. I don't know. . . . That's a real tough question. . . .

LM: But a writer doesn't want to give anybody advice, right?

BUK: Yeah, you actually don't want to, but people ask questions, you gotta answer them. A poet's supposed to know everything, like Ginsberg, those guys, they have opinions on everything, but they create that themselves. They start out writing poetry and they end up giving advice. It's a bad scene—they should just stick to the poem.

LM: But more than anybody else, your poetry contains your life.

BUK: It's true. So if you read the poems, you know all about it—you don't have to ask any questions.

LM: So everybody who knows your work, knows you. . . .

BUK: That's right. In fact, when Linda and I split, everybody in town knows it. .Then the phone starts ringing— "Hi, Hank, whatcha doin?" They don't wait long for the smoke to clear.

LM: Are you really the badass you present yourself as in your writing?

BUK: No. I used to be pretty badass, when I was in my twenties, did a lot of fighting. I was half out of my head. But now I'm really not a badass guy, it's a clown act mostly. It's an attitude that shows mostly in my earlier poems. I'm getting closer to what I really am, and not the badass clown. I realized when I broke in, I'd have to create something new to make people listen to me, so I stepped on the gas pedal, I clowned it up a little bit, to catch the public eye. Subconsciously, I knew what I was doing—I was creating something that might be noticed. But after having broken in that way, I'm drifting away from this badass, tough guy shit. I'm writing more what I actually am. Like all the girls will tell you, I'm very tender, soft, lovable.

LINDA: He's like a marshmallow. . . . But he can be badass too. He hasn't forgotten how. . . .

BUK: Once I flip, I go . . . but I only flip once every three or four years. . . . Well, maybe once a year. Then I'm completely gone—I break windows, I just flip out. But generally, I'm pretty much Mister Marshmallow. It shows in the writing—I might come on badass, but I'm really not badass. There goes my image! Looks like I just screwed myself. . . . Can I retract that? But you know, you see a lot of George Raft movies, and Humphrey Bogart, and that stuff seeps into you.

LM: You know, Bukowski, you remind me of Philip Marlowe. . . .

BUK: Philip Marlowe? I'm not up on him. . . .

LM: Raymond Chandler's detective, the hero of *The Big Sleep*.

BUK: Oh, well, I don't go to many movies. . . .

LM: Well, he reminds me of you because he's big and tough, but he's intelligent and he cares about literature and chess and like that. And in *Farewell, My Lovely*, Chandler puts down Hemingway in a way that reminds me of your story "Class," where Chinaski kicks Hemingway's ass in the prize ring. . . .

BUK: Of course, that wasn't serious. I admire Hemingway . . . But when I'm clowning it up, you'd be surprised how many people take it seriously, especially at poetry readings. Especially the female libbers. I've got one poem, "The Colored Birds," how does it end?—"This guy beats his wife every evening, one of the few real men in town." And they were hissing—they didn't know I was really putting the knock on the guy. My God, that audience was touchy.

Half the people who come to my readings, come to give me hell. When I read at City Lights, a hundred people showed up with garbage to throw at me. But they paid two dollars a head to get in, so that's pretty good. That's two hundred dollars and they never got around to the garbage. It all helps the gate. . . .

LM: Do you think audiences really hate you, or is it just a game?

BUK: Some people truly do hate me—they want to see me die, but a lot of that hatred is game-playing, too. "Let's go there and razz him"—they're clowning in a way too. But some of it isn't clowning—they actually want my balls, they really want me hanging upside down.

LM: Do you think people come to readings hoping you'll do something outrageous?

BUK: That's the trouble with poetry readings. If you drop your pants or vomit on stage or go crazy—they don't come to hear the poetry. They're looking for something. . . .

LM: I had a friend who was a bike racer—he told me the crowd didn't come to see him ride, they came to see him fall on his ass.

BUK: Yeah. Auto racing, poetry.

LM: But you're profiting from it, right?

BUK: Well, it's a hustle. I always say, if I get enough ahead, I won't do it, but how much is enough ahead?

. . .

LM: Have you ever been out of L.A.?

BUK: Hell, I've bummed all over the country. Name it, I've been there. St. Louis, Miami, Houston, Ft. Worth, Dallas, New Orleans New York, Philadelphia, Atlanta—I don't know, hell, I've hit 'em all. Little tiny rooms full of roaches, drinking wine and starving. I didn't know what I was doing, I didn't know what I wanted. I was discontented with life. I didn't want a job—I didn't want a gig, you know, that eight-hour gig. It drove me crazy thinking about it. 'Cause I saw what it did to my father.

It turned him into nothing—he just became job-oriented. He'd come home from work, sit down to the table, he'd talk about the damn job. "Oh, I told off McDonald today. No wonder they rob pennies out of that bucket—he's over talking to some woman, he's got his back turned! I went and saw Finsterwald, I told him about McDonald talking to this woman, they've been stealing money. The guy's not been doing his . . ." blah, blah, blah, blah. Every night he'd talk on into the night about his job. . . .

LM: Wasn't he curator of a museum?

BUK: He started out as a guard. Then this job offer came up. So I'd hit town and I was in this magazine *Portfolio* with Sartre, García Lorca, the whole gang. So I heard him talking to my mother, he said, "Henry writes, but he doesn't know how to use his writing. I'll show you how to use this." So when he applied for this job, he said he was Charles Bukowski, he had written that story. And, so on the basis of this, he got his hanging-picture job. And, God, I thought, people think that man wrote that story? He was such a bumbler—one of those guys who's always trying to make jokes. They thought he wrote that story? How embarrassing. . . . But that's how he got his job—he became Charles Bukowski.

LM: And it was a good job, right?

BUK: It's a good story. Yeah, I guess it was a good job.

LM: But when you finally did take an eight-hour gig, it was one of the shittiest jobs in the world—the U.S. Post Office.

BUK: Yeah. Well, I never know how to find good jobs.

LM: So somebody else used your name to get a job that was better than the jobs you got yourself. . . .

BUK: Yeah, well, of course I wouldn't go in and say, "I'm Charles Bukowski." That's corny—you just don't do that. I worked as a janitor, shipping clerk, stock boy for Sears and Roebuck, that sort of thing. You don't go around saying you're Charles Bukowski. I had lots of bad jobs. Bad jobs and bad women.

LM: I get the impression you'd rather have a bad job than a job connected with the art world.

BUK: You've got the right idea, because, if you get into that, it can suck you up. If you're too close to creation, but it's not really creation, you can lose it all. You're better off mopping the women's latrine. It keeps you straight.

LM: Did you go to college?

BUK: Two years, L.A. City College.

LM: Did you hate that as much as you hated the Post Office?

BUK: No, I kind of liked college. I'd lay around in the grass, and I had a bottle of wine in my locker, and I pretended I was a Nazi. I had a good time. People hated me—that's where I first got the taste, that being hated is kind of nice. I was the Nazi, but I was faking it, you know. People would say, "There goes that son of a bitch!" and I'd say, "Hmmm, there's something to that. . . ."

There's something about admiration that's embarrassing. Somebody'll say, "Hey, man, I really admire you. I really like your poetry." I get sick inside. But somebody else says, "You son of a bitch—" hmmm, I feel good.

LM: But you're finding more people liking you all the time, aren't you?

BUK: The last reading I gave, this guy came up, he was trembling, "Mr. Bukowski, can I tell you something?" I said, "Sure, kid." And he says, "You're a beautiful man." And I said, "Yeah? Keep buying my books, that's all," and walked off. And coming out, there's some girl, she's shaking and trembling all over and crying, "We can't let him get away with that. I don't know what you guys are gonna do, we can't let him get away with this! Those poems are terrible! Oooh! Oooh!" She's all torn up! So everything happens, man. Lots of reaction, good and bad, it's wonderful. Nothing worse than just sitting there.

LM: So you're making out all right?

BUK: Yeah, I'm making it on my writing. Never thought I would. I lucked it. I'm still lucking it. I don't make a hell of a lot of money, though. . . .

LINDA: That's gotta be the most famous poor man in the United States. . . .

BUK: But I've had a good year. I got a grant.

LM: You? How did you get a grant?

BUK: I applied. Sent in twenty poems. There were no negative votes from a twelve-man board So I'm either very bad or I'm very good.

LM: Which foundation gave you the grant?

BUK: National Endowment for the Arts. Five thousand.

LM: Nixon's foundation gave you five thousand dollars?

BUK: I guess it was Nixon. It was last year. I have no objections.

LM: It strikes me as bizarre, that Nixon would give Bukowski money. . . .

BUK: Well, I don't think Nixon read the poems. . . .

LM: Speaking of Nixon, what did you do about the draft?

BUK: What happened was, I was drinking and flopping around in this room. I never read the newspapers or listened to the radio. I was totally isolated. There was a rule, if you moved you were supposed to notify your draft board—I didn't even know that. So I was sitting in my room one night and the FBI arrived, hauls me off. But the best part was, they came back and read the stuff I'd been writing. I was twenty-one at the time, and I was writing pretty wild shit. So they went through all these papers and they read them, they figured I was crazy.

So they gave the papers to the psychiatrist. So it was all set by the time I passed my physical and I walked in to see him. He said, "Do you believe in the war?" and I said, "No." And he said, "Are you willing to go to the war?" and I said, "Yeah."

Then he said, "By the way, we're having a party at my house next Wednesday night, we're having professors, writers, doctors, lawyers, painters, creative people. It's evident you're a very intelligent man. I'd like you to come to my party. Will you come to my party this Wednesday night?" So I said no. Then he knew I was crazy—anybody who wouldn't go to a party like that just doesn't have it.

LM: That's exactly the kind of party you wouldn't go to.

BUK: Of course not. God, how painful! So he looked at me and said, "All right, you don't have to go to the war." Sweet words. . . .

LM: So you got out of the Army for your writing, and now, the government's giving you money for writing. . . .

BUK: Yeah. And I've sold options on two books that might be made into movies. Two thousand, five hundred on one and two thousand on the other. One guy's got *Post Office*, the other guy's got *Erections*. So it was about a twelve-thousand-dollar year. And for poetry, that's all right.

So I'm getting by on the typewriter. It's a miracle. But

it's not as glamorous as you'd think. The movies always show some guy with a scarf—Leslie Howard. Long cigarette holder and a British accent. Got all the answers right there. It's not that way—you've gotta hack it.

LM: And writers are very boring people. . . .

BUK: I know, because a writer is not a good talker. He's got to save the real stuff for the act. That's why, if you meet a writer who talks a lot, he just doesn't have it. You can't be a talker and a writer at the same time. It's impossible. So a good writer will never give you very interesting conversation.

He tends to be dull, stodgy. . . . Linda wrote a poem about the great poet—he stands around, scratches his ass, grunts, eats oranges and apples by the dozen. . . .

LM: What could be more boring that sitting in front of a typewriter all day. . . .

BUK: Yeah, but once you sit down, once that shit starts flowing, it feels pretty good. You got the sound of the keys, you got a beer bottle there, symphony music is on, you got a cigar in your hand, the lamp's burning, and the stuff is coming out on the page, it's actually happening, that minute you're creating something new! You hope. . . . So it feels good, you know, when the shit is rolling out. You wake up. You look at the typewriter, it looks kind of like a time clock. . . .

LINDA: What doesn't feel good, is when it don't come out. . . . That's when it's terrible—when you're just sittin' there. . . .

BUK: You've got a bad thing for going and sitting down when you're not ready. That only ties you up for another three or four days, when you do that. You put the whammy on yourself. Never get near that thing until its right up to your chin. There's some tricks I've learned. . . .

LM: Do you ever write when you don't feel ready?

BUK: On account of this deadline. Sometimes it doesn't

come out. But sometimes I've sat down when I didn't feel like writing at all, for the deadline. You've got nothing in your mind, but you write one of your best things. And if it hadn't of been for the deadline, it wouldn't have happened. Even though I had no story in my mind, you sit down, you type the first line, and it just goes. But mostly you can't force it. Somebody told me once of somebody who writes eight hours a day. Now that stuff's gotta be bad. That's pure panic. Too much.

LM: Like Thomas Wolfe.

BUK: Yeah, God, they had to junk half his stuff. His manuscripts were so large, they had to pull up with a truck to hold all the pages. Then Perkins would go through, thin it out. He was a horrible writer. Thomas Wolfe was the worst writer I can think of.

LM: Who do you like?

BUK: Oh, I like Céline, early Hemingway, Dostoevsky, early Gorki short stories. I like Jeffers, that's about it.

LM: Those guys are all prose writers. . . .

BUK: I know, I don't like poets . . . well, Jeffers was a poet. But I don't like most poets. Prefer the fiction writers. They've got more balls, more snap. Poets don't have it.

LM: Do you prefer to write prose or poetry?

BUK: Well, one helps the other. They're both good. When you write poetry, the fiction part's building—when you do the other, it reverses. The poetry tightens the short story, and the short story loosens the poetry.

They work together. They're both about the same, it's just the way you lay the line down. People ask me "What is a poem?" I don't know. You type it down, you say, "This is a poem. . . ."

LM: Are you going to stick with your tough-guy image?

BUK: Well, I've got a lot of bullshit in me anyway, and I tend to clown it up, so it's just part of a little act I've built up.

. . . But it's not entirely without truth, you know. The tough guy who drinks a lot, has trouble with women—that's not entirely without truth. But I did press the keys a little hard there at the piano. So as time went on, if you've read my stuff lately, you'll notice it's changing. Tonality—I'm moving into other areas. I get tired of the tough boy stance.

LM: At the end of that TV documentary about you, you say that the notice you're getting now came too late . . .

BUK: I mean it came too late to . . . I've already got the fat head, I've always had a fat head. I've got a natural ego, even when I was failing. But it came too late to fatten my head enough to destroy my writing. Some people get recognition and they can't handle it. Even a minor recognition like I have—no large publisher—came at a time when my insights are already built up, and can't be affected—I hope—by this little splash.

I think being known would be much harder to take when you're twenty-three, and have a lot of years ahead of you. Didn't Cervantes write *Don Quixote* when he was eighty? Now that's pretty good writing for the age of eighty. See, he held himself together in his life. Very few men can hang on for all those years and still keep it together. You've gotta know all your moves, you've gotta have instincts and everything.

LM: Is your lifestyle changing now?

BUK: I'll tell you, I have to admit it—I'm feeling better about everything. I tend to have more humor in my work, I'm not as serious or as bitter as I used to be—maybe that's good, and maybe it's bad. But sometimes it'll break down— you'll be walking around and those deep, deep blues'll jump on your back, and they've got you. And I'll lay down and say "Jesus, I feel awful." But most of the time I feel pretty good, the writing's coming along, I feel lucky. So I'm looking forward to a hell of a lot more writing, a lot more people hating me, and a lot more people digging me.

LM: Now where I come from, it's fashionable to say that Los Angeles shits. What are you doing down here?

BUK: Say, I like this town. For one thing, it doesn't have too many goddamned writers. Frisco's bad, all those coffee shops, and when you walk down the street everybody says, "Hey, there's Bukowski!" It's bad enough down here after that film. Went to get a hot dog at the track, said "Give me a hot dog," girl said "Wouldn't you rather have a cheese sandwich?" I say "What?" She says "I just wanted to hear your voice, I wanted to hear you talk." "Why's that?" "I saw you in that movie!" That's where the hatred is so nice. It sets you free. When you're hated, you can't fail, you don't have this—"Oh, somebody likes me!"

LM: But when I come down here, I feel this strong sense of deprivation—like, there's nothing to do. . . .

BUK: What do you mean—there's plenty to do. There's two race-tracks, there's bars, there's call services, you've got everything here you need—you've got Disneyland, you've got Hollywood . . .

LM: And San Francisco's got writers . . .

BUK: Yeah! You've got Ferlinghetti, McClure. The writers down here aren't very big. Although they think they are. . . .

LM: But in San Francisco the writer on everybody's lips is—

BUK: —Tell me quickly—

LM: —Bukowski.

BUK: And he lives in L.A. See, I don't have to hear that down here, I'm isolated. When the phone rings I kind of jump, I say, "Oh Christ, who's this going to be?"

LM: But you're in the L.A. phonebook. . . .

BUK: That's to get readings. Helps the hustle. I never ask to read, but somebody phones me and asks me and I say O.K., depending on the price.

LM: So you don't want people to like you, but they'll only buy your books if they like you. . . .

BUK: Or if they hate me.

LM: Why would they buy your books if they hate you?

BUK: Because they're curious. They say, "What's he written now?" I believe the haters are better buyers than the others.

LM: But isn't your writing less offensive now?

BUK: Well, if you're a good writer you're always going to disturb somebody with almost everything you write. There's that word with the capital, "Truth," you know....

LINDA: Did you read that column on shit he wrote recently?

LM: No ...

LINDA: Some woman said, "That is the most disgusting, filthy thing that Bukowski ever...." It was really funny, but she didn't pick up on that.

LM: What do you think about Mailer?

BUK: Mailer? He wrote one novel and turned into an intelligent journalist. He goes on the shows, he gets in battles with the female libbers, he's no longer a creator, he's just a journalist.

LM: Doesn't he present an image, like you do?

BUK: I don't know what his image is. Do you know what it is?

LM: Probably a badass male chauvinist pig.

BUK: Didn't he knife one of his wives? They're gonna hold that against him....

. . .

LM: In San Francisco the writers hang out together—

BUK: —That's destructive—

LM: But down here they're isolated.

BUK: Thank God. I think it was Ibsen who said, "The greatest men are the most alone." You've gotta be alone to score, you've gotta be alone to know where the hell you're at. Of course, you've gotta go out and see what's out there. But you can't stay out there and swim in it and be taken by it—you've gotta come back, close the door, and do what you have to do. But this town's fine. It's the streets without the artists—that's what any place is anyway. I just can't get away from this city. I've been on the bum, but I just keep coming back. I like it. I'm stuck with it. It's fine.

LM: What do you think of the *L.A. Free Press*?

BUK: The *L.A. Free Press* isn't much, man. I get more out of reading the *Herald-Examiner*. It's more open, there's more laughter, there's more actual news stories that are funny. The *Free Press* reminds me of the *L.A. Times*—they've become very conservative. And the massage parlor girls all have their panties put on them—it's ridiculous, good Lord—it's gotten very conservative. They play left wing, but they seem to be right wing if you read between the lines. Then they have columns for each—they've got a Mexican girl, they've got a Black column, they've got a female libber column, they've got a column to suit each person.

Then they've got my dirty stories, they put those back in the classified. The *Free Press* isn't much, man. I guess because it's so established—they've got the newsstands everywhere and people just buy it automatically because there's nothing else to do. It's not a very interesting paper, really drab fare, very lackluster. John Bryan's paper, the *Phoenix*, that thing jumps. Bryan's the best editor I know on the little paper scene. I wish he were down here stirring up some shit. He's got the touch, he's got the flare. The *Free Press* is so drab.

I wrote a story about Bryan's paper *Open City*, the way it ran, the way it folded, and he got a little miffed. He's still a little bit sore. He came charging in the door one night, he was high, and he was yelling, "Bukowski, why'd you write that goddamn story about me?" So I said, "Take it easy, John, sit down and have a beer." And he's yelling, "Oh, goddamn it. . . ." And I said, "What the hell's wrong, John, baby?" And he grabbed the door and he slammed it— almost broke the window, he slammed it so hard, and he took off. I heard his car going Brrrrrrrrrrm! It upset him so much. . . . Then the phone rang, a couple of hours later, and he said, "Bukowski, I'm sorry, I flipped my lid there." He's good for a show. . . .

When we were talking about tourist places before, it reminded me of the story about Watts Towers. During the riots I was living with Frances, they were burning and shooting and all that—you know what that woman said? She said, "Let's go down and look at Watts Towers." I said, "Now?" You could hear gunfire! She said, "Yeah." I said, "Hey, look, I'm White! All over, I'm the same color. I can't go down there." "Oh, they won't hurt you." I said, "Hell! You go down there!" That's when I started thinking I'd better get away from her. She wanted to see me destroyed, I guess.

But the Blacks usually adopted me. It takes a while sometimes, though. I was usually adopted at the factories or wherever I worked. Black cats dug me for some reason. They used to say, "We give you water, we give them sand." And I'd say, "Thanks, baby." I think it was because most White guys in the factory, their mentality isn't quite as sharp. Lots of Black guys at the factory are sharp because they have to be there but their minds are aware, so they're more interesting. So I tended to run with them because they were more interesting. So I got adopted. I had my line of shit and they had theirs, and they mixed pretty good.

LM: Well, you were like them in that you wanted to make it as a writer but you didn't want to be part of the thing, just like they wanted to make it but not be part of the thing. . . .

BUK: What's that? You talk like a jazz musician. . . .

LM: I'd love to be, but I don't have any talent. . . . Anyway, if you wanted to be a real writer, you'd have finished college and gotten a Ph.D. . . .

BUK: Oh, is that what a real writer does? Why is it the professors can't write, then?

LM: Maybe it's educated out of them? Anyway, in San Francisco the big University writers are people like Wright

Morris, and Wallace Stegner.

BUK: Oh, yeah—professional, smooth, polished . . . Actually I write very badly when you come to think of writing. I'm sloppy, careless, and I use any word that comes to my mind—I'm not very professional. I'm craggy. I'm not very good, basically. . . .

LM: You've got a different kind of style. . . .

BUK: I've got my own style. I guess you might call it careless, or I don't give a damn. I just write it down, if there is a style, I don't choose it but it's there. I'm not a smooth, professional writer at all.

LM: But you're going to get right up there with those "professionals" anyway. . . .

BUK: I don't know. I wouldn't mind staying right where I'm at. Getting the work done. I really have no plans to move to New York, get big . . . I'm just pumping it from this position, and it's O.K. Shit, I'll take fame and a best-seller and a couple of million, yeah, if I could have it I'd take it. But this is O.K.

LM: Do you think one of the universities will hire you one of these days?

BUK: Oh, they're too scared of me. I might start talking about shit or something like that. . . .

LM: What if somebody like UCLA asked you to teach there?

BUK: I'd ask them how much, how many days. . . . If the price was right I'd be corrupted a while. I can be bought any time. I'll sell my literary ass to the highest bidder. . . .

Berkeley Barb, April 26–May 2 and May 3–9, 1974

Craft Interview for
New York Quarterly

Interview by William Packard

Hello Packard, Bill:

No, the women don't write my poems for me but kriste knows they caused me to write some, good and bad, but write some. Regarding crafty interview, I am not going east if I can help it, seems Italy is next, September, I guess, got drunk with Inge Feltrinelli who told me some Hemingway stories, and she says she'll put us up at her place, there's a bookstore downstairs that Fellini hangs around in; trouble is I don't like bookstores and I have a book of Fellini movies that I haven't read, but, wait, what are we talking about here?

You know I feel foolish about craft interviews and the telephone is out and a cassette tape, no, but if you insist like send a list of questions and I'll try to make it sound like I'm in the room with you: sound of belches, moans, and laughter. I mean, we can try it and if it works for me I'll send it to you and if it works for you and yours you can run it maybe with a picture of me cueing up over a rabbit's ass? You know, I think the poets are just a little too precious with themselves and maybe when they stop getting so holy and precious a few readers might follow along. Whitman said that to have great poets we must have great audiences first. I think maybe we ought to have fairly good poets first, then maybe we'll get somebody in the grandstand besides our relatives and our whores. I think if I had to choose between making money writing poetry and not making money doing the same thing, I wouldn't have to flip a coin.

all right, then lemmee here,
Buk

Dear Charles Bukowski:

Okay we're on. Here is a list of 16 questions set up so you can run them through the typer and give answers directly on the page, together with simulated background noises, moans, barfs.

If you don't like any of the questions kick it off the page, add any you want to add.

We'll need some photos, send me 5x7 black & white, three if possible, the way we set up interviews in *NYQ*, other issues.

The question I'm most interested in is #14. By "persona" I mean recognizable mask, that's a "Bukowski" poem, meaning there are certain characteristic things, but is that "Bukowski" in any relation to what you consider the real Bukowski. Like for example, Robert Lowell sometimes presented us with a persona of Robert Lowell which was very moving but it wasn't always the literal Robert Lowell. I guess maybe I'm talking about license, literal truth versus poetic truth, and how that impinges on you the man versus you the poet. Li Po you know was the great Chinese poet who always got high on rice wine & wrote his poems & then dropped them from a bridge onto a river so they would float downstream god knows where. Better than sending them out to the *Paris Review*.

I didn't ask any question about what you think of *NYQ* as a magazine, the other poems in it (besides your own). But feel free to talk about that.

If you need extra space type on the back of each page.

I feel like I'm administering a mid-term.

Good luck and keep your eyes on your own paper.

Best,

Bill

How do you write? In longhand, on the typewriter? Do you revise much? What do you do with worksheets? Your poems sometimes give the impression of coming off the top of your head. Is that only an impression? How much agony and sweat of the human spirit is involved in the writing of one of your poems?

I write right off the typer. I call it my "machinegun." I hit it hard, usually late at night while drinking wine and listening to classical music on the radio and smoking mangalore ganesh beedies. I revise but not much. The next day I retype the poem and automatically make a change or two, drop out a line, or make two lines into one or one line into two, that sort of thing—to make the poem have more balls, more balance. Yes, the poems come "off the top of my head," I seldom know what I'm going to write when I sit down. There isn't much agony and sweat of the human spirit involved in doing it. The writing's easy, it's the living that is sometimes difficult.

When you're away from your place do you carry a notebook with you? Do you jot down ideas as they come to you during the day or do you store them in your head for later?
I don't carry notebooks and I don't consciously store ideas. I try not to think that I am a writer and I am pretty good at doing that. I don't like writers, but then I don't like insurance salesmen either.

Do you ever go through dry periods, no writing at all? If so how often? What do you do during these periods? Anything to get you back on the track?
A dry period for me means perhaps going two or three nights without writing. I probably have dry periods but I'm not aware of them and I go on writing, only the writing probably isn't much good. But sometimes I do get aware that it isn't going too well. Then I go to the racetrack and bet more money than usual and come home and drink much more than usual and scream at and abuse my woman. And it's best that I lose at the track without trying to. I can almost always write a damn near immortal poem if I have lost somewhere between 150 and 200 dollars.

Need for isolation? Do you work best alone? Most of your poems concern your going from a state of love/sex to a state of isolation. Does that tie in with the way you have to have things in order to write?
I love solitude but I don't need it to the exclusion of somebody I care for in order to get some words down. I figure if

I can't write under all circumstances, then I'm just not good enough to do it. Some of my poems indicate that I am writing while living alone after a split with a woman, and I've had many splits with women. I need solitude more often when I'm not writing than when I am. I have written with children running about the room having at me with squirt guns. That often helps rather that hinders the writing: some of the laughter enters. One thing does bother me, though: to overhear somebody's loud TV, a comedy program with a laugh track.

When did you begin writing? How old? What writers did you admire?
The first thing I ever remembered writing was about a German aviator with a steel hand who shot hundreds of Americans out of the sky during World War II. It was in longhand in pen and it covered every page of a huge memo ringed notebook. I was about 13 at the time and I was in bed covered with the worst case of boils the medics ever remembered seeing. There weren't any writers to admire at the time. Since then there has been John Fante, Knut Hamsun, the Céline of *Journey*; Dostoevsky, of course; Jeffers of the long poems only; Conrad Aiken, Catullus . . . not too many. I sucked mostly at the classical music boys. It was good to come home from the factories at night, take off my clothes, climb on the bed in the dark, get drunk on beer, and listen to them.

Do you think there's too much poetry being written today? How would you characterize what you think is really bad poetry? What do you think is good poetry today?
There's too much bad poetry being written today. People just don't know how to write down a simple easy line. It's difficult for them; it's like trying to keep a hard-on while drowning—not many can do it. Bad poetry is caused by people who sit down and think, "Now I am going to write a Poem." And it comes out the way they *think* a poem should be. Take a cat. He doesn't think, well, now I'm a cat and I'm going to kill this bird. He just does it. Good poetry today?

Well, it's being written by a couple of cats called Gerald Locklin and Ronald Koertge.

You've read most of the NYQ craft interviews we've published. What do you think of our approach, the interviews you've read. What interviews have told you something?
I'm sorry you asked that question. I haven't learned anything from the interviews except that the poets were studious, trained, self-assured, and obnoxiously self-important. I don't think that I was ever able to finish an interview; the print began to blur and the trained seals vanished below the surface. These people lack joy, madness, and gamble in their answers just as they do in their work (poems).

Although you write strong voice poems, that voice rarely extends beyond the circumference of your own psychosexual concerns. Are you interested in national, international affairs, do you consciously restrict yourself as to what you will and will not write about?
I photograph and record what I see and what happens to me. I am not a guru or leader of any sort. I am not a man who looks for solutions in God or politics. If somebody else wants to do the dirty work and create a better world for us and he *can* do it, I will accept it. In Europe where my work is having much luck, various groups have put a claim on me, revolutionaries, anarchists, so forth, because I have written of the common man of the streets, but in interviews over there I have had to disclaim a conscious working relationship with them because there isn't any. I have compassion for almost all the individuals of the world; at the same time, they repulse me.

What do you think a young poet starting out today needs to learn the most?
He should realize that if he writes something and it bores him it's going to bore many other people also. There is nothing wrong with a poetry that is entertaining and easy to understand. Genius could be the ability to say a profound thing in a simple way. He should stay the hell out of

writing classes and find out what's happening around the corner. And bad luck for the young poet would be a rich father, an early marriage, an early success, or the ability to do anything very well.

Over the last few decades California has been the residence of many of our most independent voice poets—like Jeffers, Rexroth, Patchen, even Henry Miller. Why is this? What is your attitude towards the East, towards New York?

Well, there was a little more space out here, the long run up the coast, all that water, a feeling of Mexico and China and Canada, Hollywood, sunburn, starlets turned to prostitutes. I don't know, really, I guess if your ass is freezing some of the time it's harder to be a "voice poet." Being a voice poet is the big gamble because you're putting your guts up for view and you're going to get a lot more reaction than if you're writing something like your mother's soul being like a daisy field.

New York, I don't know. I landed there with $7 and no job and no friends and no occupation except common laborer. I suppose if I had come in from the top instead of the bottom I might have laughed a little more. I stayed three months and the buildings scared the shit out of me and the people scared the shit out of me, and I had done a lot of bumming all over the country under the same conditions but New York City was the Inferno, all the way. The way Woody Allen's intellectuals suffer in N.Y.C. is a lot different than what happens to my type of people. I never got laid in New York, in fact, the women wouldn't even speak to me. The only way I ever got laid in New York was to come back three decades later and bring my own with me, a terrible wench, we stayed at the Chelsea, of course. The *New York Quarterly* is the only good thing that has happened to me out there.

You've written short stories, novels. Do they come from the same place your poems come from?

Yes, they do, there's not much difference—line and line

length. The short story helped get the rent and the novel was a way of saying how many different things could happen to the same man on the way to suicide, madness, old age, natural and unnatural death.

You have a fairly distinct persona in most of your poems, and your strong voice seems to come out of that persona. It's the mask of a bored, dirty old man who's boozing it up in Li Po manner because the straight world isn't worth taking seriously. Usually there's a hysterical broad banging your door down while the poem is taking shape. First do you admit to this persona in your poems, and then to what extent do you think it reflects Bukowski the man? In other words are you the person you present to us in your poems?

Things change a bit: what once was is not quite what it is now. I began writing poetry at the age of 35 after coming out of the death ward on the L.A. County General Hospital and not as a visitor. To get somebody to read your poems you have to be noticed, so I got my act up. I wrote vile (but interesting) stuff that made people hate me, that made them curious about this Bukowski. I threw bodies off my front porch into the night. I pissed on police cars, sneered at hippies. After my second reading down at Venice, I grabbed the money, leaped into my car, intoxicated, and drove it about on the sidewalks at 60 m.p.h. I had parties at my place which were interrupted by police raids. A professor from U.C.L.A. invited me to his place for dinner. His wife cooked a nice meal which I ate and then I went over and broke up his China closet. I was in and out of drunk-tanks. A lady accused me of rape, the whore. Meanwhile, I wrote about most of this, it was my persona, it was me but it wasn't me. As time went on, trouble and action arrived by itself and I didn't have to force it and I wrote about *that* and this was closer to my real persona. Actually, I am not a tough person and sexually, most of the time, I am almost a prude, but I am often a nasty drunk and many strange things happen to me when I am drunk. I am not saying this very well and I'm taking too long. What I am trying to say is that the longer I write the closer I am getting to what I am. I am one of those slow starters but I am all hell in the stretch run. I am 93 percent the person I present in my poems; the other 7 percent is where art improves upon life, call it background music.

You refer to Hemingway a lot, seem to have a love/hate thing for him, what he does in his work. Any comment?
I guess for me Hemingway is a lot like it is for others: he goes down well when we are young. Gertie taught him the line but I think he improved on it. Hemingway and Saroyan had the line, the magic of it. The problem was that Hemingway didn't know how to laugh and Saroyan was filled with sugar. John Fante had the line too and he was the first who knew how to let passion enter in, emotion in, without letting it destroy the concept. I speak here of moderns who write the *simple* line; I am aware that Blake was once around. So when I write about Hemingway it's sometimes a joke thing but I'm probably more in debt to him that I'd care to admit. His early work was screwed down tight, you couldn't get your fingers under it. But now I get more out of reading about his life and fuckups, it's almost as good as reading about D.H. Lawrence.

What do you think of this interview and what question do you wish we'd asked you? Go ahead and ask it of yourself and then answer it.
I think the interview is all right. I suppose that some people will object that the answers lack polish and erudition, then they'll go out and buy my books. I can't think of any questions to ask myself. For me to get paid for writing is like going to bed with a beautiful woman and afterwards she gets up, goes to her purse and gives me a handful of money. I'll take it. Why don't we stop here?

New York Quarterly 27, Summer 1985

Gin-Soaked Boy

Interviewed by Chris Hodenfield

. . .

Have you known people who've worked in movies?
Fortunately, I have not. Oh, people have come by, even before this shit started. Godard. Werner Herzog. James Woods—before he became big time. We met a lot of these people through Barbet [Schroeder]. Harry Dean Stanton. Sean Penn and Madonna. Elliot Gould. They all come by.

Harry Dean's a strange fellow. He doesn't put on much of a hot-shot front. And I make him more depressed. I say, "Harry, for Chrissakes, it's not so bad." When you're feeling bad and someone says that, you only feel worse.

Barbet just showed up one day. Said he wanted to make a film about my life. He kinda talked me into it. I was very reluctant, because I don't like film. I don't like actors, I don't like directors, I don't like Hollywood. I just don't like it. He laid a little cash on the table—not a great deal, but some. So I typed it out. That was seven years ago.

I started writing dirty stores and I ended up writing a fucking screenplay. And now I have Godard, Werner Herzog, and Sean Penn coming by. The little girl next door says, "Oh, Hank, is it true that Madonna came to see you?" I said yeah. "But why would Madonna come see you?"

Sean [Penn] wanted Dennis Hopper to direct, and I wanted Barbet. Because Barbet put seven years into this. They gave Barbet a pretty lush offer, to be the producer, a whole deal. But he said, "No! I must direct this myself."

. . .

What was your first reaction to Mickey Rourke?
I hadn't met Mickey, but I heard many stories about him. I thought, "This guy will be a complete prick. I better not get drunk and take a swing at him. I better watch my drinking. I could ruin the whole move by getting into it with this kid and being completely honest."

But he was so nice. His eyes were good. Even one time Linda and I were walking onto the set, they weren't shooting. Mickey was being interviewed, they had the cameras on him. He saw me and said, "Hey Hank, c'mere! Help me!" They got me on, talking.

I think we just liked each other. One time Linda and I were sitting in the bar when they were shooting. We were getting plastered, which was a mistake. The bar was still open while they were shooting around the corner. I saw Mickey and I said, "Hey, c'mon, have a drink." He said, "No, I can't, we neeeeed you!" Just like a little boy. He needed me to watch him act.

The guy was great. He really became this barfly. He added his own dimension, which at first I thought, this is awful, he's overdoing it. But as the shooting went on, I saw he'd done the right thing. He'd created a very strange, fantastic, lovable character. When it comes out, I can see all sorts of kids acting like him. All the kids are gonna start drinking!

How was Faye Dunaway?
I saw her in *Bonnie & Clyde*. She filled the role. Period. She wasn't exceptional. She wasn't bad. She just filled the role. [To the microphone.] Sorry to say this, Faye, you want me to lie? I just made an enemy. That's one of my problems—I can't lie.

Is [Barfly] pretty much as you wrote it?
Yeah. Barbet wrote in the contract that nothing could be changed without my permission. It's pretty good for a screenwriter. Never heard of that before.

Barbet has a lot of respect for what I write. He even phones from the set when I'm not there and says the actors can't say the line. You know, sometimes you write a line and it looks good on paper, but with the human voice it doesn't work. So I give him another line. So we've been working together that way. It's right down to what I wrote. If the writing's good, you've got a good chance for a good movie.

He's been improving the pace. The first cut I saw was very slow in the beginning. It's marvelous what they can do to pep it up just by cutting here and there—you get a sense of rhythm. A certain zip develops, you can feel it, like a horse galloping. When you get these deadly pauses, you can just sense them. We saw that in the beginning; it just bothered me, "This is so labored." They'd just put everything together, with no music.

He's really pushing it. He sent the Cannes people a rough cut, and they liked that. The last I heard, they had seven rooms with people working on it in each one, and he's running from one to the other.

The whole movie was shot in six weeks. And what's the cutting time, four weeks? We're working under the mad whip here, but instead of detracting, it seems to be giving it more jazz.

Did you get some screenplays and study the form?
Hell, no. [Disgusted.] Well, you know, it's just dialogue, people walking around. You don't have to study that. I can't see taking instruction on anything. . . .

I guess it was because I had a tough childhood, with my father telling me what to do all the time. So if anybody tells me, "This is how you do this . . ." I don't ever like to be told how you do this. I just want to do it, whatever has to be done. If somebody says, "You do it like this," I immediately cut off and go cold. And it extends to trivial areas of life. . . . Things must come through joy and wanting to do them. I don't like instruction. I can't handle it.

· · ·

If the promise of screenplay fortunes had come at a more pressing time, might it have been a more distracting lure?
It did come at a pressing time, and that's just why I did it. Because I was living in a dive and just barely getting by. I really hadn't been lucky until three or four years ago. And I'm not rich. And I'm not poor. Neither are you, right? So the money looked good. And I think they got a bargain—for what they paid for.

And if the movie's a success, you'll participate?
It will be a success, because Mickey did a great job of acting. He really did it.

Had you ever given a thought as to who might play you in in your life story?
No, because I never thought anyone would do my life story. I did think, well, maybe I'll die sometime and somebody will take a shot at it. Usually they fuck it up. There was a thing about Kerouac on TV the other night—it was awful. You can't watch it too long. This guy smiling. We were switching back and forth between F. Scott and Kerouac; we finally had to stop watching both of them.

Most writers' lives are more interesting than what they write. Mine is both. They meet on an equal plane.

I just wrote it and said it was in the hands of God, they'll fuck it up. I didn't expect a great deal. So I was ready for when they fucked it up. Fortunately, because of Barbet Schroeder's directing and Mickey Rourke's acting and all the barflies—took them right out of the bar—they got a great cast and it worked. It's going to be a fine movie. It might even win a fucking Academy Award for Mickey. For screenwriter? Well, maybe. I'll get a tuxedo.

. . .

You once wrote a regular column in the L.A. Free Press, and in a column on how to pick the ponies you said, "Having talent but no follow-through is worse than having no talent at all."
I was thinking of horses when I said that, but I guess it applies everywhere.

Have you been following through?
So far. With minor fame. That's what I've got now. Minor fame is bad.

What is the effect of fame on a writer?
Depends on your age, brainpower, and your guts. I think if you're old enough, you have a better chance to overcome what they put on you. If you're a genius at 22 and the babes

come around, the drinks . . . How old was Dylan Thomas when he died, 34? It can come too soon. It can never come too late, I guess. I think I'm safe.

I get letters from women who want to show their naked bodies. "I'm 19 years old and I want to be your secretary. I'll keep your house and I won't bother you at all. I just want to be around." I get some strange letters. I trash them. Even before Linda and I got together.

Nothing's free. There's always problems, there's always tragedy, madness, bullshit. There's a big trap waiting with all these dollies who send letters about what they're going to do for me. They just want you to walk into it and put the clamp on you. No way. So I'll answer, "Good God, girl, give it to a young man who deserves it and leave me alone. And drive safely." Never hear from them again. . . .

As Ezra said, "Do your W-O-R-K." That's where the vigor comes from, the creative fucking process. Puts dance in the bones. Like I said, if I don't write for a week, I get sick. I can't walk, I get dizzy, I lay in bed, I puke. Get up in the morning and gag. I've got to type. If you chopped my hands off, I'd type with my feet. So I've never written for money; I've written just because of an imbecilic urge.

Even when you were writing for porno magazines?
That was for the rent. [Grins.] That was sicker. I didn't have the urge, but I did it. I enjoyed that. I would write a good story that I liked, but I would find an excuse to throw in a sex scene right in the middle of the story. It seemed to work. It was okay.

Some guys manage to get hold of their creative energy when they're young, some guys wait a while.
I waited a long, long while. At the age of 50, I was still in the post office, stacking letters. I was still working, I was not a writer. I decided to quit and become a writer. When I went in to resign, the lady in the post office said [clucks tongue reprovingly]. I always remember that. It was my last day on the job. One of the clerks said, "I don't know if he's going to make it, but the old man sure has a lot of guts."

Old? I didn't feel old. You're just walking around in your body, you don't feel any age. When you get old, people say things, but there's no difference.

So that was a big blow. I said, "Oh shit, what have I done?" The landlady said I was crazy. But she was nice, and sometimes she'd leave a big dinner out for me. And every other night I'd go down and drink with them all night long and sing all night. In between I wrote my own stuff. Dirty stories. That was on DeLongpre.

I'm 66 now. That was 1970. I guess I got lucky late.

. . .

In Europe, now you are recognized on the streets. Does this get in the way?
All a drunk wants to do is have an excuse to get drunk. So if your celebrity is an excuse to get drunk, you get drunk.

I write when I'm drunk. Take away the typewriter and I'm a drunk without a typewriter. Could be some goodness left over, or some charm or some bullshit. It's all mixed together.

One of the hurtful things about fame is that you play more to a past image than to a future image.
Exactly. Especially a writer. The only thing that amounts to a writer is the next line you're going to write down. All past things don't mean shit. If you can't write that next line, you as a person are dead. It's only the next line, this line that's coming as the typewriter spins, that's the magic, that's the roaring, that's the beauty. It's the only thing that beats death. The next line. If it's a good one, of course. [Grins.] That bothers me a lot. No, it doesn't. Consider that the next line could be dead. But we're not our own best critics, are we? I imagine a lot of guys keep typing while saying, "This stuff is great."

It may be madness, but I feel I'm still growing. It's like somebody trying to push out of the top of my head. Working, working . . . A good feeling, man. The gods are good to me. They haven't always been good to me, but lately they've been kind to me.

[Raises toast.] Here's to my father, who made me the way I am. He beat the shit out of me. After my father, everything was easy.

Film Comment, Vol. 23, No. 4, July/August 1987

Lizard's Eyelid Interview

Sterling: You are a highly accomplished writer, what do you hold responsible for your success?

Bukowski: A brutal childhood, alcohol, half a dozen rotten jobs, a dozen rotten women, plus an overpowering fear of almost everything, plus a strange arrival of luck and bravery in sub-zero situations.

Sterling: Of which of your works are you most proud?

Bukowski: I'm not proud of anything. What I always like best is the last thing I've written. At the moment it is the answer to question.

Sterling: Was the character Chinaski based on anyone you know, yourself?

Bukowski: I am Chinaski. By changing my name I was able to step back and slap myself around a bit more. Maybe a half-laugh here and there. Mostly there. The "Chin" part, if you must know, was thrown in because of my chin—I was one of those guys able to absorb a terrific punch. I was not a very good fighter but taking me out was a great problem. I won a few by simply outenduring the stupid son of a bitch trying to do me in.

Sterling: What do you feel is the greatest tragedy of our time?

Bukowski: The 8-hour job. You die on it and you die without it.

Sterling: What are your hobbies, other than writing?

Bukowski: Playing the horses and knowing it is stupid but going on and playing them anyhow. I don't know what draws me to this. A half-dream of death. A reminder? I don't know. There are so many things that I don't know.

Sterling: You seem to have a fascination with sex and alcoholism. What is this fascination?

Bukowski: Sex? Well I was drawn to it because I missed so much of it from basically the age of 13 to 34. I just didn't want to pay the price, do the tricks, work at it. Then I don't know, about at the age of 35 I decided I'd better get with it, and I do suppose that playing catch-up, I overdid it. I found it to be the easiest thing in the world. I found dozens of lonely women out there. I banged and slammed like a madman. I'd be in one place or another. My car parked here or there. Dinners. Bedrooms. Bathrooms. One place in the morning, another place at night. Now and then I got caught. I'd meet one or another who'd make me feel real bad, they'd reel me in and hook me, work me over. Sharks. But as time went on, even I learned how to handle the sharks. And after a while fucking and sucking and playing games lost its reality. I screwed so much my dick was rubbing raw. Dry pussy? Sure, but mostly I knew the tricks, what to do, how to do, and then it got old and senseless. Sex is too often just proving something to yourself. After you prove it a while there's no need to prove it any longer. But in a sense, I was lucky: I got all my fucking workouts before the advent of AIDS.

Alcohol is another matter. I've always needed it. It needs me. I've had any number of beers and a bottle of wine tonight within a couple of hours. Great. The singing of the blood. I don't think I could have endured any of the shitty jobs I had in so many cities in this country without knowing I could come back to my room and drink it off and smooth it out, let the walls slant in, the face of the subnormal foreman vanish, always knowing that they were buying my time, my body, me, for a few pennies while they prospered. Then too, I could have never lived with some of those women unless they were transferred by drink into half-dreams which wavered before me. Under drink, their legs always looked better, their conversations more than the lisping of idiots, their betrayals not a self-affront. Drugs I had no luck with. They took away my guts, my laughter. They dulled my mind. They limped my dick. They took everything from me. The writing. The small, tiny flick of hope. Booze rose me up to the sky, slammed me the next morning, but I could climb out of it, get going again. Drugs sacked me. Threw me on the mattress. A bug thing. If there is an out for the disposed, it's alcohol. Most can't handle it. But for me, it's one of the secrets of existence. You asked.

Sterling: Who were you inspired by?

Bukowski: Originally, Hemingway but he faded. No sense of humor. A craftsman, got down the beautiful and uncluttered line, which I believe he got more from Sherwood Anderson than from Gertrude Stein. Sure I liked Gorky, Turgenev, Dostoevsky, then came Hamsun (see *Hunger*) but I really got blasted away when I read Céline's *Journey* . . . I read it in one reading, laughing out, thinking, now, here is a writer who finally writes better than I do. But only in *Journey* . . .

Most overrated writers: Shakespeare, Mailer, Isaac Singer, Chekhov, Tolstoy.

Sterling: Who do you consider the finest writers of our time?

Bukowski: There aren't any. Or they haven't been published.

Sterling: How does old age agree with you (I can't imagine you ever growing "old")?

Bukowski: Old age agrees with me greatly. I hammer the line in with greater luck than ever. I drink beer and wine and more of it. Things that bother most people don't bother me. One thing I can't get over or adjust to is Humanity. It's not moving, it's glued to its own shit. I love animals. Their eyes, their grace. Me, I'm 71 now, but I feel 47. But I always felt 47, even when I was 17. But I know death is at my elbow. But I don't mind. I never much cared for the game. And when it comes to take me out, I won't be sad. I've had a good strong run. Each line that I write down now is just more laughter against the impossible.

Sterling: Do you prefer to be known as a writer or a poet by conventional classification?

Bukowski: I don't care how they "classify" me. I've never searched for a place among the immortals; they haven't impressed me that much. I'm just like the plumber or the dope dealer or the jock on the 5 horse, I'm just trying to get from today and into tomorrow, somehow, trying to feel as good as possible, trying to avoid the hell-traps.

Sterling: What is your most recent project?

Bukowski: Right now, I'm working on a novel, *Pulp*, "dedicated to bad writing," a detective novel, and I'm having a right good time playing around and I might finish it, if it carries me without push.

Sterling: Your works, published as many as 34 years ago, are still increasingly popular today, does that surprise you?

Bukowski: No, it doesn't surprise me. I always knew that I had a way of slamming the line down that was bright and crazy, which carried its own gamble. As I've said elsewhere, it's not that I'm so good, it's that they are so bad. There have been centuries of graceless drivel, we've been fed pap and crap. I can hardly believe all of it. It's like a dirty trick against everybody.

Sterling: What is your opinion of religion and politics?

Bukowski: Religion is what a person builds through endurance against the forces of life. It's what he finds out is true for himself. Within and against those forces. That's all there is.

Politics is a blind horse leading a horse's ass into darkness. Politics draws the greatest fakes towards it. A true leader is either propagandized out of essence or murdered. The masses always prefer a political leader within their own likeness. In other words, an idiot.

Sterling: What is your message to the world?

Bukowski: I have no message to the world. I am not wise enough to lead, yet I am wise enough not to follow.

Lizard's Eyelid, Winter Issue, 1991